Beyond Siberia

Two Years in a Forgotten Place

SHARON DIRLAM

McSeas Books

Address for orders:

McSeas Books
1532 Santa Rosa Ave.
Santa Barbara CA 93109

www.mcseas.com

Cover design by Peggy Lindt

Cover photos by John McCafferty

Printed in the United States of America
Library of Congress Cataloging-in-Publication Data

Dirlam, Sharon
Beyond Siberia: Two Years in a Forgotten Place

ISBN 0-9712827-2-2

USA $14.00

Acknowledgments

With deep appreciation to the friends who encouraged me as this book took shape, and to the Russians and Americans who kindly answered my questions and offered their expertise, and to the people of Birobidjan, especially Vera Borisovna Vyalkova, Pavel Nikolievich Tolstogusov, Lena Vadimovna Tolstogusova and Ludmila Borisovna Vinnikova, for their continuing friendship.

American friends and colleagues we treasure from our Peace Corps days enrich these pages with their experiences, and I thank them as well.

Mara Kohn, Geraldine Kennedy, Kay Mills, Royce Adams and Patty Perrin read the manuscript and contributed valuable insights and suggestions.

Larry McLellan at UCSB advised me about the etymology of certain Russian words and names. Yelena Belyaeva at the Birobidjan Pedagogical Institute answered questions about the Yiddish classes at the college.

Thanks to friends in my writing group – Cynthia Martin, Jeannette Webber, Eleanor Jacobs, Kathleen Russell Hardin, Susan Eveler, Mara Kohn and Bonnie Hill – who offered support before, during and after our two years in Russia.

And special thanks to my husband, John McCafferty, for his love, his editing skills, and his ongoing tendency to look for the humor in humanity.

Books that were researched in the writing of this book included *Stalin's Forgotten Zion: Birobidzhan and the Making of a Soviet Jewish Homeland* by Robert Weinberg, *A Century of Ambivalence* by Zvi Gitelman, and *The Russian's World: Life and Language* by Genevra Gerhart.

Contents

For our children –
Lisa, Cynthia, Michael, Susan, Carol, Karen and John

"The beauty of Russia is on the inside."

Introduction

John and I and our children lived in Santa Barbara, California, where he was an English professor at Santa Barbara City College and I was a reporter and editor at the Santa Barbara News-Press. Then for nine years we worked at the Los Angeles Times, he as a copy editor and I as a staff writer in the Travel Section. In 1996, I earned a master's degree from the School for International Training in Brattleboro, Vermont. Then we joined the Peace Corps.

This narrative began as journals I kept during our time in Birobidjan, 1996-1998. The stories are written as I experienced them or as they were told to me. Some of the names have been changed.

Instead of using the Cyrillic alphabet, I have chosen to spell the Russian words phonetically.

1

Suspicious Russians

Our first glimpse of Russia was an unplanned stop at the desolate outpost of Anadyr, on the ragged northeastern edge of the country. The midsize jet plane taking us to Vladivostok had confronted unusually strong headwinds on the flight out of Anchorage, Alaska, and across the Arctic Circle, and landed at the first possible airstrip in order to refuel.

The plane sank beneath a layer of heavy gray clouds and teetered lower and lower over a runway made of concrete blocks. The wheels hit the airstrip with a spine-punishing thump, and its tires thwacked repeatedly at the edge of each block, with the rhythmic regularity of a jackhammer. Finally, the plane shuddered to a stop. I dared not think about the same jackhammer impact of taking off again, hoping only that we would not stay long in Anadyr.

I looked around, alarmed to see abandoned hulls of dented, rusty airplanes and the skeletons of old cars and tanks lining the runway like remnants of a failed civilization. Emaciated dogs roamed between them. On the left was a dust-covered concrete building; on the right, past the derelict planes, there was an infinite open landscape of weeds, thin trees and empty space. As we sat waiting, our seatbelts still buckled, the door of the building opened and a uniformed man appeared. From behind the building, a truck emerged and drove toward the plane.

No one was allowed to disembark, although one airport official in this godforsaken outpost climbed aboard to take a look at us, and waved a sheaf of papers in front of his face as though that explained everything. After what seemed an eternity, the plane was refueled

1

and ready to depart. I tightened my seatbelt, sank into the seat, and willed the plane back into the air. It shuddered along the runway, thumping faster and faster, louder and louder, until it seemed bolts must break loose, panels fly off, everything fall apart – and suddenly the noise abated, the ground tilted, and we were off.

We stopped again for fuel at Magadan. (I suppose Anadyr couldn't spare enough for our needs.) At this notorious home of exile for so many Russians under Stalin's rule, all passengers were ordered off the plane, herded into a cavernous waiting room, and made to stand around while our passports and visas were inspected. The officials shared a common look: unsmiling, wary, suspicious. Though we must have been a curiosity – how many planeloads of Americans could they have seen in their tenure here? – they displayed no interest beyond making sure our papers were in order.

At last, the plane took off for the final leg of the trip: to Vladivostok, a coastal city closed to all foreigners and even non-resident Russians throughout most of the 20th Century, a city romanticized by rhapsodic and nearsighted travel writers as "the San Francisco of the Russian Far East."

The brief glimpses of Magadan and Anadyr stayed with me. The Russians we'd encountered at those two stops did not seem like people I'd want to know better. I thought of intellectuals and dissidents from Moscow, St. Petersburg and elsewhere around the Soviet Union, exiled for life to this dreary, windswept, and unfathomably remote wilderness.

Millions of those exiles died. They starved. They froze. They were worked to death by their guards, who were also trapped in this vast isolation. The Russian Far East is haunted by their ghosts. And it is populated – very sparsely – by their descendants.

The immense area east of Siberia – a third of Russia's land mass, with fewer than six percent of its people – is also populated by adventurers, criminals, and ordinary people whose roots are in

Western Russia and Ukraine, people who migrated to "The Wild East" by their own choice. And there are small remaining groups of indigenous people, ignored, maligned, dismissed. And a scattering of Chinese and Koreans. Until Mikhail Gorbachev instituted the policy of Perestroika and Glasnost (reform and openness) in the mid-1980s, almost every town, factory, camp, almost every barren acre of the Soviet Union's eastern frontier, was off-limits to foreigners.

All John and I were told initially about our destination was that the Peace Corps would send us to a college or university somewhere in the Russian Far East. Seven time zones east of Moscow. Three days by train east of Siberia. Remote. "Beyond Siberia" remote. Seldom visited by tourists, seldom studied by scholars. We found precious little information to prepare us for our adventure.

In the middle of our lives, children grown, John and I had left the Southern California work force and signed up for two years in the Peace Corps. We wanted to live and work in a different culture. That was our official answer when people asked: "Why in the world do you want to take two years out of your lives at this stage?"

We loved each other, and we were happy in our second marriage, but we wanted more. We wanted to be latter-day explorers.

John said he wanted to make up for lost time. He craved the adventures he'd given up by marrying at age 19 and spending the next twenty years getting through college, raising four children, teaching English, and living with a wife who didn't enjoy traveling.

I wanted – what did I want? I also had married young (age 17), had three grown children and a good career. Now I wanted something else, something beyond the loose connection I had with my distant father and far-flung children, beyond the career and adventurous vacations.

I admired people who at this stage in life turned to politics or service to others or advancement in their field. But for myself – I was embarrassed to say it out loud, because it sounded like a cliché, or a case of arrested development – I was looking for meaning. I was looking for something I hadn't found along the career track, or in what seemed to me like our increasingly consumerist society, or in my own small efforts as one of millions who join causes to make the world a better place. I longed to go to a distant end of the earth where life might be simpler, issues less complex, my sense of purpose clearer. Maybe I also wanted to escape.

Within weeks, Peace Corps officials called, inviting us to go to Russia. They didn't specifically tell us at the time, but they had received a request from Birobidjan (sometimes spelled Birobidzhan, and pronounced Beer-a-bid-JOHN), in the Jewish Autonomous Region, for a married couple with master's degrees to teach at the Birobidjan Pedagogical Institute.

Knowing we were headed for Russia, we learned the Cyrillic alphabet and practiced listening to Russian language tapes. We said "*spokoinoi nochi*" instead of "good night." We learned how to say, "Where is the metro station?" and "Is there a good restaurant near the hotel?" although we never had a chance to use either phrase in the Russian Far East.

Five days before our departure date, the phone rang. John answered.

"Hi! This is Stacy Cavanaugh from the Russia Desk at Peace Corps," said an overly cheerful voice. "How are you two doing?"

"Oh-oh," John said. "Why do I think there's a problem?"

"What is it? Who is it?" I asked anxiously.

"Peace Corps," he said.

"It's not a *huge* problem," she said. "But your group will not be going to Russia right away." She let that sink in and then added, "There's a little problem with visas."

We were displaced. Tenants were ready to move into our house in Santa Barbara. Where would we go? When would we know?

"We're working on it," Stacy said.

It seemed that we had the choice then to just say we couldn't handle the uncertainty, and to take our names off the Russia list, or we could stand by to see what developed.

We stood by. We did the hardest thing for us to do – nothing. We were impatient Americans. We didn't like waiting, not knowing in what direction to face. We weren't used to having other people in control of our lives.

Three days later, Stacy called again. She said the Peace Corps had decided that all the new volunteers for Russia – 45 for the Russian Far East and 30 for Western Russia – would begin training in the states.

The summer of 1996 was election time in Russia, and no Russian bureaucrat knew whether Boris Yeltsin would continue as president, or which way the political winds would blow, so no one would take the risk of authorizing entry visas for seventy-five American volunteers. There were still plenty of leftover Communists in the Russian bureaucracy who regularly accused Peace Corps of being a spy operation. But the Peace Corps optimistically assumed our visas would eventually be approved. A college campus was found in a remote corner of West Virginia where we could train for a low midsummer price.

Surrounded by rolling hills and thick forests, and bypassed by the nearest state highway, the town of Athens consisted of one small college (Concord College), a few houses with swings hanging from front yard trees and vegetable gardens in the rear, a white wooden church topped by a small cross, gas station, grocery store, school bus stop and – hidden away down a winding road through the woods – a bar called the Last Resort.

As difficult as it was to get entry visas into Russia, Peace Corps found it surprisingly easy to obtain exit visas for the Russian language teachers to come to us. And so it was that 14 Russian women won a surprise trip to the United States, where none of them had ever been before. Our exposure to Russian culture began with their reaction to us.

The Russians ranged in age from 24 to 50. Dark-haired Natasha Ivanova and her best friend, blonde Katya Kostina, from Vladivostok, were beautiful women, each with a husband and son at home. These two would never readjust to Russia after their immersion in American culture. Galina Volkova, the excitable and accident-prone wife of a Vladivostok scientist, and Irina Strobykina, a university dean, cajoled and coddled the volunteers in their language classes. The pretty ones were flirtatious and the stout ones were warm and motherly. Some of the younger women wore black mascara and bright red lipstick; several had dyed or bleached their hair. Gold teeth were common – not really gold, of course, but a yellow metal alloy.

Of the fourteen, Vera Borisovna Vyalkova, in her late thirties, looked the sternest. She came from the town of Ussuriisk, north of Vladivostok. Her lips, without a trace of lipstick, were drawn into a tight line, and she stared myopically from behind round thick glasses that tended to slide down and that she constantly pushed back into place. Her dark hair was severely cut, short and straight. Wearing a simple blouse and skirt over her thin frame, she stood stiffly at attention when she was introduced to our group. I felt intimidated by her severity, but I was assigned to her language class. This was my great good fortune: My true appreciation of Russia began with getting to know Vera. Sternness was her cover for uncertainty; a barbed wit disguised her sensitive Russian soul.

How strange it was for the Russians to land in America. We Americans were getting ten weeks of intensive training to learn how to cope with Russia. They got not a single day of training before coming to us.

Some of them had never been inside a restaurant, even in Russia.

"To my mind," Vera Borisovna explained, "restaurants are for the bureaucrats and the decadent newly rich."

Vera, in her Russian accent overlaid with a British accent, told me about her first night in America.

"They (Peace Corps trainers) met us at the airport in Washington, D.C., took us to a hotel, and registered our names. Then we all walked to a small restaurant for supper. The Americans sat at separate tables from us, so we found it quite impossible to ask them questions about what to do. I am still embarrassed that we didn't know about tipping. The woman who served us our supper was the first person in America to be kind to us, and we left her nothing."

By the time the Russians were introduced to our group, a week later, several of them were wearing new American clothes – sandals, T-shirts, blue jeans. Before arriving at the training site in Athens, they had been given their first American paycheck (with a hefty increase over what the Peace Corps paid them in Russia) and they'd been on a shopping expedition to an American mall.

"Is new watch," Katya said proudly, extending her arm so everyone could see. "Big watch!"

"American jeans!" said Irina. "Kmart style!"

Galina bought an American calendar and wondered why it showed Sunday at the beginning of the week when we called it "the weekend."

Vera did not shop. She was saving her money for the trip of a lifetime – to England, where she had never been.

"I am in love with all things English," she told John and me, in her precise Russian-British accent and her brisk, flowery manner of speaking.

The Russians had also witnessed the Fourth of July celebration in the nation's capital, toured the White House and the halls of Congress, and had other travel adventures to their credit.

After she was safely back home in her apartment in Vladivostok, Galina recollected the most frightening moment of her trip to America: In Washington, she had ventured from the hotel by herself and become hopelessly lost. She walked and walked, ever deeper into the seedy part of the city, and grew increasingly frightened and hysterical. No one offered to help her; she was afraid to approach anyone.

Finally, she saw a uniformed policeman, the first time in her life she had ever encountered a black man, and in great confusion mingled with relief, she planned to say: "Help me! Help me!"

"I ran to him and cried, 'Take me! Take me!'" Galina said. "Thanks God, he was a kind boy!"

On our isolated mountain campus, during the long, hot month of July, there was a problem with the fire alarm in the dormitory.

A week after we arrived, the alarm went off at two in the morning, and seventy-five sleepy volunteers and our American and Russian trainers stumbled out of bed and trooped down the stairs and outdoors. A half-hour later we were all allowed to file back inside and go to bed.

Two nights later, the alarm sounded again, around three-thirty in the morning. This time some of us grabbed pillows and stepped into shoes before trudging outside.

The next week, in the middle of the night, it happened a third time. Still, we all filed out again, grumbling, shaking our heads.

The following winter, John and I were sitting in our kitchen in Birobidjan, talking with Vera. We asked her what had been her main impression of America.

"That would be the fire alarm incident," she said.

She and the other Russians were amazed at our compliance.

"Such an exercise in my country would result in a private tutorial in Russian profanity," Vera said. "But not a single American person expressed scorn and indignation. In Russia, we would wake up, and if we smelled no smoke we would return to our beds in a minute."

I tried to explain. "From kindergarten on, Americans are drilled to respect fire alarms, no matter what," I said. "It is just not in us to defy them."

"It is not respect," she countered. (Vera would invariably correct us, even when she was agreeing with us.) "In Russia, we are terrified of the law, but whenever possible we defy it.

"In America, you are free and uninhibited, but you keep to the rules."

2

'The Back of Beyond'

The Peace Corps decided on a deadline: If our Russia visas didn't come through by August 5, our training group would be dispersed to other countries. On August 4, Russia granted us one-year visas.

Jeff Murdock, the training director, called a meeting in the college dining hall when the news came, and announced that visas and plane tickets were on the way. A huge surge of energy swept the room; people cheered, applauded and hugged each other. Three days later, we left West Virginia.

Separated into two groups, we loaded our mountains of luggage into two trucks and climbed aboard two buses – Russian Far East volunteers on one bus and Western Russia volunteers on the other. Until that moment, everyone vaguely knew that we were headed in separate directions, but not until then was the split so clear. Many of these people, we would never see again. I looked around at the others on our bus. They ranged in age from 22 to 68; many were new college graduates; 35 were single, and there were five married couples, including John and me.

The two groups had trained together for five weeks. Friendships had formed, and romances had flourished, fed as they were by the allure of temporariness and intensified by the anticipated separation, now taking place.

"The five major couples are all going in opposite directions," according to Amy Dickerson, a warmhearted red-haired woman in the seat behind us, who was in tears, having just said goodbye to her new boyfriend.

Our children were their ages. John and I speculated what being a "major couple" might mean in their generation. Promises? Seriousness of purpose? Consummated sex?

While we were in Athens, volunteers had discovered the funky Last Resort bar. It was a rundown, rowdy hideaway deep in the woods, but the beer was cold and the music was loud, and it absolutely was the only place to go drinking and dancing for miles around. Volunteers and Russians alike crowded in with the locals on Friday and Saturday nights. Natasha, Katya, Vera and a few of the other Russians learned some things about American hillbilly culture by going to the Last Resort.

One night, there was a drunken brawl right in front of their table.

"A customer hit a girl and someone started hitting him, and he found himself by the feet of the customers, and they started kicking," Vera said. "They took him by the scruff of the neck and kicked him out of the bar."

She took a deep drag of her cigarette before concluding: "And so, well, then he started shooting."

"You had an American travel adventure," John said.

"Not an American travel adventure," Vera said. "An American cultural peculiarity."

Vera was very specific in her observations, and furthermore, she liked nothing better than verbal sparring.

It was at the Last Resort that Amy, heading for Vladivostok, fell in love with the man heading for Moscow, and Natasha fell in love with Jeff, the training director, and a feisty woman from Moscow got involved with a lawyer who, in his midlife crisis, had dropped out to join the Peace Corps. Life would never be quite the same after Athens. Couples cried and hugged, promising to remember each other, promising to write.

One of the separating couples was Lisa Cross and Brian Foster, she with wavy brown hair and dark flashing eyes, he with long golden curls and broad shoulders and a long slender body.

Vera Borisovna, whose Russian roommate was inconsolably homesick and wanted only to be left alone to cry, had befriended the two lovers. The gossip was that Brian was attracted to Lisa's beauty, and to Vera's intelligence. The three of them were often together, sometimes sitting and talking animatedly at their own little table in a corner of the Last Resort.

But Vera had distanced herself from Brian and Lisa when the red tent appeared. The tent had made Lisa and Brian the talk of the training.

Lisa's roommate, Michelle Kraviec, objected to repeatedly being locked out of their cramped dormitory quarters so Lisa and Brian could "have some privacy."

"Basically, they wanted to have sex," Michelle said. "I had no objections to that. They're of age. Who cares? But I got tired of being locked out of my own room."

Lisa and Brian suggested that Michelle move in with Brian's roommate, Adam, but Michelle and Adam weren't interested. The trainers overheard that argument and gave notice that anybody who started swapping roommates would be ordered to pack up and go home.

The next afternoon, Brian slipped away from training and hitchhiked to a shopping mall a few miles away. When he returned, he and Lisa told Michelle they had solved the problem.

That night, the lovers pitched a new red two-person tent on the lawn near the dorm, at the edge of the campus. "Don't ask, don't tell" was the policy regarding the tent. It became known as the "sex tent." It was where Lisa and Brian went when they wanted their privacy. It was rumored they also subleased the tent from time to time.

But Brian was heading for Moscow, Lisa for Vladivostok. They were the last couple still outside the buses, kissing passionately, whispering, and stroking each other's long hair, finally letting go and boarding their respective buses as the drivers revved their engines.

Until the last minute, a few of the Russian women stood on the grass smoking cigarettes, then they, too, reluctantly boarded. Vera took one last drag on her Marlboro and climbed aboard our bus. She took the seat in front of us. And she fretted about Lisa.

"She has a tendency to lose herself in drink," Vera said. "I worry about her being in a Russian village. I worry about her drinking with tractor drivers."

Before the first year of our service was over, Brian had fallen in love with a Russian woman and then, growing tired of her, he quit the Peace Corps and moved to Prague where he fell in love with a Czech woman. As for Lisa, in the Russian Far East, life breezed along: she taught village children by day, and partied with new Russian friends by night. But her friendship with Vera was another story.

We bused from Athens to Dulles International Airport and boarded a plane for Seattle where we spent a short night, then by numbing degrees on to Vladivostok – via Anchorage, Anadyr, Magadan – each stop confirming the sense that we were going ever deeper into the farthest corner of the world.

The Peace Corps first came to Russia in 1993, and established its office in Vladivostok, a formerly closed city, a Russian naval port that had been off-limits to foreigners and even to non-resident Russians. Before our group had come two waves of business volunteers – a failed experiment, pairing idealistic American business volunteers with corrupt or befuddled Russian businessmen – and one wave of English teachers.

At the Vladivostok airport, our luggage appeared from under rubber flaps onto a small carousel. Bags circled once and fell off as more luggage piled up behind them.

We got through customs eventually and wandered half-asleep into the sultry, rainy August night. Under the dim lights of the parking lot, we piled onto buses. Our luggage was jammed into the back of a big square truck, covered with a tarp and lashed down with ropes. We followed the luggage along increasingly bumpy roads up the coastline to the Solnechnui Sanitorium – the Sunshine Resort.

This was a dank, old hotel building, three stories high, surrounded by mud and weeds and croaking frogs. The place was rank with the wet-dust smell of mildew. We could hear mice scurrying about.

The hotel had once been a health spa, or sanitorium, one of many such accommodations that flourished throughout Russia in the days of Communism – places where bureaucrats went to relax, enjoy the sun, be massaged, eat well, and generally enjoy the perks of office. By the time our group arrived, it had sunk almost to the point of being uninhabitable. Set amid dense thickets and swampy earth, the Sunshine Resort was anything but.

Training resumed.

A few doubts set in. This part of Russia was extraordinarily remote. Yes, here was natural beauty – windswept ocean, rocky cliffs, vast miles of wilderness. But here also were brutally cold winters, corrupt officials light years away from Moscow and accountability, wild dogs and mosquitoes, a sense of isolation, of being lost in a place that wasn't supposed to be inhabited by humans.

The day after we arrived, a heavy rain turned the dirt road into a river of mud. Potholes became small lakes; chunks of asphalt became stepping stones.

People said there was a kiosk not too far away that sold candy, soft drinks, beer and pretzels, but which sold out of almost everything as soon as our group heard of its existence. John and I ventured outside when the rain let up and made our way along the muddy road. Carefully walking toward us was a tall and strikingly beautiful girl under a red umbrella. She wore a bright red dress and red shoes with high heels. Although her shapely long legs were spattered with mud, her blond hair was perfectly curled, her lipstick and mascara freshly applied. The sight of her cheered us immensely.

As the girl passed by, she couldn't resist glancing at John, a tall, broad-shouldered man with a well-trimmed beard and wearing a windbreaker; he was so obviously not Russian. She blushed and wobbled on the uneven path when she caught his eye and he smiled at her.

A small contingent of our predecessors visited us at the Hotel Sunny. They were an interesting group, these Peace Corps volunteers who had already been in the Russian Far East for a year.

They were jolly, scruffily dressed, and condescending, as though they had seen some blueprint that said they were survivors and we probably wouldn't be. I wondered if the group before them greeted them with the same attitude. I wondered, too, if our group would settle into a similar state of assumed superiority, and whether cloaking one's self in a groupy machismo was a necessary ingredient of survival. And these were the volunteers living near the big city, not the ones sent to remote outposts! We gleaned from them answers to some of our questions and we, in our naiveté, fed their appetite for admiration.

Clouds of mosquitoes rose as day turned to dusk. In the middle of the night, a dog began to howl. At five in the morning, we were awakened by a car radio. Below our window, a burly young man with a butch haircut drank a beer as two girls stumbled around him, laughing, in a halting, drunken dance.

The next day, training director Jeff Murdock issued a stern warning to Lisa. She had slipped away the day before and disappeared into the bars of Vladivostok where she was last seen with a pair of Russian sailors. Fortunately, Lisa returned safe and sound, having slipped back in sometime before dawn, while the trainers spent hours through the night searching for her. Lisa said she didn't know there was a curfew, and she resented being scolded in public. But she promised it wouldn't happen again.

After three days at the Hotel Sunny, we bused out to Ussuriisk, two hours north of Vladivostok. We met our "host families," Russians who agreed to house and feed us for the rest of the training. Now we were in Vera's territory; Vera was an English professor at the Ussuriisk Pedagogical Institute. She lived with her mother, a retired teacher, and "Granny," her beloved elderly grandmother.

We settled back into the training routine. Four hours a day of Russian language classes, and another four hours of work and cross-cultural training.

Our group would soon be dispersed in the widest radius and at the greatest cost of any Peace Corps program anywhere in the world because the Russian Far East is so vast. Out here, Moscow seemed a world away.

Vera Borisovna calls the Russian Far East "the back of beyond." Isolated, unknown, primeval – it's a place where, occasionally, tigers can still be seen in the wilderness, where ever fewer numbers of indigenous people cling to their traditions, where there remain thousands of Russians who have never met a foreigner. Communist cities, long closed to outsiders, opened their doors to us, just a crack, and their gatekeepers looked suspiciously at our passports and visas.

Our "host mother," Nadezhda, a widow, and her son, Andrei, lived at the edge of Ussuriisk, a 45-minute bus ride away from the college where we trained. Bus Number Nine ground along the road, swaying this way and that in a futile effort to avoid potholes. There seemed to be no laws regarding people walking on the side of the road or trying to cross it. Traffic did not stop, or even slow down for them.

"Pedestrians aren't protected," Tanya, a Peace Corps volunteer in Ussuriisk, said. "On the contrary, drivers seem to aim for them."

"I would be willing to ride a bicycle, but it is infringed with danger in Ussuriisk because of careless and reckless drivers," Vera said. She was especially critical of "the newly rich," those Russians who managed to acquire inordinate amounts of money after Perestroika, when everyone else was struggling. They invariably drove expensive cars imported from Japan or the United States.

"Our newly rich drivers are exceedingly inaccurate," she said. "You may see as evidence the corpses of cats along the road."

The first day John and I took the bus into Ussuriisk, we got off at the wrong place, lost our way and wandered for an hour, through dusty streets and past crumbling buildings, under the glare of the hot August sun. It seemed as though nothing was done to keep anything in repair. Buildings were scabby and cracked, broken concrete and asphalt lined the streets, bus stops were rusty shells. In front of every apartment building, a few old women sat on benches. Their conversations ebbed as we walked by. Some gave us toothless smiles when we said hello to them, others turned away.

In the classroom, flies buzzed in lazy circles near the ceiling. In Nadezhda's apartment, our bedroom was on the sunny side of the building and sometimes we felt like bugs trapped in a jar. There were no screens on the windows and we were covered with mosquito bites.

Galina Volkova, our Russian language teacher during our first week in Ussuriisk, spoke some English, but not enough to explain anything, and she introduced material that we had no way of comprehending. Then after loudly drilling us for a few minutes, she gave a little laugh and moved to another activity. It was very frustrating. But she was jolly and kind. I missed Vera.

17

For her part, Vera, with a doctorate in linguistics, was fascinated by the English language. She was especially intrigued by the versatility of English, such as using a noun as a verb.

"Do you think it will storm today?" John had asked her.

"'Storm' as a verb?" she said. "In Russian, such possibilities of conversion do not exist, frankly speaking."

Our host mother was a retired hat maker who supplemented her income by working as night watchwoman at a nearby factory. Nadezhda was built like a short fireplug and possessed of unstoppable energy and irrepressible optimism. Her shiftless son, Andrei, drank huge quantities of vodka and spent most of his time repairing a rusty hulk of a car that he hoped someday to be able to drive. At first, we thought Andrei spoke no English. Nadezhda knew three English words: bye-bye, okay and dollar. They had a cat which they called, simply, *Koshka* (female cat).

One of the host families lived in an apartment building with no running water. In its five years of existence, it had never had running water. But housing was in such short supply that people lived there anyway. Everyone in the family had to haul water from an outside faucet up to their fourth-floor flat whenever they came in.

Michelle had a host sister with a jealous boyfriend who circled the apartment by the hour to make sure she didn't go out.

Mike Hinken's host mother was a television newscaster. The first time we met her, a bleached blonde with bright red lipstick, she was wearing skin-tight pink shorts, a halter top and tall platform sandals.

"You win for the sexiest host mother," John told Mike, a conservative young man from Illinois.

"She's really nice though," Mike said. "She even irons my underwear."

One Saturday, Nadezhda took us by bus five miles into the countryside to her *dacha*. Her large plot of land sloped to the south and lay baking under the August sun. Near the top was a little blue house, about ten feet long and eight feet wide, minimally constructed and uninsulated, like a child's playhouse. Cozy and worn. An ancient couch filled half the space. Nadezhda said when she was too tired to go home, she would sometimes spend the night there. Gardening tools stood in a corner; onions and corn were laid out to dry for seed. The surrounding garden, mostly harvested, had yielded its first corn and its last raspberries.

Nadezhda changed into an old dress and muddy shoes, then pumped water into a bucket and mopped the cabin floor with a rag, chuckling as she worked, chatting to us in Russian. We nodded in agreement though we had no idea what she was talking about.

We strolled around the garden, watching, trying to help, as she picked cucumbers and eggplant, one misshapen tomato and another half-eaten by bugs or worms, and a few ears of still-green corn. The year's harvest was not very good, she said. Too much rain too soon, then hot and dry for too long. She pulled a few weeds, filled a sprinkling can several times and wet down some of the plants, stuffed the vegetables into a burlap sack, took off her gardening shoes and washed her feet under the pump, stepped into her everyday shoes, slung the sack over her shoulder – no, John could not carry it for her, he was tired, she declared – and led us back to the bus stop.

Late one night, in the apartment, when Nadezhda was feeling restless, she knocked on our bedroom door just as we were getting ready to sleep.

"*Moshna*?" she said, smiling. (May I?)

"*Konyechno*," I said. (Of course.) Whatever it was, how could we object?

There was a refrigerator in our bedroom that seemed to be fully stocked, loaded to the far corners, mainly with packages of food from the *dacha*. Nadezhda took everything out of the refrigerator. She said she wanted to move it to another room, but, of course, first she had to empty it.

When everything was out of the refrigerator, she called Andrei to help her move it. But Andrei had crept out of the apartment while she worked. She absolutely would not hear of having us help her move it. Practically in tears, she began reloading the refrigerator. Defeated in her purpose, she finally allowed us to help her put everything away again.

Another night, at 10 o'clock, the indefatigable Nadezhda began grinding three bucketfuls of yellow currants for juice. Andrei was scrubbing out the sink.

On the rare occasions when Andrei worked alongside his mother, we knew he was guilty of something, doing penance. His sister, Nadezhda made sure we understood, was a successful doctor in the port city of Nahodka, while Andrei – well, we could see for ourselves, she would shrug. Andrei would grow silent. Sometimes he was able to quietly slip out the door while she explained to us how shiftless and worthless he was. But other times, like this one, he would be forced to work until her dark mood lifted.

We closed our door and tried to sleep.

3

People Sent Away

Many of Nadezhda's neighbors used to work in the factory where she was the night watchwoman. Like most factories in the Russian Far East since Perestroika, it no longer produced anything. It had been turned into a scrap metal warehouse. Most of the neighbors were unemployed. Nadezhda, who worked three overnight shifts a week, would come home just about the time we left for the training center.

On other mornings, Nadezhda prepared breakfast for us, usually leftovers from the dinner we had eaten the night before: fish and pickles or wieners and cabbage salad or potatoes and fried onions. When she was at work, we could make our own breakfast: boiled eggs, when there was gas to light the stove (utilities often disappeared for hours at a time, sometimes days), bread and cheese. We ate at the small kitchen table which had benches attached to both sides. Nadezhda kept a hot plate handy for when the gas went off. Electrical power was fairly reliable.

With us, Nadezhda would laugh and bustle about, a dynamo of jolly energy. Andrei was intimidated by her. His sister, the doctor, had a husband and two children whose pictures were displayed on top of the television set. But Andrei, after a short-lived marriage, was divorced and unemployed.

Both mother and son seemed to genuinely enjoy helping us work on our Russian, even when we were too tired to make any sense of their coaching. The more trouble we had understanding something Nadezhda was saying, the louder she would say it, until she heaved herself back into her chair, yelling, laughing, and gasping for air.

Andrei was more helpful. Once he got used to our presence, he let us know that he had learned a few English words in school. He liked drawing pictures for us. Stick figures. And telling us the Russian words to go with them. "Daughter – *Doch*." "Woman – *Jenshina*." "Car – *Machina*." "Money – *Dengi*." He had a daughter, age seven, and a girlfriend, Olga, who wanted to marry him, which he didn't want to do, and the big old car that he wanted us to see. Time and again, he promised to come and visit us when we moved away, and when he got his car fixed. He paid rent for a tin shed a mile away where he kept his car.

Some nights, Nadezhda came into our room to talk. She would kneel on the floor, with us propped side by side on the fold-out couch which was our bed, where we sat to do our homework and prepare lessons for the next day. (By this time in training, we were teaching English to small classes of college students.)

These talks with Nadezhda gave us a chance to practice our Russian. We would talk about what time to have breakfast, our schedule for the next day, whether it might rain, was supper adequate, and anything else the three of us could think of. These were funny talks, full of gestures, noise, laughter. One evening, she described her sister's shopping binge at the Ussuriisk Chinese market, and concluded, "Bye-bye, *dengi*, bye-bye!" which, by the end of a long and fractured conversation, struck all three of us as hilarious.

One night, we got home from training around 7:30. Nadezhda was working the night shift. Something was propped in front of the door, so that even after unlocking it, we had to push our way in. We hit a wall of noise. Not the big-orchestra Dvorak or Tchaikovsky records Nadezhda liked to play, but heavy metallic rock, at maximum decibel, bouncing-off-the-walls, reverberating-in-the-chest loud.

John headed for the kitchen where we could see Andrei and three other men sitting around the table, and I headed straight through the living room, passing by the couch where a man and a woman were locked in an oblivious embrace. The music blasted from the radio and a game show blared from the television set. I reached for the closed door, anticipating the relative sanctity of our tiny bedroom.

I heard John yelling, then the music dimmed a little, and he came toward me. Andrei toppled out of the kitchen behind him. Our bedroom door was locked. I pounded on it. There were at least four drunken men in the apartment, and we couldn't get into our bedroom. I stood by the locked door, anxious and displaced.

"Moment," Andrei said, putting his hand out as though to protect the door from me. "Moment, *poshalusta*" (please).

"I want to get in!" I cried.

"Andrei," John said, with more patience than I had. "Andrei, open the door."

"Moment, moment, *tovarish*" (comrade), Andrei mumbled. He took one of our hands in each of his, and tried to pull us away from the bedroom door, pushing me toward one living room chair and John toward the other. The couple on the couch sat up and straightened their clothes. The woman patted her hair and the man grinned at us. I kept saying I wanted to get into the bedroom. If it hadn't been a six-story climb up the stairs to get to the apartment, and we hadn't been so tired, and if there had been someplace – anyplace – for us to go instead, we probably would have gone there.

Finally, we heard shuffling and scraping, and the bedroom door opened. A woman stumbled out, tucking in her blouse, her hair a wild tangle, her purse slung over one arm. She barely looked at us, or at the pair on the couch, or at the tall, gaunt, red-faced man coming out of the bedroom behind her. They headed for the front door, fumbled with the lock, and, kicking Nadezhda's cat out of the way, stumbled toward the stairs.

23

We heard a crash in the kitchen. I ran into the bedroom and closed the door behind me; John and Andrei headed for the kitchen.

I dropped our books on the floor, tucked my wallet behind the fold-out couch, just in case, and opened the door onto the scabby little concrete balcony. The bedroom smelled of sweat and sex. One plaid sock lay in a little heap by the couch. I stood and stared vacantly at the concrete block building across the way. A man came out onto a balcony, scratching his bare stomach. He lit a cigarette.

Suddenly I realized the apartment was quiet. The bedroom door opened.

"Come and see," John said.

Reluctantly, I followed him to the kitchen. A gray-haired man lay slumped under the table, his head resting sideways on the bench. Andrei sat on the bench opposite him, his hand wrapped around a shot glass.

"*Smishno*" (funny), Andrei said, an irrepressible grin playing on his face. "*Ochen smishno*" (very funny).

The man under the table was Andrei's former boss, the man he had worked for the last time they both had jobs. They were having a party to celebrate something. We never learned what. A birthday, maybe. Or a new job.

The boss stirred, moaned. He flopped over, rose to his knees, and managed to crawl out from under the table. Then he heaved himself up to the bench, curled his fist around an empty shot glass and slammed it on the table.

"*Vodka!*" he said.

Andrei grabbed the vodka bottle and turned it upside down. Not a drop left. The gray-haired man tipped to one side and passed out again, on the bench this time, his head against the wall. The two other men and the couple on the couch had slipped out of the apartment. It was decided to let "The Boss" sleep it off where he was. He was already snoring.

Andrei put his finger to his lips and made a shushing sound. He shook his head back and forth, willing us to understand. *"Nyet, Momma. Shhhh. Nyet, Momma."* We got the message: Don't tell Mama.

The next morning, we woke up to the sound of thumping and banging and Nadezhda yelling at Andrei. We didn't have to keep his drunken party a secret. "The Boss" was still asleep on the bench. Nadezhda was chasing Andrei around the apartment, hitting at him with her short-handled broom. When we emerged from the bedroom, momentarily distracting Nadezhda, Andrei took the opportunity to unbolt the door and flee. We didn't see him again for a week. The man under the table stumbled away, too. As he left the apartment, *Koshka* slipped in, purring.

Crystal clear skies and perfectly comfortable weather came to Ussuriisk.

Vera said the Russians call this time of year *"Baba Leta,"* which means "old woman's summer." She explained: "This compares to the last blooming of a woman's beauty." Vera's birthday is during this season. "The trees, forest and taiga are colorful, the sky is transparent and crystal," she said. "This is the time of my birth, and so my favorite season."

Ussuriisk celebrated its 130th anniversary as a city. Helicopters dropped leaflets and roses, girls recited poetry from a large stage erected on the main square, young male dancers performed those fantastic Russian dances in which they kick one foot forward while dropping to the floor balanced on the other. A group of women with gold teeth sang loudly into a blaring microphone (we had to hold our hands over our ears as the high notes screeched like throbbing sirens). An old war veteran with medals halfway down his jacket spoke for some minutes and the crowd drifted away. Seven couples exchanged wedding vows, lined up in front of a local official.

John taught a class on poetry to Russian students of English, with Vera, Natasha Ivanova and Galina Volkova observing him. They were very impressed with his presentation on imagery and metaphor.

"You moved my soul," the beautiful Natasha said, stroking his arm. "Oh, John, I wish you had been my teacher." She was so appreciative and cozily familiar, I could easily understand how Jeff, the Peace Corps trainer, could become infatuated with her.

Vera wrote a haiku, along with the students. Hers compared a butterfly's wings to the sweet smell of iris blossoms.

Near the end of training, Andrei decided that he and we should drink together. He poured cognac into three jelly glasses, offered a toast, and before we had raised ours to our lips, he had swallowed his in a single gulp, then poured another. He made toast after toast whether we joined him or not.

In the morning, before Nadezhda returned from her overnight factory shift, he turned up the radio to full volume. Shouting over the thudding beat of the music, he announced, "Hard rock!"

That night, Andrei argued with John over some music John was trying to tape for a lesson. Andrei reached out and pushed buttons on the tape recorder. John, muttering to himself, popped out the tape, came into the bedroom and closed the door. Soon Andrei knocked on the door, peeked in, and asked to borrow the English-Russian dictionary. I handed it to him and he backed out, carefully closing the door behind him.

Twenty minutes later, he returned, and said, "Am I disturbance you?" Then he enjoyed trying out the English variations on the Russian word he had looked up: "Derange, disrupt, bother, annoy?"

We resisted being drawn into another "evening with Andrei," and finally he grew tired and left the room. A few minutes later he returned, asking if he could go through our room to have a cigarette on the balcony. "Am I disturbance you?" he said again, smiling.

The following night, to our relief, he appeared briefly and announced, "I sleep Olga today night." Peace at last.

John and I did not know until near the end of our ten weeks of training that we would have the privilege of being the first Peace Corps volunteers to go to the Jewish Autonomous Region – which was never quite autonomous and never securely Jewish. At the Birobidjan Pedagogical Institute, we would be the first Americans, even the first native speakers of English, many of our students had ever met.

We set about trying to find out something about this place that was to be our home for two years. There wasn't much information available, and after we got there we were relieved to find that the starkest description of Birobidjan we had found was an exaggeration. A writer named Ben-Ami, in "Between Hammer and Sickle," described it in 1982 as a "ghost town," from which all traces of Jewish culture, other than Yiddish street signs, were "blown away by the cold Siberian wind." Writers have since repeated this conclusion. They didn't look closely enough.

What we found instead was a town of about 60,000, including a few thousand Jews – among them a newspaper publisher, a bartender, a baker, city officials, and some of our students and friends. We also found a small and growing reconstruction of Jewish culture.

Of the hundreds of Jews who settled here when the autonomous region was first established, many came willingly. They were oppressed by poverty or discrimination in their homeland, but they envisioned a better life than they had left behind. In a latter-day way, I identified with them: They had come here by choice, most were more political than religious; they were looking for a brand new start.

Decades of tragedy and terror followed those promising beginnings. The land was harsh and the terror of law even harsher. For half-a-century, any form of religious activity was stifled. But by the time we came, in 1996, middle-aged Birobidjan Jews and their children were busy studying the Torah, many for the first time in their lives, struggling to learn and practice the rules and rituals of their ancestors. The street signs were still in both Russian and Yiddish, the main street being named for world-renowned Yiddish writer Shalom Aleichem. A wooden house on a side street had been made into a makeshift synagogue and plans were being developed to build a new synagogue. About ten percent of the students at the college claimed a Jewish heritage.

It was on March 28, 1928, that the Soviet government decreed Birobidjan was "to be given over exclusively to the colonization of Jews."

The historic document declared that the "Soviet policy in regard to nations had as its purpose the placing of all hitherto suppressed minorities on a sound foundation. So in regard to Jews, the government, after ensuring for the Jews the right to work in field and factory, as well as political equality, and the opportunity for education, did not rest satisfied, but decided to ordain a new phase in the solution of the Jewish problem."

What Stalin called "the Jewish problem" was multi-faceted. The Jewish community was plagued by anti-Semitism, grinding poverty, lack of opportunities and high unemployment. Jews and Russians resisted the integration of Jews into Soviet society. The adherents of both Zionism and Judaism were considered a threat by the Soviets. The search was on for a place to resettle the Jews.

The document promised: "This meant making available to the Jews land upon which they might become an independent people; land upon which to develop their own state, and efficient government, and an indigenous culture; a territory large enough to furnish all necessities to a numerous population."

Historians cited two reasons for the placement of the Zionist settlement in this far corner of Russia: fertile soil, and, except for a few Kazakhs and Tungus, the lack of an indigenous population. Creating a human buffer zone on the long-disputed Russia-China border was never officially stated as a reason for the settlement. However, having bought the region from the Chinese in 1858, Russia had no secure hold on the land, and Chinese and Korean nomads were gradually moving in, along with Ukrainians and Russians who had moved to the region around the turn of the Twentieth Century.

"The settlement of the area with trustworthy and responsible people is a basic requirement in strengthening the defenses of our Far Eastern frontier," Semen M. Dimanshtein, a Soviet spokesman, was quoted as saying.

Jews in Western Russia and Ukraine were told that if they settled Birobidjan, they would be pioneers in a "Jewish republic," a "homeland of their own," or as one enthusiastic Jewish woman imagined it, "the Land of Israel in our own country."

Birobidjan was envisioned by some as a homeland not only for Soviet Jews, but for other Jews as well. In New York, IKOR (Organization for Jewish Colonization in the Soviet Union), a Communist organization, described Birobidjan as an opportunity for Jews "to realize their 2,000-year-old dream of becoming a nation."

Birobidjan was to be a center of Jewish culture with Yiddish as the official language. Postmarks and street signs were in Yiddish. The Shalom Aleichem library built up a collection of Yiddish works. By one account, the Soviets planned for 60,000 Jews to migrate there in the first year.

But the Jewish settlers came slowly, not by the thousands but by the hundreds, and many soon left. The Jews who had farmed in western Russia and Ukraine found a very different kind of soil in this isolated region. Far being from a promised land, the reality of Birobidjan consisted of a harsh climate, swamps, blood-sucking insects, heavy rains, and anthrax, a disease that killed hundreds of their horses. Of the 654 Jewish settlers who arrived in 1928 in the spring, 325 remained by the first of October.

Gradually, migration increased. A famine hit western Russia. Hitler rose to power. Some people were forced to relocate to the Far East, others were driven there by the hope for a better life. By 1933, there were 8,200 Jews in the autonomous region, though even at that time they were just 20 percent of its total population.

The government proclaimed: "For the first time in the history of the Jewish people, its burning desire for the creation of a homeland of its own, for the achievement of its own national statehood, has been fulfilled."

The rhetoric impressed foreign audiences who mobilized financial assistance. An IKOR leader wrote: "The Jewish masses are getting a large and beautiful land. They will become its masters and use their language in it. The Jewish people will be members of the great family of nations building a new world for themselves, without exploitation and without national and racial oppression."

Jews came from Poland, Argentina, the United States and elsewhere, as well as from the Soviet Union. Most of them, never having been farmers, preferred to settle not on the collective farms, but in the growing town of Birobidjan.

Jewish culture blossomed. Jews moved to top positions in the local government. Yosef Liberberg, head of the Jewish section of the Ukrainian Academy of Sciences, became chairman of the regional executive committee and inspired others to follow him to Birobidjan. Agriculture became more successful. On May 7, 1934, the region's status was upgraded from "National Okrug" to "Jewish Autonomous Oblast," two steps below "Republic," in spite of the fact that the Jewish population continued to be less than 20 percent of the total.

This peak of Birobidjan's Jewish status ended abruptly in 1937, when the Soviet government turned toward totalitarianism and Stalin's purges began. Professor Liberberg was arrested as a "Trotskyite," then secretly killed. Many of the Jewish leaders of the region were convicted of espionage. Others were purged. Some historians believed the purge was an aberration as the secret police temporarily got out of control; others said Stalin systematically used purges to maintain control.

After World War Two, the Jewish population of Birobidjan increased and Jewish culture again flourished briefly, but another purge in 1948 destroyed practically every vestige of the Jewish culture: a Yiddish theater, a publishing house, a literary magazine. The teaching of Yiddish was banned. The Yiddish books in the library were burned. The Jewish writers of Birobidjan were arrested and killed.

Between 1948 and Stalin's death in 1953, in Birobidjan and throughout Russia, Yiddish culture was all but destroyed by the arrests of several hundred Jewish cultural leaders – writers, actors, artists and others. Most were sentenced to ten years of hard labor on charges of "bourgeois nationalism" or slander of the Soviet Union for asserting that anti-Semitism existed, or espionage. The Jewish Section of the Soviet Writers Union was dissolved.

In the Jewish Autonomous Region, by the end of the next decade, only ten percent of the population were Jewish, none of those in a position of leadership.

On the last day of training, Galina Volkova brought champagne and a big chocolate candy bar to class. This was both to celebrate the end of our training in Ussuriisk, and to celebrate her husband Anatoli's homecoming. Anatoli Volkov, a respected marine scientist, had been out to sea on a research expedition for four months. This was the first of many champagne and chocolate celebrations we would have in Russia.

We were all relieved to see training end. It was not only difficult being in class six days a week, but a constant strain living in small apartments with Russian people and not being able to speak their language. No space. No privacy. I'm sure the families were glad to return to their normal lives, too. The Peace Corps insisted on trainees having a private bedroom, though this often meant displacing someone in the family. The Peace Corps paid well for locals to make room in their lives for us, and it was enlightening for us to be immersed in their culture. Still, it wasn't easy.

At the swearing-in ceremony, Jeff Murdock made a long speech to the Russians who had hosted us. The pretty, dark-haired Natasha stood at his side, translating, her voice quavering with emotion, her eyes filled with tears. Jeff was going home to America; she was returning to her husband and son in Vladivostok.

The day after we were sworn in, our group departed by bus and train, to destinations as far flung as Vladivostok at the southern tip of the Russian Far East, to Gorin, a village north of Komsomolsk, east to Dalnegorsk on the Sea of Japan and west to Birobidjan.

Russians have a custom when someone is going away on a trip. After everything is ready and you are about to leave, everyone in the household sits down and holds hands for a couple of minutes of silence. And then you go. That silent moment brought our emotions to the surface as nothing else could have done. It also made me realize that there are many times when we don't stop and make room for emotions. I couldn't help shedding a tear.

When we stood up, we hugged and kissed each other. Nadezhda gave us yet another quart of jam to add to our load, which was well over its original weight of ninety pounds each by now, with the addition of the water distiller and the textbooks issued to us by the Peace Corps.

Andrei helped us load our baggage into a taxi. Although we couldn't imagine both of us fitting in the remaining space, John and

I did manage to squeeze in, and then Andrei miraculously insinuated himself in as well. Nadezhda stood in the yard of our building, looking after us to the last minute. She waved, and wiped her face with her hand, as the overburdened taxi backed out of the yard and clanked away, shuddering and swerving down the bumpy, potholed road to the train station.

Andrei waited for the train with us, smiling, nodding, keeping an eye on us. Nadezhda must have ordered him to be sure we got aboard without any problems. The big, green trans-Siberian train pulled into the station, right on time, and Andrei helped us pile our belongings aboard. He stood on the platform until the train moved, then he hurried off to the garage to work on his car.

The biggest surprise of training was when John and I told Vera we were going to Birobidjan.

She had a funny, eager look on her face, as though waiting a firecracker to go off. Then she pushed up her glasses, grinned, and announced:

"It is not only the two of you who are going to Birobidjan," she said. "It is also my humble self."

I was astounded and delighted. John was, too. Vera told us she had decided to accept a position at the Birobidjan Pedagogical Institute; she would join us there in October.

"Vera, this is such wonderful news!" I said.

Vera said that for years the college had been trying to lure her to move from Ussuriisk to Birobidjan to teach English. Most recently, she had been offered the position of English Language Department chair.

"I visited there just before coming to America," she said. "Anatoli Surnin, the director, made me feel welcomed and appreciated. He spent the entire day showing me the sights. He promised me my own apartment. At that time, I couldn't make up my mind about it. Now that we are going there, I feel excited. Not only that, I feel exhilarated!"

Her eyes were dancing, and she was jittery with anticipation.

"I don't mind telling you: It was you Americans, with your sense of adventure, that gave me the courage to say yes," she said.

And in Birobidjan, clever, passionate, stubborn Vera would become our dear, unforgettable friend.

4

Hello, Birobidjan

The horizon was beginning to lighten in the east when the big train clattered to a stop. Looking out the window, John and I could make out the whitewashed train station topped with the town's name in both Cyrillic and Hebrew letters: Birobidjan.

Although the sky was still gray with night, the air was sultry with a wet, oppressive heat. We climbed down onto the platform, collected our luggage and looked around, wondering which way to go and whether there would be anyone to meet us.

Fog hung in the dark air. Or was it moisture drifting upward from the swampy land the town was built on?

Suddenly a million mosquitoes surrounded us! I gasped. It was as though they had been lying in wait for fresh foreign meat and they quivered with excitement over every inch of our exposed flesh. We both instinctively waved our hands wildly in front of our faces, trying to keep the horrible whining little beasts out of our nostrils and mouths and ears.

John yelled, "Come on!" and bolted for the station. I followed closely behind.

A pale man, handsome and as tall as John but built like a sprinter rather than a football player, stood inside the station door, looking benign and amused. I realized later that Sergei Mikhailovich Turbin, deputy director at the college, always seemed to be smiling, even when he wasn't.

"You are the Americans," he said in Russian, grabbing hold of both our hands. "I have been waiting for you."

"Yes," we confirmed, feeling very obvious with our big backpacks, our Western-style clothes and our reaction to the mosquitoes.

John had blood on his forehead where he had swatted one and I noticed blood on my hand, too.

"Follow me," Sergei Mikhailovich said. "Car waits for you."

We stuffed our bags in the trunk and got in. The car turned two corners and stopped outside a two-story L-shaped tan building.

Sergei Mikhailovich told us to wait outside the locked and barred front door while he went around to the back and woke up the night watchwoman. We could hear her approaching the door with a clanking of heavy keys, and soon we were ushered inside. Then the watchwoman, Elvira, hurried off to telephone Kommandant Valentina, the building superintendent, who lived in a nearby apartment with her husband Uri.

While we waited, we heard much commotion, excited voices, doors banging, someone scurrying about, a car approaching the back of the building. In the dark hallway, we could hear a long and intense conversation between Sergei Mikhailovich and Valentina, a short, stout woman who walked with a swagger and had bleached-blonde hair. We would come to know Valentina all too well over the next two years. Though their voices were low, it was obvious that the discussion was heated, that Sergei Mikhailovich was out of patience, and that Valentina wasn't about to take the blame for whatever the problem was.

Eventually, Sergei Mikhailovich returned to us and grinned. There was great embarrassment over the fact that the apartment which had been prepared for us was already occupied by someone else. Americans were obviously in short supply, and a small dark man from Seattle, Washington, had shown up the day before we did, made his way to our building, and Valentina mistakenly assumed he was the American husband, coming for some reason without his wife.

The confusion intensified when John and I showed up. If we were the Americans sent by the Peace Corps, then who was the man from Seattle?

Finally a compromise was reached. We were shown a larger apartment, at the end of the hallway, even though it wasn't ready for guests. Valentina jiggled the key in the rusty lock and opened the apartment door. Forced from its wedged position in the door jamb, the door swung heavily inward and sagged against the wall, its upper hinge hanging by a bent screw.

We looked around. Cobwebs draped the living room, spiders and cockroaches were everywhere, along with dead flies and the droppings of mice. There were no kitchen cupboards. Bubblegum-pink silky cloth draped the walls in the living room from the high ceiling to about four feet from the floor where it met a metallic wainscoting; in the bedroom, a similar cloth, but in baby blue, hid the whitewashed plaster walls. This cloth probably did more than add to the decor. It probably kept the plaster from flaking into dust and covering the room, judging from the amount of powdery white plaster that was lodged behind the fabric where it met the wainscoting.

Propped on one piece of a brown vinyl sectional couch was a huge stuffed boar's head, a grotesque black thing with a long snout, black lips revealing sharp teeth, and, curling from its lower jaws, a pair of curved fangs. Its beady black eyes stared dead ahead, its bristly hairs were coated with dust. The head was attached to an oval-shaped wooden plaque, painted brown, with curlicue edges. It was the homeliest thing imaginable. John loved it. Seeing us gazing at the thing, Valentina promised to remove it immediately.

"Leave it here," John said. "I'm going to name it Gorky Pig."

Valentina and Sergei Mikhailovich both stared in bewilderment, possibly embarrassed, sure that they had misunderstood, or that John was making a joke, but he persuaded them to leave it, and Gorky Pig stayed.

Sometimes I hid the heavy thing behind the couch for weeks before John noticed its absence; other times I would come home from class to find it propped in its original place on the couch. John had Vera take our picture with Gorky and labeled it "The Nuclear Family." Having Gorky around marked us as eccentric right away, since no proper Russian would have such a joke prop sitting in the living room. Hanging on the wall of a *dacha* or a country house, maybe, but not behind the desk or in a chair.

We left our bags in the apartment. Valentina promised they were safe because she was calling her husband immediately to come and repair the door. And she would call one of her other workers to clean the apartment which had apparently not been entered for months. And she would have sheets and pillows brought for the bed. And she would order a bottle of propane gas to stand next to the small gas stove in the kitchen.

Sergei Mikhailovich took us downstairs to the cafeteria. Breakfast was strong black tea and triangles of wheat bread with thick slabs of cheese and butter, and slices of tomatoes. We left uneaten the thin gray salted herring swimming in oil on a cracked saucer.

He apologized for the fact that the director of the college, Anatoli Surnin, was not on hand to greet us.

"Anatoli Surnin is having a treatment for his cancer," he said, in such a nonchalant tone that I almost didn't grasp the importance of what he was saying. Smiling, he gestured vaguely at his abdomen.

Sergei Mikhailovich, second in command, apologized, too, for not being able to speak English with us; though his English was certainly far better than our Russian. And he mentioned that his girlfriend, Larisa Belichenko, couldn't be here to meet us because she was in America on a post-graduate fellowship. Larisa was the English Language Department chair, he said. "My girlfriend. Your boss."

"But I thought Vera Vyalkova was going to be the chair," I said.

Sergei Mikhailovich smiled and shook his head. "Larisa," he said.

He left the table abruptly, saying he would return at noon and take us to a banquet that was being prepared for us, and there we would meet Anatoli Surnin. He pointed out the direction of the town center, half a block away. So at seven in the morning, we were free to go anywhere, except where we longed to go: to bed for a nap.

We decided to take a walk around town, first slathering bug repellent on our faces and arms. But the oppressive, sultry, bug-ridden September heat that was our first impression of Birobidjan had given way to a slight breeze that brushed the mosquitoes back to their swamps.

Our building, housing both our apartment and the classrooms of the Foreign Language Division, was on Pushkin Street, which intersected half a block to the left of our building with Birobidjan's main thoroughfare, Shalom Aleichem Street. In the other direction was Lenin Street and the one beyond that was where we had just come from the train station.

We headed left, across Shalom Aleichem Street, toward the Biro river. The river loops and winds along a broad flat expanse through Birobidjan. Here in the center of town, a wide and well-tended pathway lined our side of the river. A bridge a mile to the north connected to the west side of town and to a military base twenty-five miles beyond. In places, there were grassy areas where people picnicked and sunbathed. Nothing anywhere in town resembled the green lawns of England or America. The vegetation was native weeds and wildflowers, dandelions and meadow grasses.

(Besides being environmentally sound, this meant there were no lawnmowers, edge trimmers, leaf blowers, or any other motorized lawn-care tools. When the grass in the parks got too high, goats and cows were temporarily brought in to graze.)

Along the rocky shore of the river, that day of our first impression, boys stood with long fishing poles. Girls strolled in pairs, holding hands. Tall birch and poplar trees shaded the path. Willows grew along the bank. As in many Russian towns, near the river there was a playground very much like an old-time amusement park, with a metal merry-go-round painted red and pink, a small yellow Ferris wheel, a stage with two tin soldiers standing atop the backdrop, swing sets, and a big barn that held an old bumper-car operation that was set in operation on Sundays and holidays.

We wound our way back to the central outdoor marketplace – the *rinok* – and strolled around. In the middle section, Russian vendors at rows of metal tables sold foods ranging from fresh produce to imported coffee. Off to one side, in makeshift stalls or at tarps laid out on the ground, Chinese vendors sold cheaply made but expensively priced clothing, plastic toys from China, boots and belts, shoes and hats, also from China, piles of used car parts, tools, American cosmetics, dishes, pots and pans, and pirated videos, an ever-the-same and ever-changing array of imported goods.

A severed and skinned cow's head at the rear of the *rinok* marked the meat shed. Inside, a pig's head on a bloody metal table signaled the sale of pork. Large men and women in stained aprons stood behind their raw offerings, knife at the ready, to carve meat off bloody haunches, ribs or backbones. Dark red organ meat lay piled in metal pans. A giant stood at the back of the shed, occasionally wielding a huge axe against sides of beef or pig. Carcasses hung from hooks behind the butchers.

In the central food area, about half of the selection was locally grown vegetables and fruits in season, jams and canned vegetables, eggs, homemade pickles and garlicky hot sauce. Other vendors sold imported foods – bananas and oranges in season, various kinds of instant coffee, tea, powdered soups, sugar and flour, rice, foreign canned vegetables, chocolate candy, bubble gum, and a varying assortment of other things.

The vendors, all women, stood behind long metal counters, each one responsible for an eight- or ten-foot section, her stacks of goods arranged in front of her, with price tags, and boxes of goods behind her. The woman next to her would be selling a similar assortment of things, and so on down the rows, each one selling little and earning little.

Twice a day, a man in an expensive foreign car would stop in front of a vendor, collect money from her and count the merchandise she had sold; few of the hardworking vendors were in business for themselves.

We were shown into the apartment again just before lunchtime. By then its large kitchen contained a table, two stools, a small refrigerator, a small cupboard that would soon be nailed to the wall, and an empty propane gas canister that stood beside the two-burner gas stove.

The size of the apartment was impressive. There were three large rooms including the biggest kitchen of any that we saw in Russian apartments. It was large enough to seat eight or ten people around the table, and we could always round up as many little four-legged stools as we needed from our classrooms. (Students sat not in chairs at desks, but on little square stools, two to a table.)

Our apartment would never be mistaken for a normal Russian apartment, Vera assured us later, when she first saw the place.

"We would never have the toilet in the same room as the sink and tub," she said, disapprovingly. "It is the sure mark that you are living in a hotel."

As we sat in the apartment and waited for Sergei Mikhailovich to come and take us to lunch, we listened to Valentina's small husband, Uri, wrestle with the broken door.

Uri was no handyman. He was sweating furiously, muttering as he worked, a little shaky as he tried to hold the heavy door in place and insert some oversized screws into the heavily screw-pocked door jamb.

John offered to help, but Uri seemed positively alarmed at the idea. His dark eyes widened with fright and he nervously glanced over his shoulder, to see if there were any witnesses, or, most likely, to see if Valentina was in the vicinity.

Uri was a military man, which gave our building good security and gave Valentina some clout with local authorities, but he was also short and slight and mild-mannered, and Valentina exerted great power over him.

We left Uri to his struggle when Sergei Mikhailovich showed up. We marched downstairs, through the long dark hallway past the cafeteria, and past Elvira, the woman posted at the entryway to the building. Besides guarding the gates, she also served as janitor. She mopped the classroom and hallway floors, dusted, changed light bulbs, and once a week she would change our sheets and run a mop around the kitchen floor – until she was fired a year later by Valentina.

Lunch was served at the college's main building, in a dining room reserved for important occasions. The table was set for seven people: Sergei Mikhailovich; Elena, a young teacher called upon to be our translator, who asked us to call her "Ellen"; John and me; Sergei, the foreign affairs officer; Anatoli Surnin, the director, and the mysterious other American.

Everyone was there except the director. We took our seats and waited for him. Meanwhile, the other American rose from his seat across the table and heartily shook the hand of Sergei Mikhailovich. Then he reached over to shake John's hand.

"I am very happy to meet you. You will love it here. These

people are incredible," he said. "They love Americans. Are you also American?"

John and I both nodded.

"Let me introduce myself. My name is Eddie Creek. I am from Seattle, Washington, and I am here on business." He narrowed his eyes suddenly and squinted at us suspiciously. "And you have told them you are teachers, yes?"

"We *are* teachers," John said. "How about you?"

"Well, I will be direct," he said, lowering his short, heavy body back onto the chair. "It has been my experience in Russia that most foreigners who say they are teachers are missionaries. And would this be true, do you think?" He narrowed his eyes and squinted at us suspiciously.

"No, we're really teachers," John said. "We're Peace Corps volunteers."

Ellen whispered something to Sergei Mikhailovich and the two of them got up and left the table, motioning us to stay put.

Eddie's upper lip twitched. He grinned slyly and bent towards us as though to impart a secret. "I am a business entrepreneur," he said. "I can smell a good thing when I see it."

I'm sure John and I both looked puzzled. Eddie glanced at me briefly and turned his attention again to John.

"This is the Jewish Autonomous Region, am I right?" he said. "And where there are Jews, there is money, can you deny this? And where there is money, there is opportunity."

He put his fingertips together and proclaimed: "We are in the right place at the right time."

Sergei Mikhailovich returned to the table. He still wore that inscrutable grin. I was beginning to realize that his smile was seldom an expression of his mood.

Eddie sighed happily and rearranged himself on the wooden chair.

At that moment, the director rushed into the room. Anatoli Surnin was a strikingly handsome man, in his forties, rail thin, with wild gray hair and heavy black eyebrows that shot out at sharp angles from his face. The moment he appeared, he dominated the room with his intense energy. He was immediately followed by Ellen and then three stout cafeteria workers came from the kitchen carrying trays of food.

We all rose from our chairs, as if we were in the military and required to stand at attention. Anatoli Surnin briskly shook hands with John, then me, as Sergei Mikhailovich introduced us. He looked confused for a moment at the fact there were three Americans instead of two, and after a brief, animated conversation with Sergei Mikhailovich in rapid-fire Russian, he turned his attention to John and me. On this first meeting, he was extremely cordial and solicitous.

Eddie, he ignored completely. Eddie turned his attention to his plate. He ate voraciously, as though it might be his last meal for a week.

We were served a huge lunch, beginning with a champagne toast, then generous portions of baked salmon coated with a mayonnaise sauce, fresh green beans, cold beet salad, new potatoes slathered with butter, olives and pickles, dark bread spread with cheese and caviar, and a brownish-yellow berry juice that our hosts insisted was very healthful. They called it "compote." Tea and cake completed the feast.

We ate heartily. It had been a long time since breakfast. The director hardly touched his food. He toyed with an olive, broke the crust off his bread, sipped a little tea.

Anatoli's dynamic intensity could be frightening. He was a master of intimidation, we were to learn, to everyone from janitors to professors, except for two people: his beautiful second wife, who was much younger than he and who ruled their domestic life with an iron hand, and old Mr. Levin, an important local official whose support he needed to keep the college running.

As the cake was served, Eddie wiped his mouth with a napkin, and settled back to chat with the Russians who had so warmly welcomed him with a free apartment and a first-rate lunch with the top people.

But as suddenly as he had entered the room, Anatoli abruptly rose from the table.

"*Do svidaniya!*" he yelled at us, shaking John's hand again and clapping me on the shoulder. "We are glad to have you here!"

To Eddie, he said nothing.

After lunch, Sergei Mikhailovich motioned for us to follow him. He told Eddie to stay at the table with Ellen and Sergei. We never saw Eddie again.

Sergei Mikhailovich and his driver took us on a tour of the town. He pointed out the post office, the children's cultural center, the philharmonic hall, the sports hall, and other attractions, and then he took us back to our building.

He walked us through the now-empty smaller apartment where Eddie had spent the night, and told us we had a choice. Which apartment did we want? The big dirty one at the end of the hall, or the smaller but nicer apartment that was already prepared for habitation.

Curious, I asked where the other American had gone.

Sergei Mikhailovich gave a dismissive wave of his hand, claiming not to know.

"Maybe hotel," he said. "Maybe train. No problem."

We decided to keep the larger apartment.

The first story we heard about the Birobidjan Pedagogical Institute was that it had been founded some seven years before by a wealthy Russian Jew, Lev Rachmilovich Levin, who required that

Yiddish be taught. Mr. Levin, people said, worried that the Yiddish language was fast disappearing from the world.

Later, we learned that Mr. Levin was not quite the noble figure we had been originally told. He was chief of the local building department, and therefore his support of the college was crucial. Some people called him "Mister Money." But far from being a benefactor, according to a friend speaking off the record, Levin may have even reaped substantial profits from his dealings with the college.

At any rate, the college had originally been founded in the mid-1930s, when the Soviet government perceived Yiddish as the bedrock of a non-religious, Soviet Jewish community in the region. Yiddish was taught in Birobidjan's schools, by teachers trained at the college.

But a few years later, the college was shut down in a terrifying purge and the Jewish roots of the city were trampled.

In 1989, as the Soviet Union opened up under Mikhail Gorbachev, a new Jewish cultural center was set up in Birobidjan to teach Jewish music and dance for children and Yiddish for children and adults.

Also in 1989, under Levin's mercenary eye, the Birobidjan Pedagogical Institute was re-established, and once again the Yiddish language was offered as a course of study, along with Russian, English, French and Chinese. As for the limited extent of Levin's role, one friend said with some authority: "At that time, nobody in the Soviet Union except the state could establish anything by his own means."

This was the college where we would live and work.

It fell to Ludmila Sergeievna Tsimbalyuk to show us around the Foreign Language Division and figure out what to do with us. She was the temporary department chair – until Larisa returned or until Vera arrived; we weren't sure which. In either case, her indifference stunned us.

Sergei Mikhailovich had told us to be ready for work first thing Monday morning.

Ludmila Sergeievna, a woman of about forty, knocked on our door precisely at 9 a.m. Her blonde hair was beautifully cut and styled, her dress fashionable and perfectly tailored, her pretty round face carefully made up and neutral of expression.

"How do you do?" she said, in her cool and cultured voice. "It is my duty to introduce you to the faculty."

She declined our invitation to come in, but offered her hand to John and then me, just the tips of her fingers, pulling away after scarcely making contact as though she had encountered wet paint or worse. Then she stepped back into the hallway, nodding for us to follow her.

Russians do not like to stand in doorways – it's either in or out, and in this case, our visitor preferred to wait in the hall.

We quickly collected our things and followed her to the teachers' office at the other end of the building, where the faculty awaited us – all of them Russian and all women but one: five teachers of English, two teachers of Yiddish, two teachers of French and two teachers of Chinese, including the one male. Just outside the closed door of the teachers' office, her hand on the doorknob, Ludmila Sergeievna turned to us abruptly and said, "What shall I call you?"

"Sharon Dirlam," I said. "And please, tell us your name again?"

"Just a minute," she said. "Again?" She cocked her head to one side and strained to understand my name.

"Shar-on Dir-lam." I knew it was a tough name. I tried "Deer-Lomm," which is closer to how Europeans generally pronounce my name. As for "Sharon," it usually comes out "Sharr-Own." In any case, my name did not set well on her tongue, nor did she want to struggle with it at the moment. She turned to John. "And please, your name?"

"I'm John McCafferty," he said.

She tried: "Mick-Mick-Mick-Cough-Mick-Cough..."

"May we say we are John and Sharon?" he asked.

"Well," she said, visibly relieved. "I suppose you may. Shall we enter?"

We could smell the tension in the room when Ludmila Sergeievna opened the door. The man stood. The ten women sat rigidly at attention – six behind their desks and four lined up on the couch. As if at a signal, they rose to their feet and leaned toward us like flowers in a gentle breeze, including Ellen, whom we had already met.

"Please introduce yourselves," Ludmila Sergeievna ordered us, and we did so.

Then she nodded to each teacher in turn. As they introduced themselves to us, each gave a slight formal bow. The teacher of Chinese was a frail young man named Oleg; his thin blonde wife, Svetlana, taught English.

Svetlana turned beet red and seemed to all but forget the English language in her nervousness.

"I am wife Oleg, man by me," Svetlana said, causing Irina Alexandrovna, a short chubby teacher of English, to burst into a fit of giggles. Oleg, who didn't understand a word, simply looked bewildered.

Immediately when the circle of introductions had been completed, Ludmila Sergeievna clapped her hands once and snapped, "You may go now!" as though she needed to wake them all from a hypnotic trance.

Abruptly and noisily, they rushed off to their waiting classes, and Ludmila Sergeievna turned to us. In all this time, she had not smiled once, nor did she then.

"Have you got any idea what you might be able to do?" she said, as though at a loss to imagine how we could possibly be useful.

"Didn't Anatoli Surnin tell you?" John said. "We are here to teach English."

She sighed. "Well. Yes. Hmm. I doubt that you would be able to teach grammatics." She paused, as though deep in troubled thought. Then she continued: "Or stylistics, or phonetics." Then she hit upon a possibility. "You might be able to teach home reading. Yes, I think home reading is the thing. Oh, and perhaps you could guide polylogues."

I could sense John bristling at her condescending attitude, and I was trying to think of something useful to say, when he gave his blunt reply:

"Grammatics is not a word. Nor is polylogues. As for phonetics, I hope you don't think your pronunciation of English is correct."

Now there were two people bristling, but at least John had claimed an equal footing. Ludmila Sergeievna reddened perceptibly, turned to the huge weekly schedule posted on the wall and ran her finger up and down the hours and days, whispering to herself. When she addressed us again, it was to suggest that I teach home reading and polylogues (dialogues for three or more people). John suggested that he start out teaching English poetry and American culture. Ludmila Sergeievna erased some entries and penciled in our names.

This was our introduction to the casualness of the schedule. It was posted on Friday, usually, but subject to change on a daily, sometimes hourly, basis. Those erasures would cause some confusion. As we worked our way into the faculty routine, we were never sure how often our classes would meet or when they would end. However, if a class inadvertently got dropped from the schedule, it had to be made up. We learned to be vigilant.

Before city officials would allow us to have the propane gas canister filled so we could cook, John and I were required to attend a lecture on the dangers of gas under pressure.

This meant that Valentina, Ellen as translator, and John and I had to make a trip to the Birobidjan Office of Gas and Electrical Power. We rode there in style – Valentina and her husband, Uri, had somehow acquired a huge black Lincoln Continental that they proudly proclaimed had formerly belonged to Eduard Shevardnadze, onetime Soviet foreign minister and later president of the Republic of Georgia (Stalin's birthplace). Such were the mysterious connections between high government and low bureaucrats, and between Moscow and the Russian Far East.

A big-breasted woman, with dyed red hair swept into a bouffant bun on top of her head, sat filing her nails in the dreary little office. She wore a low-cut beaded sweater and a plaid skirt. Black file cabinets behind her desk bulged with folders and plans and thick documents. She directed the four of us (Uri waited in the car) to sit on a row of chairs at her right.

After ten minutes, she put away her nail file and hoisted herself to her feet, sighing wearily. She reached up and tucked some stray hairs back into the unruly bun, giving John a sidelong look which I noticed but he didn't. He was too busy trying to decipher the Russian letters on some leftover Communist wall posters to give her the attention she might have expected. She shrugged and motioned for us to follow her.

She led the four of us into a small room and directed us to sit down again. The walls were lined with huge gruesome photographs which she proceeded to describe, one after another, in elaborate detail, with Ellen translating.

The photographs depicted disasters that were caused by the careless use of bottled propane gas. There were graphic shots of mutilated bodies, the wreckage of kitchens after explosions, a dead dog which was apparently a victim of such a blast, a close-up picture of a severed arm – all in stark black-and-white. In case this wasn't enough to persuade us of the dangers that faced us, the woman launched into a long lecture, read from a manuscript, tediously

50

translated by Ellen. She warned about the dangers of propane tanks, improper venting and unsafe cooking practices. She cautioned us against using the gas oven for heating the apartment, drying clothes or drying our hair. Valentina gave all appearances of listening closely, as though fascinated.

Next, we were directed to rise, and escorted into a third room, this one filled with actual debris from gas explosions – twisted pipes, bent canisters, exploded stoves, and, strangely, an old gas mask that looked like something left over from a war. The lecture continued on the chemical properties of propane gas and the pressure at which it is stored.

After two long hours of being warned and educated, the woman took us back to her desk. She ordered us to sign some papers, which she then stamped with an official seal, and sent us on our way.

It was another week before the empty canister was carted away and one with propane gas was wheeled into our kitchen and connected to the stove. Signs on its side warned: "Danger!" and "Under Pressure."

When we tried to use the oven, rather than just the two top burners, the smell of sweet scented gas was overwhelming, and worried students rushed to our door to check on us.

At the end of our first year, city officials declared that propane gas was unsafe for domestic use, and Valentina had to dump the old gas stoves and buy new electric ones. They weren't as sturdy, and the electric heat was impossible to regulate. The stove would just keep getting hotter and hotter. But at least the only smells were of scorched food, and we didn't have to fear lighting a match.

5

Isolation and Intrigue

As we came to know more about our corner of Russia, we were puzzled at how little we had ever heard about this autonomous region – the biggest geographic area in the world designated as Jewish.

Birobidjan, a small, pleasant city, was created out of swampland and forest and rock. In the distance, to the north and west, low mountains create a natural barrier, and to the south the Amur river defines the Russia-China border.

"They drained the swamps and built a city," a local historian wrote of the early Jewish settlers. A huge black-and-white photograph in the local museum shows these heroic men and women marching forth into the wilderness to plant crops – their bright, idealistic faces turned to the sun, their feet ankle-deep in mud.

At its height, according to local records, the region boasted 128 elementary schools with Yiddish as the language of instruction, the Museum of Jewish Culture, the teachers' college, a medical school, a music school, and 27 Jewish and state collective farms.

Museum records mention both the pre-war purge and another post-war purge in 1948. For decades, residents of the Jewish Autonomous Region had found it extremely unwise to openly declare a Jewish heritage. During those years, there were no local synagogues. In the 1970s, a one-room *shul* was allowed to open.

Perestroika and Glasnost opened the door not only to the reconstruction of Judaism, but also to escape. By the mid-1990s, people with a Jewish heritage were allowed to emigrate to Israel. Suddenly there were several versions of who was Jewish and who was not, and in any case Birobidjan was losing population, Jewish and otherwise, as people tried desperately to find a place to go where they could make a living.

By the time we arrived, local estimates varied from 5,000 to 10,000 Jews still living in Birobidjan, of a population of around 86,000. They were among the leaders of the community. Total population of the Jewish Autonomous Region was estimated to be 218,000.

Perestroika wasn't working out very well as far as ordinary people were concerned. Factories had closed; industry and manufacturing, of everything from textiles to electronics, had all but come to a standstill; many people had lost their jobs; others, still employed, often went unpaid. On the books, the teachers at our college were paid $200 a month. But they hadn't received any money for four months, then just after we arrived they were notified that money had arrived from Moscow; they all lined up at the cashier's barred window in the main building of the college and were handed $20 each, with the promise of "More. Soon."

(Our young translator, Ellen, immediately spent the $20 on a new beige dress she'd had her heart set on.)

Old-age pensions, once enough to get by on, were worth less than $5 a month. Outside the *rinok*, an elderly woman had homemade braided rugs for sale, which nobody seemed to want except John and me; on the street corner, an elderly man hawked newspapers. Many people had *dacha*s, garden-size plots of land in the country, which they farmed, and, like our Ussuriisk host mother Nadezhda, they cooked, canned and preserved all of the vegetables and berries they grew there for the long winter ahead. Their *dachas*, and, in this part of Russia, food sold in the marketplace by Chinese vendors, kept them going.

Ellen said the suicide rate was extremely high among young men, especially in the villages.

"Russian women are stronger than men," Ellen said. "I don't know why. It's possible that women have less ego and they are more accustomed to being oppressed."

Even though the college got precious little money from Moscow, the law didn't allow it to do anything enterprising to raise money because it was a public institution. As an important local official, Mr. Levin seemed to keep a tight rein on the flow of money. At the corner of our building was a paint and wallpaper store which he owned and operated. (It would have been an ideal location for a college bookstore.) Gossip was that the sexy brunette at the front desk of Anatoli Surnin's office, who did little but sit and file her fingernails, was Levin's current girlfriend.

Most people seemed to plod along day after day, one foot in front of the other, hoping things would get better. "*Zhag za Zhagem*," they would say (step by step).

The textbooks we used were very droll – dry British dialogues and apolitical stories from the turn of the Twentieth Century (O. Henry was a favorite author), which the students would recite in unison, paying careful attention to intonation and stress. The students were extraordinarily good at memorizing. We heard them recite flawlessly, from memory, page after page of their favorite poet, Aleksandr Pushkin, as well as Shakespeare in both English and Russian.

As modern-day language teachers, John and I came as a shock to them, with our emphasis on creative communication. Many of our students had an astonishingly large English vocabulary, though it was as outdated as their books for home reading, and their comprehension of written English was excellent. Their grammar skills were also incredible (in more ways than one; they were taught that English has 26 verb tenses). But other than memorized dialogues, they didn't *speak* English very well.

54

The home reading textbooks, held together by string and willpower, contained hundred-year-old British short stories whose common theme was their complete insipid innocuousness. The most exciting tales in them were the O. Henry stories. There were occasional passages from Jack London and W. Somerset Maugham, but not enough for plot or even dramatic tension. Only the complete text of "The Great Gatsby" came close to providing content worthy of discussion, and its inclusion in the old Soviet college curriculum was no doubt due to its depiction of American decadence and materialism.

We felt very isolated without a telephone, without e-mail. Letters took three weeks or more to arrive from America. As of October, we hadn't received any mail. Coping with daily life was practically a full-time occupation. We devised conversational activities for our classes. I washed our clothes in the bathtub and hung them on racks in the kitchen and bathroom to dry. We walked every day to the *rinok* to shop. We studied the Russian language.

For the first time in our lives, we had to cope with long johns and mosquitoes at the same time. But as the weather changed course – winter descends from the Arctic Circle and sweeps eastward across Siberia while summer wafts up from the Yellow Sea and across the Gobi Desert – the long johns soon won out.

Peace Corps volunteers in the smaller villages around the Russian Far East confronted more primitive conditions than we did. Birobidjan was a nice little city, with tree-lined streets, kind people, concerts and other cultural events, and wonderful breads, fresh every day, wheaty and substantial. And the berry preserves, fresh from people's gardens, were delicious.

One afternoon, with much excitement, Kommandant Valentina presented us a new television set. She called us to the office downstairs and motioned for John to lift the TV and carry it upstairs to our apartment. I ran ahead to unlock the door. John set the TV down in the living room, then we trooped back downstairs and were on our way out the door to go shopping.

Just as we reached the front door, a red-haired girl, a very thin boy and another young man came rushing in and had an excited conversation with Valentina. Then Uri, Valentina's husband, came along and joined the conversation, and Ellen the translator showed up and got involved as well. We tried to leave, but they motioned for us to stay.

After they continued their animated conversation for another few minutes, Ellen informed us that a mistake had been made; the television set was not for us. But we might get one later. Meanwhile, the one John had just carried upstairs needed to be removed immediately. We all marched back up to our apartment and the young man unplugged the TV and carried it out, the red-haired woman took the remote control, and the skinny boy followed them down the stairs. We went shopping.

We ate supper at a simple restaurant across from the train station. A young woman slouched back and forth from behind the counter to the tables, with not a word or a smile to anyone. She served us *pelmini* (Russian dumplings) on chipped plates, cabbage-and-carrot salad, and tall bottles of sour beer. As we ate the steaming, doughy dumplings, filled with cabbage and meat, a boy, nine or ten years old, drifted in and out of the doorway. He was very thin, with a solemn face and dirty clothes. When a man got up from the next table and left the restaurant, the boy slid quietly to the table and regarded the dish. Empty. When the woman came to clear away the dishes, he darted back to the doorway. He said nothing to the three people sitting at another table, eating and drinking; they ignored him as if he weren't there. A woman and her son, about the same age as the beggar boy, entered, ate quickly and left, walking hurriedly by him.

John and I began to understand why the teachers focused on reading and writing rather than listening and speaking. They never heard English spoken outside of class. They taught English as we would teach Latin, like a dead language. All over Russia, people were teaching English who themselves had never heard a native speaker of English. No wonder they preferred the written page.

Ludmila Borisovna Vinnikova (we referred to her "the sweet Ludmila" as opposed to "the cold Ludmila") was the first faculty member who was unconditionally friendly to John and me. A beautiful woman, slim and graceful, Ludmila was also new to the department. She proudly told us that her husband, Alexander, nicknamed Sasha, was Jewish and that he worked for the Birobidjan city administration. Their son, Daniel, was away studying at a military academy and their daughter, Masha, attended a local high school and played the accordion.

"It is very interesting to hear English spoken by people whose native language it is," Ludmila said. She added, blushing, "During the years of Communism, we had a saying: to study English in Russia was as sensible as to study belly-dancing theoretically."

Given their isolation and lack of funds, it was impressive that the teachers spoke English as well as they did. The school had little money, the teachers went unpaid for months, the books were worse than obsolete, and the methodology was as antiquated as the books.

Spelling mistakes in cheap Russian textbooks became distorted facts that were taught class after class, year after year. For example, a phonetics book discussed at length "the necleus of the word" (nucleus). And, in a Russian complication of English grammar, "the future in the past" was considered a verb tense, as in: "He said he would come tomorrow."

We were welcomed by most of the students with open arms, along with the hope that we would find books, somewhere, somehow. I brought along a textbook called "Understanding and Using English

Grammar" by Betty Azar (they were very suspicious that it listed only twelve verb tenses). We wrote letters to schools and friends at home, asking for books. We needed everything: American and British literature, short stories, poetry, especially sets of books we could use for our classes.

Each day was marked by a trip to the post office where we found our newly rented mailbox empty.

The college sponsored an annual "day in the country" for its teachers and staff and their families. I saw Ludmila Tsimbalyuk at a distance, but she didn't return my wave. Ludmila Vinnikova invited John and me to sit with her and her husband Sasha and their daughter Masha, a tall girl blessed with her mother's delicate beauty instead of her father's ruddy roundness. And we became acquainted with another family who would become close friends: the Tolstogusovs – Pavel Nikolaievich, a professor of Russian literature, his beautiful blonde wife with large ice-blue eyes, Lena Vadimovna, who taught English, and their sons Kolya, 12, and Vanya, 5.

The college rented two buses for the Russian holiday honoring teachers. (Each profession has its own Russian holiday.) We rode for about a half-hour into the countryside, then through a gate. The gatekeeper asked some questions, then pulled down on the iron bar across the road to unlatch it and let it swing up.

We crossed small rivers, ponds and bogs. A few yellow and brown leaves were still clinging to the trees, oak and maple, larch and fir; there were occasional patches of bright red sumac. At the end of the trail, we all got out. People scattered to gather wood. Several bonfires were lit. Cloths were spread on the ground and foods was taken out of bags and baskets. People sat with their own groups, administrators in one area, the English faculty some space away under a tree, and elsewhere the psychology department, the mathematicians, the philosophers, assorted children, husbands and wives, and a gray French poodle named Dali, after Salvador Dali who had a Russian wife.

The hardy teacher of physical fitness dropped her clothing to reveal a black tank suit. She alone took a swim in the bracingly cold Biro River. She swam proudly by, her head in the air, doing a version of the breast stroke, and got out downstream where admiring secretaries waited with a towel and her clothes. Vodka toasts were offered and picnics were eaten – pickles and cutlets, kolbasa and other sausages, wheat bread with butter, crackers with mayonnaise and cheese, tomatoes, hardboiled eggs, smoked fish, puffy potato-filled pastries.

Late in the afternoon a relay race was set up. Each team began by collecting sticks and grasses, and, when there was enough, they put their pile of weeds on a rock and set fire to it. As soon as a monitor declared that the fire was burning well, the team ran to the next station, where another monitor stood. They were handed a compass and told to point to the north. Having accomplished that task, the group raced to a series of planks propped on poles; each person had to snake between the poles without knocking over a plank. Next there was weight-throwing, then an obstacle course running the length of two boards (one had to lift the first board while standing on the next and place it in position to step on again), then a race to the finish line.

Winners drank bottles of beer. Then there was a tug-of-war. The professors, secretaries, administrators and janitors all participated in these events with vigorous enthusiasm.

Someone rang a bell and we all headed back to the picnic area for a huge kettle of fish soup that stout women from the cafeteria ladled out and served with slabs of dark bread. Another round of food – cheeses, cookies, pastries, cabbage rolls, cold meats, hard candies – and drink – water, brandy, more vodka, orange drink, beer – with more toasts.

Pavel Nikolaievich poured himself some vodka and raised his glass. With his wife translating, Pavel said to me, "You could be Russian. You have a sweet face, like a Russian woman, and a quiet voice, like a Russian woman." Then he turned to John and said, "She never yells at you, right?" Lena giggled and added her own comment to Pavel's. "Pavel is saying to me, 'Be sweet, like Sharon.' But how can I, when he is so outrageous?" I basked in the glow of their kind words, exaggerated as they were.

At the end of the afternoon, a man played the accordion, Pavel led a group in singing, and all the young women danced exuberantly, their faces flushed. People yelled and hugged each other, girls wandered about in pairs holding hands, little girls danced, trying to imitate their older sisters. A few of us went for a walk up the southern slope of a nearby hill. From the top we could see for miles around, the golden-tipped expanse of scrubby wilderness spread out before us, low blue mountains in the far north, Birobidjan to the east.

"There are tigers left," Anatoli Surnin told us. "And snakes. The snakes of local legend." He offered a toast: "To our health – It's everything. It's all we have." We clinked glasses with him and drank and remembered that he was battling cancer.

On the way home, all the people on our bus, led by a rather drunken Pavel, sang loudly and lustily: "Moscow Nights," "*Oy, Moroz, Moroz*" (Oh, Frost, Frost), and other songs every Russian knows by heart.

The city fathers turned on the heat in our building in mid-October. By midwinter temperatures would drop as low as 40 below zero, and people said the wind would be even worse than the cold.

We were treated kindly. People at the college liked having us here; we got a lot of stares and whispers on the street. Our students in those first weeks were shy about speaking. They were reluctant to try English, but they thought our attempts to speak Russian were hilarious.

Tatyana Makedon, the slender, high-cheeked beauty who was dean of the Foreign Languages Division, insisted that John and I speak English exclusively with our students; I could see that our Russian would not progress very fast at this rate.

It was customary for the students to rise when the teacher came into the room, and not sit again until the teacher directed them to do so. Students stayed together in a small group from their first year of college until the last. Each group traveled from class to class, always with the same six or eight other students. Many such intensely close friendships, forged by proximity day after day for five years, lasted a lifetime. In our classes, we watched romances start and stop, resentments fester, silent treatments in progress, pairs trading places, friendships flower and fade and bloom again.

The students whispered together in class, especially when another student was speaking, and they saw nothing wrong with copying each other's answers when taking a test.

Two of the students were especially eager to practice their English. Denis Kopul, slim and handsome, quicker to grin than most Russians, would stay after class and linger in the hallway, hoping to have a word with John or me, though he was shy about speaking in front of his classmates. Lena Tsimbalyuk, on the other hand, disappeared immediately after school each day, but in class she was happiest when she could speak at length. She always sat in the front row, and was always eager to whisper and help her beautiful best friend, Olga, who sat next to her. When Olga was absent, Lena sat alone.

Lena, who was Ludmila Sergeievna's daughter, looked remarkably like her mother, same attractive round face, same elegant style, same queenly self-confidence. The two were as close as sisters. They came to school together and left together, whispering and laughing like schoolgirls. Unlike most of her classmates, Lena didn't have a boyfriend. She had bigger plans than settling down and spending the rest of her life in Birobidjan.

Behind Lena sat a shy, sweet girl, Masha Voroshbit, whose English writing was both creative and error-free, but who blushed furiously whenever I called on her and spoke barely above a whisper.

Having learned English from antiquated textbooks, the students would say such things as "to be sure, my dear fellow," "we are ever so pleased," and "oh, jolly good."

"I am not a Birobidjan native," Lena Tsimbalyuk said in her first speaking assignment in my conversation class: a five-minute presentation about oneself. "My home is Sochi, on the Black Sea, and when my father retires from military service our family will return there." She paused, and then added firmly, "We will gladly return there."

Neither Lena nor her parents felt connected to Birobidjan though they had lived in the Jewish Autonomous Region since Lena was four years old.

Happily for us, Vera Borisovna arrived in Birobidjan and took up her position as the new chair of the English Language Department. Larisa Belichenko was definitely out, Vera assured us.

This was the first time since her university days that Vera had lived on her own, and not with her mother and grandmother. Anatoli Surnin kept his promise to Vera: There was an apartment waiting for her. However, it was in a horrible state. It was a one-bedroom apartment near the edge of town, on the first floor of a six-story building, but there were no bars on the windows, as was usual for first-floor apartments. Three of the windows were broken. One corner wall was stained and cracked from a plumbing leak in the apartment above. Debris covered the floor. A layer of dust covered the debris.

Anatoli Surnin's excuse was that he had some other apartment in mind, but its occupants had changed their minds about moving out, and now that Vera was here there was nothing to do but grab the first available place. He hoped she would agree.

"I have no other choice," Vera said. "Unless I turn around and go back to Ussuriisk."

And that, Surnin begged her not to do.

Ludmila Sergeievna had not relished acting as the department chair after Larisa Belichenko left for America; there were problems in the department that only a strong, involved leader could mend. Furthermore, Vera was already scheduled to teach three classes as well as run the department. (No one seemed to know whether Larisa was aware she had been replaced.)

Surnin proposed an immediate solution to the housing problem: Vera would stay in a room on the first floor of our building for two weeks, during which a contractor would make the necessary repairs to her apartment.

"It is agreed," Vera said.

Vera knew it was a momentous step that she had taken, but, she said philosophically, "I would rather have regrets for an action I have taken than regrets for doing nothing at all."

Vera didn't know it yet, but by taking the job, she made an instant enemy of the smiling Sergei Mikhailovich Turbin. His girlfriend would come home in the spring to find Vera in her place. We started to hear rumors about why Larisa might have lost her position: she had made many enemies.

One of them was Pavel's wife, Lena Tolstogusova. She had taught in our department until their second son, Vanya, was born.

"Larisa declared that because I had to take care of my new baby, I was not dedicated to my work," Lena said. "She forced me out of my job. I had to transfer to the Department of Languages for Other Majors."

This was a less prestigious position. The students in Other Majors only studied English because it was a general requirement, not because they wanted to learn the language.

"Of course, as you can see, I survived the battle," Lena said. "Some of her other victims were not so fortunate."

Vasili Nikolaievich Ivchenko, a popular teacher in the department, had clashed with Larisa over a pregnant student's right to continue her studies. This particular student was not one of Larisa's favorites. And since Larisa had control over all of the students' grades, she forced the young woman to leave. Vasili fought the expulsion, and lost his job. However, being bright, personable and well-connected, he landed a good job in the city administration. Though he missed the classroom, the city paid more money, and more reliably, and this pleased Irina, Vasili's new young wife, enormously.

A third rumor concerned a male student who had fallen out of favor with Larisa when he married a woman she didn't like. She forced him out of school in his fifth and last year. In this case, the parents' connections were stronger than Larisa's. Being friends of a local judge – they took the matter to court and won the case. But meanwhile, this had created a furor that split the department. Then Larisa won her fellowship and left for America.

Three of the teachers in our department – our translator Ellen, the short chubby Irina Alexandrovna, and a tall woman named Alexandra from Sakhalin Island – had studied under Larisa at the Khabarovsk Pedagogical Institute and had been hired by her in Birobidjan. They remained loyal to her; the other teachers were glad to see her gone.

Vera stopped by her new apartment at the end of the first week to see how the repairs were progressing.

"Imagine my surprise!" she exclaimed the next morning over coffee. "There was a woman, my age, supervising the repairs! I am scarcely able to hold a hammer, and this admirable woman, Faina, can do everything! She even knows how to force two common laboring men to do a proper day's work! I witnessed this spectacle myself."

Vera was completely impressed by her contractor's expertise. The repairs were on schedule; already the apartment looked bright and cheerful, the debris was cleared away, the walls were patched and painted, and rolls of colorful linoleum stood ready to lay on the kitchen floor.

"There is one more thing about Faina that impresses me," Vera said. "She has the most original ideas about everything. Not from books, not from education, but from life itself. She is an orphan; she raised herself up."

In late October, we received our first batch of mail since leaving the States.

As I washed laundry in the bathtub, I thought that life in Birobidjan was probably a lot like life in small-town America in the 1930s or so, with few private cars, primitive washing machines (if any), daily shopping, creaky plumbing and not many telephones.

As I hung my satin pajamas over the radiator in the kitchen to dry, I thought of my mother who died the year before. They were her pajamas: white, with tiny blue flowers. She had never worn them.

When my mother got such presents, she always saved them "for good" because she didn't like using up fine things for everyday, though I don't know where she would ever wear satin pajamas for good. After she died, the clothes my sister and I went through, clearing out her closets, could be categorized as those she saved for good, which were like new; those she wore constantly, to a state of soft, shapeless comfort; and those that were hopelessly out of style, but too good to throw out.

Routine household chores, that took so much time in Birobidjan, were good for the mind, I liked to think. As I scrubbed and wrung the laundry, my thoughts ranged over years and decades, remembered images and creative possibilities. I recalled that ten years earlier, when John and I were thinking about going either to Beijing, China, or Paris, France, my mother said her choice would be China, "because it's more different from America than Europe, and so there would be more to learn." Although she traveled mainly to the popular tourist places, she encouraged me to seek out the unusual experience, the road less traveled, the chance to have the mind tested.

Writing travel stories for the Los Angeles Times had also had an impact on my thinking. I traveled to exotic places, but never for time to do more than touch the surface – see the sights, talk to people, absorb enough color and history to write a story. The desire grew to stay in one place long enough to get below the surface.

Our Russian was improving by the day. When we shopped, the vendors seemed amused by our linguistic efforts, but we managed to communicate our needs.

Vera was a patient tutor. She would drill me for an hour, using my green "Russian for Beginners" textbook, and explain to me the idiomatic expressions and the complicated Russian cases. But when my lesson was over, John would join us and we would immediately switch to English and have some real conversations, animated and interesting.

"Did you notice that Vera has a tendency to refute whatever I say?" John asked me once after she left.

"It's just her mannerism," I said. "She does it to me, too."

"I say something, and I wait for her to say: 'It is not this, it is that,'" he said.

He had mentioned that history might consider Mikhail Gorbachev the "George Washington of post-Communist Russia," and Vera argued, "No, John, I disagree. You see, Gorbachev tried to treat the consequence, not the reason."

I recalled that one day I had praised the movie, "Doctor Zhivago," and Vera countered: "Yes, well, you see, a foreigner wrote the film based on a novel that is ambiguous to Russians. What can you expect? We know it is not true."

When John observed that some of the smartest people in America were Russian Jews, Vera snorted. "There are no such people as Russian Jews," she said. "They are either Russians or they are Jews."

John said it seemed that many Russians were xenophobic. "No, we are not," Vera said firmly. "We are quite hospitable to foreigners." But then she paused and added, "We don't like Chinese traders."

And yet Vera also said, with great pride: "I hate to boast, but everyone has found the Russian Far East to be more free, more tolerant, even more cultivated and cultural, and more perceptive than the conservative belt around Moscow."

I enjoyed working with the students, having lessons go well. With classes of only ten or twelve students, who mostly seemed interested, teaching was very satisfying.

I reread Solzhenitsyn's "One Day in the Life of Ivan Denisovich." It was easy to imagine the barren landscape, the sense of isolation, and time forgotten. A line from the book paralleled our experience: "He had sent his last letter in July and got an answer to it in October."

6

Getting to Know Them

We walked every day along Birobidjan's tree-lined streets, passing quaint old wooden buildings, plus a lot of scabby-looking concrete apartment buildings. The two-story wooden buildings, we learned, were actually slum housing, with a few small shops tucked in between apartments. They had no plumbing. Water was carried in by buckets from a corner pump. A row of outhouses served as toilets. And there were a couple of public bathhouses not far away. The tallest apartments were at the edge of town, eight stories high and eight apartments wide, each exactly the same as the one below, the one next door, the one beyond that. There were neighborhood parks, a children's center with an indoor swimming pool, a movie theater and a stadium. As for cultural life, there were museums, an art gallery, a small cadre of artists, a local bi-weekly newspaper, occasional concerts by local and visiting musicians, student music recitals, and dramatic productions by traveling troupes.

In Birobidjan, there were also the local militia, occasional corrupt officials, endless bureaucratic hassles (which for us meant a constant tug-of-war with our passports and visas), a few mean young thugs, many extremely poor people, and small gangs of children living on the streets, who had to beg and steal in order to survive, and hundreds of other children who lived in the three large orphanages in the area.

We searched for signs of a Jewish presence. There was Mr. Levin, of course. And there was the big bakery owned by a Jewish businessman that supplied most of the bread sold around town – crunchy, dark rye bread and the more popular crusty wheat loaves, bought fresh every day for about twenty-five cents. And various college and city leaders we knew were Jewish, including Boris Fineman, a self-important college official who was now wearing his winter hat, a hoary and hairy piece of fur that John said "looks like road kill."

But when we asked, no one seemed to know, or want to tell us, whether there were religious services. The usual Sabbath hours were not visibly observed. Was there a temple? Did a Jewish community exist?

We visited the massive concert hall near the river, the *Philharmonium*, fronted by a huge metal sculpture that depicted at one and the same time a treble clef and a menorah. We found the office of the weekly newspaper, *Stern* (Star), and learned that it was Jewish-owned. Seven of its eight pages were in Russian and one page was in Yiddish.

Finally, at the west edge of town, near the main building of our college, we discovered a hand-painted menorah on the door of a small wooden building, a sturdy but weather-beaten structure that had endured sixty long winters. Here was proof that something tangible remained of the Jews' religious heritage. People shrugged and said indifferently that the tiny synagogue no longer contained a Torah and was seldom used. But there was a caretaker, they said. We knocked, and there was no answer. There had been a real synagogue nearby, but it was destroyed in 1956.

Yes, Jews did meet to observe holidays, I was finally told, reluctantly, when I continued to press one college official for information. This person said they met privately, discreetly, in each other's apartments. Another person said no, that was not the case; they met at the little house with the menorah on the door. We were strangers in the community and we were not invited.

For so many years, such meetings had been forbidden, and the people who attended them were accustomed to keeping their religious activities strictly among themselves. If outsiders wanted to think no such activities existed, the Jews were contented to let them think so.

Still, there were stirrings of renewed vitality in the Jewish community – importantly, the fact that our college taught Jewish literature and Yiddish, classes were offered around town in Jewish history and culture, and several Jewish organizations had sprung up, including a sports club and a youth group. At the *Philharmonium*, the Children's Cultural Center and other venues around town, Israeli folk dances were often performed. A couple of years before we arrived in town, the Jewish Autonomous Region officially established a Department of Jewish Culture and appointed a chubby, bald man as the Minister of Culture.

Yet an element of identity confusion or outright denial continued to exist. One afternoon I was chatting with Natasha, a teacher of Yiddish. "Are you Jewish?" I asked.

"No," she said. "I am Russian."

"How did you happen to become a teacher of Yiddish?" I asked.

"My grandparents were Jewish."

"But Natasha, how can you have Jewish grandparents and not be Jewish yourself?"

"My grandparents were Jewish in Ukraine," she said. "I am Russian."

Vera moved into her apartment, though she had hardly any furniture or any other household supplies. Having no other jobs lined up, Faina wanted to help her settle in, to Vera's great relief and delight. In Ussuriisk, Vera's mother and grandmother had always taken care of the daily chores while Vera's life centered around her work and her students. To have a friend who knew how to hang cupboards on the kitchen wall and, furthermore, fill them with dishes and cups and sacks of flour and rice and other necessities of life, was an answer to those nagging questions about domestic practicality

Vera had dared not ask before precipitously packing her bags and moving to Birobidjan.

The friendship between Vera and Faina that began at their first meeting quickly flourished. Within weeks, anyone seeing them would have thought they'd known each other for years.

The late October weather was sunny and brisk, most of the leaves blown from the trees, but no snow yet.

On a Friday evening, we were invited to a reception for the opening of a new exhibit at the Birobidjan Modern Art Museum. Vera went with us. There were at least 200 people crowded into the small gallery, milling around, admiring the local art, seeing and being seen. We and Vera were invited into the back room to join a select few patrons who toasted each other with vodka and champagne and ate cookies and nuts and cheese. I bought a little painting by Boris Kosventsev, the museum director, for 60,000 rubles – $12 at the current exchange rate. Boris smoked like a chimney, kept people's glasses filled, and thoroughly enjoyed his self-proclaimed role as genial host; his wife, with a disapproving scowl, disappeared in an angry huff as the back room grew boisterous and loud.

Vera hadn't been able to quit smoking, though she had said in America that she wanted to quit when she got back to Russia. But now she was much too preoccupied to even consider it. She claimed she hated being the boss, but she took the job very seriously and, in her energetic way, established her authority.

Even the director withered under her wrath when he crossed her. People said Anatoli Surnin didn't mind yelling people into submission, intimidating them with his forceful personality, but Vera yelled right back at him, tapping her foot angrily as she spewed rapid-fire Russian at him when he failed to deliver on a promise, as he so often did.

"I can be rather persistent and impudent," she said, smiling.

In those early days of her power, Vera usually got her way, and the department benefited greatly.

One night we went to dinner at the Tolstogusovs' apartment. Lena, a beautiful blonde woman with round light-blue eyes (John and I remarked frequently how many really good-looking people lived in Birobidjan) taught English to students of other disciplines; Pavel taught Russian literature and spoke little English but was a fan of the Beatles and Simon & Garfunkel. Pavel and Lena met when they were university students.

"The first moment I met her, those eyes of hers went straight to my heart," Pavel said.

Lena came from the mountainous Urals region of western Russia; Pavel grew up in a village on the rugged coast of the Russian Far East, so impoverished that sometimes his mother, his brother and he had nothing to eat but bread and red caviar.

Lena brought course after course from the kitchen – cheese and bread, then a platter piled high with baked chicken, then salads and homemade pickles, more vegetables, a Russian rice casserole called *plof*, and later, chocolate candy, cookies and tea. After dinner, Kolya and Vanya were allowed to run into the next room and play computer games while the adults sat around the table singing songs – Russian, American and Beatles songs.

Pavel read and wrote in English though he wasn't comfortable speaking the language. But he knew all the words of all the songs the Beatles sang in the 1970s.

"In Russia, in our college days, the Beatles were subversive," Lena said. "We weren't allowed to listen to them. And so, of course, they were our favorite singers."

The songs Pavel sang most often were "Yesterday" and "Bridge Over Troubled Waters," Lena sometimes harmonizing with her soft, soprano voice.

Pavel videotaped us, smiling and waving at the camera, our arms around each other, John waving a drumstick, and little Vanya running back into the room, jumping into his mother's arms, singing a nursery song in English for the camera.

An intellectual, quick-minded and articulate, Pavel was also fun-loving and natural. He was handsome in an odd way. Behind his thick glasses were one bold blue eye and one eye clouded to blindness when he was a child; during a fight, a boy had poked him in the eye with a knife.

Pavel was wiry-thin and had a thick mop of light brown hair. He never sat still for long. If he wasn't aiming the video camera at us, he might jump up and dash to his computer for a quick answer to some question in his mind, or go out to the balcony for a cigarette, and then return, full of intensity, to redirect our conversation to something he'd just thought about. He would struggle to express himself in English, I would try to say something in Russian, Lena would translate.

A piano had stood in Pavel's and Lena's bedroom for years.

"Pasha plays beautifully, but he will never play for us," Lena said.

"I am not performer," Pavel said. "I don't like piano. I sing, I play guitar. That is enough." He suddenly amazed us all by sitting down at the piano and playing a tricky Chopin mazurka.

A few weeks later, Pavel sold the piano, and that was the end of that.

We had first met Pavel the week we arrived, when we went to the main building of the college to try and find the alleged Internet access that was supposed to exist. He also was looking for it. Pavel had spent the summer in Moscow, doing post-doctoral studies, and when he returned it was to find that the Internet access, upon which he relied heavily, no longer existed.

He spent hours at a computer in a corner office, where a secretary deposited us in our search, fiddling with the keyboard and phone lines and wires and various commands, as if to try and will the Internet access back into existence.

"Please, wait," he said to us, over and over. "I think here is problem." He would try one thing, then another. "No, I think here is not problem. Wait. Maybe ..."

Finally, he said, "One moment, please," and left the room. John started to follow him. "Please," he said, putting his hand out, palm up, like a traffic policeman. "Wait."

We waited. Our lives, it seemed, were often stalled by the comings and goings of others, seldom with any explanation. We were trying to learn patience. I wrote in my journal. John fiddled with the keyboard. After an hour, Pavel returned, clutching an official looking document.

"Here is problem!" he said, victorious with his discovery. "Telephone bill!"

The college had not paid its phone bill for four months, and the line to the computer had been disconnected.

Alexander, one of my students, offered to send messages for us from his computer at home. An aspiring businessman, he charged two dollars per message. I printed out a message to my father and gave it to Alexander, with no results. His English wasn't good enough, nor was my Russian good enough, to communicate what the problem was. Had he sent the message and gotten no answer? Had the message been returned? Had he even sent it?

But thanks to Alexander, we had plenty of practice hearing the Russian words for "tomorrow" and "maybe" – *zaftra* and *moshet buit*.

Although they attended a teachers' college, many of our students said they hoped to be translators or go into business; others simply said they hoped to get out of Russia. Only a few said their goal was to be a teacher.

Their attitudes were often jaded and naive at the same time. Perestroika, coming just as their generation passed childhood, had left them floundering. They went from being true believers, as only children can be – aspiring Young Pioneers singing the hymns of Communism, saluting Lenin and Stalin – to an adolescence in which their childish ideals were crushed by a disillusioning reality.

"We truly believed that the outside world was even more impoverished than we were," one of my students said. Svetlana Belokrinitskaya was a strikingly glamorous girl, with flawless makeup and jet-black hair. "We believed we were a united force, creating a better world. Now I feel embarrassed because everything we were told was a lie."

But there were people who admitted that they missed the sense of a mission, the belief in a greater cause. They missed the parades, the uniforms with little red scarves, the camaraderie of working together for the common good.

Vera spent the summers of her college years picking potatoes on a communal farm. And in the mid-1980s, other college students worked on the construction of Birobidjan's *Philharmonium*, now a vibrant center of the town's cultural life.

Our friend Ludmila Vinnikova, about forty, looked back on the innocence of her childhood with nostalgia.

"We worked together. We believed together. As children, we were happy," she said. "After all these years, I still have my red scarf."

Vera sat silently sipping her tea while Ludmila reminisced.

Later, in one of our kitchen talks, Vera told John and me, "I was certainly not happy during the time of my childhood. My father died when I was seven. There were neighbors who disappeared, and we were forbidden to talk about them." Then she stopped, lost in thought. "There is more to say about that theoretically happy time. One day, I might say more."

Vera seldom dwelled upon her past. She took a deep drag on her cigarette and stared at the crown of the poplar tree outside our second-story window, its few remaining leaves swirling in the wind.

"My granny survived those times, but I cannot say she was happy."

Our three large rooms were sparsely furnished but comfortable enough. Elvira, the dotty old watchwoman with dyed red hair, doubled as janitor. She included our apartment on her rounds, coming in to dust and mop once a week. Our kitchen looked down at the courtyard where students went to smoke, and where, after classes were through for the day, children came to play and fight. Sometimes an older couple sat on a bench under a tree and drank vodka. Russians never drank out of the bottle, which was considered a sure sign of alcoholism, but they poured it into shot glasses, clinked their glasses in a toast, and tilted their heads back to swallow it in one gulp, then poured another.

Since our classes were just down the hall, we enjoyed knowing we wouldn't have to go out on those 30-below-zero days promised in the dead of winter, except to buy food.

The local marketplace had everything we needed. Some things could not be found: good wine, popcorn, Parmesan cheese, plastic bags, paper towels, to name a few. Brand names were seen – Ajax, Head & Shoulders shampoo, Crest toothpaste – but they were fakes. Furniture was expensive but schlocky; small appliances were scarce; clothing and shoes, often of poor quality, were also expensive.

The twenty dollars worth of rubles that our teachers were paid in September was the first pay they had received since May, and there had been no money since. Their housing was provided, and medical care, but we never knew quite how they managed.

76

Many of them had a big garden in the country. A *dacha* was not just a place where families went to enjoy the countryside; it was where they worked every weekend in season to plant, tend and harvest their crops. Most people didn't have cars; they took long bus rides, unlocked the gate to their *dacha* (hoping scavengers hadn't stolen the fruits of their labors, and the vegetables too), filled cloth and plastic bags with cabbages, berries, corn and potatoes, and went home to cook and can, preserve and store foodstuff for the long winter.

Some *dacha* owners, including our janitor, Elvira, supplemented their income by selling their vegetables and canned goods at the *rinok*, the open-air market.

Kommandant Valentina was embarrassed to find Elvira selling her jams and preserves in the market. She told her to stop or she would fire her.

"I pay you enough money to live on," she said.

"Six months, no pay!" Elvira shot back.

People were very generous. What they had, they shared. When Pavel and Lena invited us to dinner, they put more food on the table than we would serve at Thanksgiving. And Elvira often brought us food – crabapples (which I made into jam), some unfamiliar but edible greens, a bag of potatoes.

On the down side, there was in the region a palpable depression, a sense of despair and hopelessness, a failure of belief that anything would ever get better. If a person tried to start up a small business, and managed to make a little money, the criminal element took notice and began to extort, or bureaucrats moved in to tax it to death. A small business that seemed to be thriving would close its doors; the ranks of the unemployed expanded.

Our young translator Ellen had told us earlier about the high suicide rate among young men. Now she told us her own tragedy.

"My former boyfriend hanged himself last year," she said. She had broken up with him because he had "very bad manners." She didn't elaborate.

"A few days after I refused to see him again, he hanged himself from a rafter in his father's barn. He left a note blaming me for his death."

Ellen fell silent for a minute, then said, "Of course I was very shocked. But I don't blame myself. He was only one of many young men who have killed themselves. When times are bad in Russia, the women grow strong; the men grow weak."

Of her high school class in a nearby town, she said, one-fourth of the boys were dead already. Ellen was 24 years old.

Her new boyfriend was a veterinarian.

"But I won't marry him because he has no chance of ever leaving the countryside."

Ellen had ambition beyond the life of a teacher in a small town; she had applied to a university in Moscow to continue her post-graduate studies.

The education system didn't have the state support that it had in Soviet days, and with few jobs to look forward to, many courses of study had closed down. Former professors worked as shopkeepers and office clerks. The receptionist at the Peace Corps office in Vladivostok had once been a professor of metallurgical engineering. The brightest students, who once could count on a state-funded university education and guaranteed employment, competed for scholarships wherever they could find them. After graduation, they grabbed jobs wherever possible, though this might mean living permanently in a remote village.

Most of our students were bright and ambitious. But a few were the spoiled sons and daughters of the "newly rich" (corrupt bureaucrats and criminals, in some cases), and they seemed to be untouchable: their parents were paying tuition. Some of these youths came to class and talked to each other, failed to turn in homework, clowned around and disrupted lessons, and apparently nothing could be done. Others seldom showed up at all.

"After spending two academic hours in their company, I always have a splitting headache; I grow catty," Vera said.

Ironically, some of the less academic students were non-Jewish Russians majoring in Yiddish. These students had little interest in studying Yiddish (and the Jewish students hoping to emigrate to Israel would have preferred to study Hebrew) but anyone who agreed to major in Yiddish, and pay tuition, was accepted as a student.

One rich young man, Andrei Sergeievich, already 26 years old, had failed his exams six times and still sat in classes and made life miserable for the long-suffering teachers. But he had a good reason for being there: As long as he stayed in school, he avoided the military draft.

Many of our students talked to each other during class, even immediately after being asked to be quiet. It was strange to us. But then we noticed that when we went to concerts, as well, we could hardly hear the music for the buzz in the audience, so we thought maybe Russians had a different sense about paying attention. I began to grade the students in my conversation class on "listening comprehension" as well as on talking. They were shocked at the concept.

Several of the college girls (at our institute, they outnumbered the boys five to one) dressed like movie stars or Barbie dolls, in sheer polyester, plastic coats and fur hats, spiked heels and tight dresses. Many of them were beautiful, with long legs, good skin, lovely profiles, eyes that were strikingly light blue or green or gray. They wore bold red lipstick and heavy eye makeup, yet they were still fresh-faced and childish in some ways. They looked like Hollywood starlets, yet in this "back of beyond," what would be their future? For many, an early marriage – their big dream – one or two children, and too often a swift slide into middle age, with missing teeth, wrinkled skin, and hands coarsened by hard work.

A few would manage to get to Moscow or other large cities – those whose parents had connections. (Resumes and job applications were unheard of.) Some would return to nearby villages and become underpaid teachers, recalling their student days as the highlight of their lives.

John taught writing to the fifth-year students in the group majoring in Yiddish. This class, due to graduate in June, was the oldest class and the only one in our department dominated by males. There were several Jewish students among the group; his favorites were Stanislav (Stas) Tarnovski and Igor Plotnikov.

Stas, a tall, lean youth with a hawkish face, drove an expensive sports car. He had a good sense of humor and wrote well-crafted English essays when he tried, which was infrequently. Whenever Stas saw us waiting at a bus stop, he invariably stopped – sometimes having to back up or make a U-turn across the street – and insisted on giving us a ride wherever we wanted to go.

Igor was a hulking brute, having lifted weights for years, and with his butch haircut he looked like a Russian thug, but he was shy and sensitive, and was the only student in the class who completed every assignment. Igor spoke English deliberately, but correctly.

"I was advising him that as a teacher he would need to make sure the children knew when it was time to stay in their seats and be quiet," John said. "Igor nodded and said, slowly, 'I make them be quiet. No problem.'"

Sergei was the class clown, a small, unkempt youth who always looked bewildered, as if he had just been pushed into a snow bank. The other students wrote about Sergei's misadventures, such as the time he sank his boat in the shallow Biro River, and the night he camped out with his friends but got caught alone in a driving rainstorm when his friends drove away and left him behind, sleeping in the grass.

"Sergei's just funny. He says funny things, and people can't resist playing jokes on him," John said. "But everyone likes him. When he comes into a room, the mood lightens."

Arkady, whose father owned the big Jewish bakery in town, came to class wearing fine tailored suits, black or dark blue flannel, topped by an expensive black overcoat, with a white silk scarf, and gloves, as though dressed for a role in a movie about the mob in old New York.

"Arkady showed up today with a beautiful shiner," John reported one Monday evening as we were preparing dinner. "He said he didn't remember what happened, but the other boys said there was a brawl after the dance Saturday night. Stas said the fight was Russians against Jews, but Igor said it was just that everyone was drunk on vodka."

Stas had a girlfriend, Anna Romanova, a statuesque girl with frizzy blonde hair and heavy makeup. She spent no time doing homework. In class, she drew elaborate pictures in her notebook of palm trees and orchids. She talked dreamily about when she and Stas would emigrate to Israel.

One day the beautiful Svetlana, whose mother was a television personality in Komsomolsk, came to my class wearing a black bra and lacy see-through blouse, a shiny black skirt split from knee to crotch in front, in back and on both sides, shiny satin-like stockings, and spiked-heeled boots. Interestingly, the boys didn't gawk, or even, for that matter, seem to notice.

Yet sexy Svetlana would blush and stammer and turn beet red when I called on her to speak.

Many of the students faithfully watched the TV show "Santa Barbara," an evening soap opera about rich people. The show died after a short run in America but was still popular in Russia. When they learned John and I were actually *from* Santa Barbara, they were impressed. We tried watching the show, hoping to discover why it was so popular. The characters were one-dimensional and they spent all their time arguing or telling each other how much they loved each other. Where was the drama? The tension? The plot?

But people were hooked on it, maybe because it purported to show how the beautiful rich people of Santa Barbara lived. The settings were sumptuous, the fashions fabulous.

When we introduced ourselves to people, saying we were from Santa Barbara, their mouths would drop open in amazement. That would be followed by bewilderment, disbelief, or possibly disappointment – we were so obviously not like the characters on the screen.

One day a young Siberian sailor stopped in the middle of the street – not a safe place to stand – and stared at us. We may have been the first Americans he had ever seen. (How could people tell? Our shoes and backpacks, most likely. Maybe the way we dressed, the way we walked.)

He followed us into the *rinok*, so we decided to be friendly and practice our Russian with him. We asked him where he was from and what his name was, then we told him our names and home town.

When we said "Santa Barbara," he laughed and shook his head, then reached out to touch us, as if to see if we were real. John, amused by this youth in his cap and jacket and black-and-white-striped sailor's shirt, handed him an embossed business card with our address on it and a little palm tree in the corner. He looked at the card and ran his thumb over it as if it were a treasure, then tucked it safely away in an inside pocket of his jacket.

He reached into another pocket and handed John a small plastic icon of Saint George, his patron saint, and insisted that he keep it "for good fortune."

I hoped his saint would not abandon him.

"More likely," John said, "some day a former Siberian sailor will show up at our door in Santa Barbara."

7

Fur Hats and Winter Picnics

Winter approached. Early in November, temperatures dropped to 15F by night, but days were sunny and dry. People gathered for winter barbecues along the river. Already children were sliding around on the thick ice at the edge of the river, near our building. The river was shallow there, but in the middle, where it ran widest and fastest, patches of torn earth with icy weeds flowed by like rafts, covered with snow from the nearby hills.

The saddest sight was the gangs of beggar children on the streets, tough little boys and girls dressed in rags who tried to get money (often for their drunken parents to buy vodka, it was said). Sometimes people would buy bread for them, sometimes they would bring them into the cafeteria for a hot meal. Some of the little boys, ten years old or so, already had bashed-in noses and scarred faces; they were as tough and wary as feral cats. They had the look of old men, with weathered skin and hollow eyes. It was heartbreaking to know that some of them were already doomed. They didn't go to school, they smoked cigarette butts from the gutter, some of them drank vodka. By night they slept in cellars like stray animals, snuggled together to keep warm and survive; by day they bullied schoolchildren and stole from old women.

On a Saturday night, from downstairs in the cafeteria came the rhythmic thump of rock music, interrupted by occasional loud cheers. A wedding party was in full swing, and it fell to us to hide the bride in our apartment. This was an old custom; the bride would be whisked away from the wedding party by friends and relatives, and the groom would have to find her, then pay "bribes" to reclaim her.

The bride was Oxana, the 19-year-old daughter of one of the cooks in the cafeteria. Her brother and a friend, along with building superintendent Valentina and her husband Uri, brought her to our door.

Oxana kicked off her high-heeled white shoes in the hallway outside the door, which made it very easy for her new husband to locate her. Breathlessly, she pushed into our hallway and closed the door, then stopped and looked at us like a frightened child.

"*Moshna?*" (May I?), she asked in a high squeaky voice.

We motioned her to the wide brown-vinyl couch. She bounced onto it, like a little girl, and sat there in her puffy white dress, hands folded in her lap, her legs spread wide and her bare feet dangling several inches above the floor.

Not a minute later came another banging on the door. We opened it a crack and in came Kommandant Valentina with a bottle of vodka and accompanied by several other members of the wedding party – the two sets of parents, we guessed, and an assortment of gold-toothed matrons and pot-bellied men with red faces.

Stout Valentina, laughing wildly, her face bright red, ran to our kitchen cupboard, grabbed several glasses and cups, slammed them on the desk near the computer, and poured vodka into them.

There was nothing to do but hold our cups out for vodka as toasts were made to the bride, while Valentina kept yelling our names and saying "Okay!" and "Bye-bye!" – her two English words.

Finally, the bridegroom spotted Oxana's shoes outside our door and came to claim his "kidnapped" bride. As directed by Valentina, we demanded a bunch of grapes, a bottle of wine and a piece of wedding cake before we would release his bride to him.

On my birthday, November 6, the other teachers gave me a box of candy and some flowers, my students sang "Happy Birthday" to me, and we had Lena Tolstogusova and her sons over for dinner, along with Vera. Pavel was in Moscow for a conference.

"Pasha hates Moscow," Lena said. "Everything costs so much in Moscow, and he has no money to spend."

John's Russian language tutor, Ludmila Anatolievna Buistrova, the college librarian, turned 29 a week after my birthday. Traditionally, the person having the birthday gives the party. At the end of the day the desks in the teachers' office were cleared off and pushed into the center of the room to use as a makeshift table. Ludmila, who was several months pregnant, baked creampuffs herself and proudly served them, along with spongy pastries from a bakery, two bottles of champagne, nuts and cheese, slices of apple and orange, and a box of chocolate candy. Everyone liked Ludmila; all of the teachers stayed for the party.

Ellen presented Ludmila with three roses and she put them in the vase that we and the other teachers gave her. (A Russian bouquet always contains an odd number of flowers; except for funeral arrangements.) Because we were there, everyone sang "Happy Birthday" in English, and later they sang a Russian birthday song to her, and Ludmila Anatolievna joined in the singing.

Some jokes (*anekdoti*) were told, and otherwise people just sat, ate, and enjoyed the respite from their usual routine. Chat was minimal. Silences were just as they were, periods of not talking, not signs of social failure. Ludmila Anatolievna was pleased and happy. Her husband, Sergei Buistrov, and their little daughter Nastya came by to join the party.

Later that same day, workers from a department store trooped off a bus at the front door and filed into the cafeteria downstairs for another party. The round tables were set with the tin forks and chipped plates that our students used for lunch, but each table had a bouquet of flowers and a glassful of napkins; the colored disco lights overhead were lit and the place looked almost cheerful.

There was an increasing number of parties in the cafeteria; Kommandant Valentina and the kitchen help made extra money for themselves by catering such events.

In the early evening, we heard a drunken-sounding man and woman fighting in the hallway, outside the door of our apartment.

We didn't want to open the door, although they banged against it in their struggle, but we worried because a huge mirror, six feet high and eight feet long, had recently been propped against the opposite wall, and could easily be shattered. The pair yelled and pushed each other around. We were torn between the desire to avoid trouble and the desire to interfere, to help the woman, or try to end the fight. But the fear of getting hurt or making matters worse won out; we stayed inside, hoping the door would hold. We heard a loud slap, the woman cried out, they yelled some more, then they stumbled away.

Kommandant Valentina told us the next day, when we went to her office to ask that the mirror be moved somewhere else, that the party had actually been a wake, and the couple outside our door were a brother and sister fighting over their father's will.

The Russians seemed to be fatalists – their general attitude about life being that they would endure. They would have feasts and parties, sing and dance and laugh, raise their children, read and play music and memorize poetry, but they seldom took political action. When we asked the teachers why they didn't go on strike over not being paid, they replied, "It wouldn't do any good." When we commented on the unfairness of the new tax laws, they said, "It's true, but there's nothing we can do."

Back in Ussuriisk, Vera had commented on the unpleasant taste of the local water. "If I had a choice, I would mind," she said. "But I have no choice, so I don't mind."

A Russian proverb was mentioned to us more than once: "God's in his heaven and the Czar is so far away." Another adage holds that "he who rises above the crowd gets his head chopped off."

In some ways our Russian friends were better educated than many Americans, especially in history and the classics, maybe because there were fewer distractions, entertainments, diversions. But I had the impression that they saw no other choice but to outlast the hardships, first of communism, now of nascent capitalism. Not all of them did endure. Some drank themselves to oblivion, or committed suicide. Or left the country.

I was stunned by people's generosity. I knew they couldn't afford it, but they lavished gifts on us, and the more we tried to do for them the more they did for us. People seemed happier to have us bring a bunch of flowers and a bottle of Moldovan wine from the *rinok* than gifts we had brought from America; they reciprocated with homemade jam or pickled cabbage. John had carried from home eight bottles of Tabasco sauce, theoretically to use as gifts, but he hadn't given a single one away. (It wasn't a problem though; he averaged a bottle a month to spice up his Russian food.)

By mid-November, the temperature had already dipped as low as forty below zero. I wore a fur hat in the bone-chilling freeze of the Russian winter. Fur hats and coats were not mere fashion statements, they were necessities. We saw an old woman from a village wearing boots made of antelope hide. Kommandant Valentina had a new fur hat made from the skins of two minks. Or so she said. Whatever it was, it sat atop her wild bleached hair like an osprey's nest, and, unlike any mink I've ever seen, its hair was stiff and uneven. Valentina was proud of her hat. She said it was made expressly for her: skinned, shaped and sewn by special order.

Many of the fur hats around town were fashionably shaped, jaunty, snug and warm. There were no animal-rights activists in Birobidjan to throw red paint on otter, sable and mink.

Fashions at the school went into winter mode. The girls who paraded about in tiny skirts and polyester lace blouses began wearing bulky woolen sweaters, long skirts and tights under their fur coats, and, for those who could afford them, high leather boots. The other girls wore vinyl boots, thick stockings, and coats of fake fur from China.

Boys walked down the street with their arms slung around each others' shoulders. A pair of girls were just as likely as a boy-girl pair to hold hands, whisper together, and lay their heads on each other's shoulders. In class, when I put my finger to my lips to signal for quiet, they giggled and blushed. The students were affectionate with each other. Even students and teachers unselfconsciously touched each other affectionately. And when I walked with another teacher, she would take my arm or I would take hers. A friend would stroke my shoulder, straighten my collar, or take hold of my hand as we listened to a concert.

I would miss this casual friendly connection in America, where such close physical contact seems threatening, and sometimes is.

Svetlana, who had always sat alone at the front of the class, had a new friend. Katya. She and Katya, a rather large and dowdy girl, were constantly together. For the first time since I met her, Svetlana looked happy.

People at home wrote to us asking what our Russian friends thought of President Boris Yeltsin. People in Birobidjan didn't care much for him, but they considered him to be the only alternative to Communism. Most of our students didn't want to go backward, but many of them didn't see how to move forward either. Some people who managed to make money fell prey to extortionists, criminals, or, at the very least, heavy taxes, though there were the few "newly rich" Russians who ostentatiously flourished.

It amazed me how so many people kept on working without a paycheck (though they did have their housing, often connected with their workplaces). With closed factories and empty stores, the economy seemed to be at a standstill. And yet, people said more goods were available than five years ago, and maybe things were starting to improve.

We learned a new Russian expression, actually an old proverb: *Nadezshda umeryat posledni* (Hope dies last). It's a different spin than the parallel American proverb: Hope springs eternal.

Elvira came rushing up the stairs and knocked on our door late one afternoon. Out of breath, she insisted that one of us hurry downstairs.

"Vladivostok," she said, making circular motions around her ear.

"Telephone?" John shouted, excitedly.

Since the college wasn't allowed to make long-distance calls, it was imperative that incoming calls be answered, and the sooner the better, before the connection was somehow cut off.

"*Da*! *Da*!" Elvira was ecstatic that she had managed to communicate. Much of our successful communication was in one-word sentences with elaborate hand signals.

Ten minutes later, John returned, grinning. "That was the Peace Corps," he said. "They have our boxes."

There were eighty pounds of books and teaching materials from friends at home awaiting us in Vladivostok.

The Peace Corps office would hold them until we could make the trip there to pick them up, since to ship them by train would likely have meant their disappearance. We still hadn't received a single one of our monthly packages of bills and mail from the tenants at home, although some single letters had arrived intact. One envelope had been ripped open. It contained a letter mentioning that a packet of powdered chili pepper was enclosed. The letter arrived, but no chili pepper.

"I hope whoever took it thought it was an exotic drug and took a deep sniff," John muttered.

We decided to go to Vladivostok in December to pick up the boxes.

Near the end of November, we spent a day in the country. Viktor, maintenance chief at the college, was our guide. We were going on a winter picnic. Originally, we were supposed to go for a weekend of cross-country skiing, but Viktor said there wasn't enough snow, although the snow was deep and blinding.

I don't know where we would have slept if we had stayed overnight. If it was in the big, drafty, old lodge where we spent the day, it's just as well we went only until dark.

Viktor, a short, fat man, with boundless, breathless energy, raced from crisis to crisis as a matter of routine. The picnic was a major event involving foreigners, so along with John and me came Sergei, the foreign liaison man, with his wife, Ira, and their daughter and son, about seven and four, and Viktor's own six-year-old daughter, Tanya, and our friend Vera.

First we stopped at the public square in the village of Waldheim to look at a large bust of L. Gefen, the man who set up the village in 1928. Waldheim, which started out with 32 settlers living in tents, was the first Jewish collective farm in the Jewish Autonomous Region. "Yiddish was spoken everywhere," a man who lived there in the 1930s told an interviewer decades later.

Although the swampy area was muddy and mosquito-infested, he recalled feeling "more comfortable" than he had in his hometown near Moscow. But others reported horrendous conditions in Waldheim and other communal farms in the region, inadequate shelter and food, and land unsuitable for farming. In the mid-1990s, Waldheim still had a school, an orphanage with its own garden tended by the children, a few concrete apartment buildings and a scattering of old wooden houses, a general store, and a small museum run by an elderly Jewish man.

After another few miles, we arrived at our destination, a very rustic resort with a wood-fired sauna. The van was unloaded; Ira had brought bags and boxes of food, and Viktor provided several bottles of vodka, a couple of bottles of champagne and soft drinks for the children.

After brushing the snow off a badly weathered wooden table, we piled the boxes and bottles on it and Viktor popped open the champagne. He poured it into little cardboard cups and we toasted each other. We drank quickly because the champagne leaked through the cardboard onto our mittens.

Sergei, meanwhile, collected branches and twigs and pieces of scrap wood from a nearby pile of lumber and arranged them in a big rusty iron grill.

Viktor and John and I played a free-for-all game of snow soccer, kicking and batting a ball back and forth between goals, children running and kicking and falling and getting up again. The snow was so cold it didn't stick to their well-padded snowsuits. John and I laughed and yelled with the children, to the great amusement of the other adults.

"Everyone knows Viktor is a wild man," Vera told us later. "But until you Americans came, we never saw people over 40 cavorting this way."

The quiet little foreign liaison man, Sergei, coaxed a fire in the grill with an ancient bellows, which shot icy air at the small flame as he pumped on the foot pedal. Eventually a cheerful blaze drew us to the grill where we pulled off our mittens and warmed our hands.

Viktor unscrewed a bottle of vodka. By now, glasses had been unpacked and we could sip at a normal pace. But the Russians toasted and immediately tossed down their vodka in one gulp. Viktor laughed and poured himself another, yelled, "*Za vasha zdarovia!*" (to your health!), and gulped down his second shot. Sergei abstained. He was the designated driver.

The vodka burned our throats and was soon followed by thick slices of crusty bread, fatty *kolbasa* sausage and hunks of cheese, accompanied by a pickled salad of cabbage and hot peppers.

Viktor gulped down a third shot of vodka with a toast to Russia, and directed us all to return to the wintery playground. He climbed the ladder of a tall slide, stood on the icy platform high above us, then, squatting, he gave a high-pierced yell, and barreled down the slide and out onto a slick strip of packed snow that doubled the length of the ride.

The three children raced to follow him, shouting as they shot along the icy runway, then eagerly awaiting the inevitable collision with the next well-padded child.

"*Pa-shlee! Pa-shlee!*" Viktor commanded, waving to us. (Come on! Come on!)

Accepting the challenge, John, then I, scaled the icy steps cautiously, slid down the slide and along the ice, and quickly rolled out of the way because big Viktor followed closely behind us.

Once was enough.

Sergei, Vera and Ira stood by, smiling and waving and whispering together. We imagined Vera explaining to the others that, yes, Americans were certainly different than regular Russians, but we were all right once you got to know us.

Viktor, in his 30s, as wide as he was tall, presented a formidable bulk, barreling through the afternoon, drinking vodka, chasing children and rolling down the slide. After enough vodka, he also displayed his prowess as a dancer, leaping into the air and kicking out both feet as though he were a slim boy instead of a very fat man.

But Viktor's bulk was at its most spectacular when it came time for the sauna.

First, the men and the women separated, each group going into a large room lined with cots, to have a rest. We women lay on our cots, in our long johns and covered cozily with cotton sheets and woolen blankets. The three children fell blissfully into afternoon naps. Ira, Vera and I talked about Russian customs and shared verses and limericks we recalled from our childhoods. Vera was fascinated with English limericks, so I reconstructed several as well as I could from memory.

When the innkeeper knocked on the door and announced that the sauna was ready for us, we women wrapped ourselves in bed sheets, and padded barefoot down the hallway while the children slept on.

We stepped out of our sheets and tiptoed into the incredibly hot sauna. It took my breath away. I gingerly climbed to the middle bench and lay down, wondering how long I might last. Ira pulled a clump of oak leaves out of a bucket in the corner, and swatted my back and legs with them – to improve the circulation – then I in turn swatted her, smacking the soggy, fragrant broom against her fair skin, already pink from the heat.

The heat in the sauna was regulated only by opening the door frequently, as otherwise the temperature just kept rising, fueled by a roaring wood fire beneath the floor. I could only stand it for five minutes.

Then we went steaming into the next room, where there was a deep, square pool of cold water.

Viktor, Sergei and John had already been in the sauna. We arrived at the pool in time to see Viktor plunge into the cold water, gasping and sputtering, then hurl himself out again, laughing, to have another swig of vodka.

After he left, I stood on the step to the pool and lowered first one foot and then the other into the icy water, just up to my ankles. That was enough to cool off my entire body. Vera and Ira dipped into the cold water, then right out again.

Wrapped in our sheets, we sat for awhile on a wooden bench, drinking hot, sweet tea, then we returned to the sauna, for another few minutes, and finally, spent, back to our cots for a real nap.

An hour later, Viktor pounded on the door, waking up the children, calling us all to dinner.

The innkeeper had brought in our food from outside, before it froze as hard as ice, and had heated a kettle of delicious oily chicken stew Ira had brought. This was ladled onto our plates along with steaming-hot potatoes. There were more Russian salads, heavy with mayonnaise, followed by cheese and bread. Moldovan wine was poured. More toasts were made – to friendship, to picnics, to winter, to Russia, and to "America, our ally during the Great Patriotic War." Grapes and walnuts, apples and pears were passed around, then, cookies and jam and chocolate candy. Viktor demanded that everyone drink more vodka. When no one agreed, he shrugged, and poured some for himself alone. He ignored the disapproving looks from Vera and Ira. More tea was served.

Viktor drank to oblivion, stumbled off to another room, and passed out.

The innkeeper brought in a tape recorder and played some Western disco music at the far end of the room.

"Well, it's a pity that Viktor is dead drunk," Vera said sarcastically. "We are probably playing his favorite music."

The children danced in front of the fireplace, and we danced a little, too. Night fell. Time to go home. Sergei and John and the innkeeper hauled Viktor out the door and stuffed him into the back seat of the car.

Back into our warm clothes, back into the cars, back into town. We were both exhausted and incredibly relaxed. We slept around the clock, like babies.

As the temperature continued to drop, snow fell and stayed on the ground, and more snow fell every few days. The days when there was no snow were bright and sunny – and icy. We learned to walk carefully. The air was dry and with factories shut down there was little pollution. The snow stayed white. The roads were occasionally sprinkled with dirt for traction, and a few places were plowed, but generally the snow on roads and sidewalks got tamped down into a solid sheet of ice. Driving was treacherous (Peace Corps volunteers aren't allowed to drive), but it was a prettier scene than the blackened walls of plowed snow that banked up on the curbs of New England towns.

At dawn one day, the thermometer read –17F. Snow lay thick on the ground, rising in windswept banks up the sides of buildings. The air was brilliantly clear. Orion was a major presence in the pre-dawn sky.

The courtyard below our kitchen window had filled with snow, and all the concrete chunks and piles of debris scattered there were covered with snowdrifts. The drifts were lovely, curving white, and they caught windblown snow as it swirled along on its way to corners and crevices. It was more picturesque than a flat yard full of snow would have been.

Thanksgiving weekend, we hosted a crowd of eighteen (a few Russians, but mostly other Peace Corps volunteers). We couldn't find a turkey – John found one frozen turkey leg in the market, and cooked it as a token – so we made do with a feast of sage-flavored stuffing covered with chicken drumsticks. (Frozen chicken drumsticks were imported from the United States; the Russians called them "*Bush nogi*.")

The Americans brought pumpkin pies, cookies, ice cream, and even one can of cranberry sauce someone's mother had sent. The Russians brought winter salads, nuts, champagne. Amy Dickerson, our group cookie maker, brought me three jars of peanut butter, three boxes of brown sugar and a giant package of chocolate chips, all from a Western-style store in Khabarovsk.

All of the Americans stayed overnight, so Anatoli Surnin told Kommandant Valentina to open a couple of the empty rooms on the floor below us, and between these places and our living room floor, everyone managed to get a night's sleep.

We were glad to see the other volunteers, for the first time since training, and hear about where they lived and worked. One young woman said she was living with a family in a village, in a house with no running water; they all visited a local bathhouse once a week to bathe and, of course, they had to use an outhouse.

Someone brought a guitar and we sang old American songs like "My Darling Clementine" and "She'll Be Comin' 'round the Mountain" and old Russian songs like "*Oy, Moroz, Moroz*" and "Moscow Nights."

There wasn't a clean towel in our apartment after the crowd had left. (There were only four to begin with. They had to share, and were still grateful.) Our shower was the most popular place in the building that weekend. Some of the villages and cities were having regular power outages, hours – sometimes days – of no heat or no water; Birobidjan had been spared that. It was becoming clear that our city government functioned quite efficiently, for Russia.

We were glad, too, when Saturday afternoon came and we saw everyone off on the train and peace descended once again. We had all enjoyed getting together. And it was good for us to view Birobidjan through the appreciative eyes of the other volunteers.

The older volunteers agreed that living in the Russian Far East was like going back in time: "Few people have telephones or cars, everyone takes the bus or walks, no one has much money so there's more socializing at home than going out, people sit around in the evening singing songs after dinner. They all have gardens and they can their own fruits and vegetables."

The younger Americans listed the down side: "They get married too young, they have babies too young, and they grow old too fast.

They have harsh living conditions, poor dental care, maybe not a very good diet. Sometimes too much vodka."

And John added: "Not to mention the huge amounts of mayonnaise they eat on everything. Russians buy mayonnaise by the four-liter jug."

Mayonnaise, he declared, "is the drug of choice in the Russian Far East."

As we walked back to our apartment from seeing everyone off on the train, Vera said firmly, "I will never forgive Lisa."

"Come on in and have a cup of coffee," I said.

And Vera told me about the end of her friendship with Lisa Cross, with whom she had spent so many hours in West Virginia.

Vera had invited Lisa to stay overnight with her on Friday, and Lisa said yes. Vera imagined that they would talk for hours about life and love, about Brian Foster and Russia, about Vera's new job and Lisa's life in the village. Lisa was to be the first overnight guest in Vera's new apartment. In fact, Vera had never had an overnight guest of her own before in her life because she had always lived with her mother and her granny.

"The problem began Friday afternoon, when we went to the modern art museum," Vera said.

Several of us went, and we hadn't noticed any problem. But we were looking at the new art on the walls, while Vera was watching Lisa and Boris Kosventsev, the art gallery director.

"Boris immediately fell in love with Lisa," Vera said, taking a deep drag on her cigarette. "I noticed this right away."

She flicked the ash off her cigarette and tapped her foot nervously, as she did when she was holding back an intense emotion.

"Lisa thought nothing of it, because men are always falling in love with her, but the plot thickened when Boris brought out a bottle of vodka and motioned her into the back room."

This was both a storage room and a makeshift salon where Boris frequently hosted exhibiting artists, local dignitaries and honored guests. We had been among the chosen people who crowded in and squeezed together on chairs and couches surrounding a low table laden with cheeses, wines, bread, various snacks and vodka.

"Well, it was too early for drinking vodka, as everyone well understood, and you and John and the others left.

"But, of course, Lisa wanted to stay and drink with Boris, and laugh and talk. And have Boris make love to her, for all I know."

Vera stayed at the gallery with Lisa and Boris, for an hour, then another hour, and finally, sometime after dark, she left.

"I abandoned her to her fates," Vera said bitterly. "I do not know where she spent the night, but I know it was not in the bed I prepared for her."

And that unforgivable slight ended the friendship they had begun in West Virginia.

8

Deep Freeze

Temperatures dropped to –33F some December nights. At noon, though still bitingly cold, the outdoor market was open and crowded. We made the mistake of staying outside too long, and missing lunch, and we both felt chilled and shaky.

We bought tickets for the Monday overnight train to Vladivostok to buy supplies that weren't available locally and to pick up our boxes of books. The trip would be a nice change, we thought.

The train was stiflingly hot and bumpy (the Okean had this reputation), sealed tight, not drafty like the older Russian trains. We slept fitfully. The Americans called this train the "shake and bake."

Usually on time, the train was an hour late arriving in Birobidjan; we boarded at 7:30 p.m., and got to Vladivostok, two hours late, at 11 the next morning. We spent another two hours standing in line in the cold train station to buy our return tickets. Then we waited on the platform in bitter icy wind to catch the *electrichika* (the local train) for the ride past junkyards and wild empty beaches to a suburb called Chaika (seagull). After a long walk from the track, we arrived at the Peace Corps headquarters just in time to miss lunch. The cafeteria closed at two. By three o'clock, I knew I had a severe case of the flu. John did, too.

Antonina Salinon, the program manager, pointed out our boxes to us. We packed the books into our backpacks and suitcases, left them in the office overnight, and made our way back downtown, met a volunteer named Andy who gave us the key to our friend

Nicole Crabtree's apartment – she being out of town – and went to bed.

In the morning, we wrote a thank you note to Nicole for her hospitality, and for the homemade vegetable soup she had left on the stove for us. And a note thanking Andy without whom it would have been impossible, in our stuporous state, to find her apartment in the first place.

Harry Anderson, another volunteer, came by Nicole's apartment, we had tea, and he took us to the U.S. Consulate library where we picked up some free maps and books. We bought steamed potato pies from a street vendor, ate them, and made another stop, at a Western-style food store where John bought a five-pound carton of Parmesan cheese.

"We'll never use it up," I said weakly. "Don't they have the little green and yellow cans?"

"This is all they have," he said. "And Harry says buy now, because this is the first and maybe the last time they'll have it."

We trudged back to the train station in the late afternoon and climbed aboard an extremely crowded *electrichka* back to Chaika. We almost failed to get off at our stop, it was so hard to muscle our way through the immovable mass of Russians between ourselves and the exit. I thought I did not have the strength to reach the door. When I managed to get through, the feeling was like being born – a long laborious struggle through an inelastic opening in an otherwise solid body.

I popped out as the door slammed shut.

John was already on the platform, breathing heavily, ready with his story of heroically applying a collegiate football shoulder block to free his trapped arm, keeping an iron grip on his shopping bag which otherwise was sure to plunge to the tracks below, his arm possibly following.

We propped each other up, A-frame, and recovered our senses, then trudged on.

Now I had a visceral understanding of why the Germans lost the Great Patriotic War, as the Russians call World War Two. Russians endure. They do not give way. They are an immovable, stoic, enduring, solid wall of human resistance to force.

Finally, we arrived once again at the Peace Corps headquarters. We went straight to the medical office. Sarah Farrell's warmth and sympathy gave me a renewed sense of connectedness to life. She also provided cough syrup, aspirin, antibiotics, and an invitation to go home with her for dinner. Sarah and her husband John demanded nothing of us. We sat in their dining room like two lumps, full of humility and gratitude, as they fed and soothed us. Later they drove us in the Peace Corps van to the train station to catch the 11 p.m. train back to Birobidjan, and helped us lug our books, videos, clothes, supplies, and Parmesan cheese, across the station, down the stairs, and onto the train. I felt like a sick, dependent child. I don't know how we could have coped without them.

Unlike the Okean, this train was barely heated. We found our bunks in the open second-class car, burrowed under heavy woolen blankets and went to sleep. At 1 a.m., the train stopped in Ussuriisk. I heard the shuffle of people climbing aboard, entering our car. I felt a chill on my face.

I opened my eyes. Three stout female vendors, with passive, mournful faces and snow-covered coats, stood facing my bunk like emissaries from the underworld. They stared at me.

They said these bunks were theirs.

In what seemed like a miracle of good fortune, Vera also got on the train at Ussuriisk and found us in this predicament. As the heavy metal wheels creaked into motion and the train moved north, Vera arranged for the vendors to find other bunks. The negotiations were as slow and noisy as our progress along the tracks, and involved the interference of several other passengers and a grim-faced conductor. At last, the vendors agreed to move, and Vera settled in across from us.

"After you left Birobidjan, I decided to get on the next train and visit my mother and granny for a couple of days," she said.

"We are so glad to see you, Vera," I mumbled, pulling the blanket closer around my neck. I was in my usual berth, on the top bunk, John below. The train was very cold, but a bit warmer near the ceiling. Vera put on her knitted hat because frost was flying in through the cracks around the window onto her head.

It was a slow train home. Instead of the usual fifteen-hour ride, it was twenty-one. And bumpy. I got sicker. I was too weak to move. I cried. I felt helpless and useless. John slept.

The train arrived in Birobidjan at eight the next evening for a five-minute stopover. I despaired that we could get our mountain of luggage off in that short a time. But we underestimated our network of Russian connections.

Kommandant Valentina, it turned out, knew an Army colonel who happened to be coming in on the same train. We would never know how he knew we were on the train, too, but he found us, and helped us unload our bags and boxes.

John, feeling somewhat recovered from the flu by this time, noticed that no one else was allowed to get off the train until we and our luggage were on the platform. Then the handsome and imperious colonel signaled a taxi for us, shook John's hand, snapped his heels and strode to the nearest bar. We sank into the old taxi and collapsed for the two-minute ride to our guesthouse. Vera waved goodbye and headed for her bus stop.

Elvira, the janitor and sometime night watchwoman, and Valentina and her husband Uri all met us at the front door and helped us lug our supplies down the long dark hall, up the stairs and into our apartment. They were excited by the amount of luggage we brought back with us.

"*Podarok?*" Valentina said several times, laughing, and finally frowning. We learned later that the word means "gift." Naturally, she was expecting something for her troubles. We had no idea.

I crawled into bed and slept.

Friday the Thirteenth. I couldn't raise my head, let alone get out of bed. The flu wracked my body; my mind was a blur.

I dreamed I might die before morning, and I dreamed of an old mother pulling her children through to death with her, an unbearable trip to make alone for an old woman – can't leave those children behind, don't want them left behind, pull them through.

I dreamed of a wretched poisoned cockroach pulling behind her the translucent sack of eggs, waddling on spindly legs, dragging the burden of her progeny.

However, I lived. I got well. Later, I made some notes in my journal.

I jotted down some differences between America's and the Russian Far East's transportation systems. In America there are the trucks and cargo trains, the transportation corridors, the lanes of traffic and lines of rails, crisscrossing the country, bringing everything from everywhere to everywhere. Giant trucks, long trains, filled with cars and cereal, grain and tools, clothes and shoes, steel beams and tall timbers and prefabricated houses, cans of peas and corn, frozen pizzas and ice cream, cotton, polyester, nylon stockings, computers and magazines, drums of ink, tubs of oil, barrels of beer and all the rest. In America, there are drivers of all shapes and sizes, wearing baseball caps and cowboy boots, blue jeans and denim vests, leather jackets lined with sheepskin. They drive along listening to rock music, talking on their cell phones, warning each other about speed traps, stopping at truck stops to shower and eat big platefuls of roast beef and mashed potatoes and drink coffee, and gas up and drive on.

But in the Russian Far East, the transporters were heavyset women with veined legs and whiskered lips, their heads wrapped in burlap scarves, their round bodies in quilted cotton coats, their wide feet in woolen hose and felt boots. They climbed on the night train in Ussuriisk, having paid off some customs officials, and heaved aboard their overstuffed plastic duffel bags full of Chinese merchandise. They bribed a train official to let them carry their overweight luggage: a couple of giant bags per woman, the maximum amount each could manage to carry.

John saw a train conductor grope one of the women; she did not even bother to turn around or show a reaction. They carried from Ussuriisk – where there is a Customs office – dishtowels and kitchen implements, Mandarin oranges and toilet paper, jars of instant coffee and packages of powdered soup, trinkets and gadgets, metal nails and plastic lids, scrub brushes and sweat suits and fake Rolex watches.

The car we were on was full of these middle-age and older women with their heavy bags. They helped each other settle their freight, and, finally, they settled themselves for the night. They didn't buy the blankets and pillow cases from the conductor as we had (for about two dollars a person) but made do with the free quilted pads and their own well-padded coats. They slept. We slept. In the morning, they helped themselves to hot water from the samovar at the end of the car and stirred it into their instant soup. They ate soup and cold dumplings, and slurped tea, and slept most of the way.

Winter. Deep cold winter. While summer was hot and muggy and mosquito-infested, winter was crystal clear and cold. The snow was so white it was almost blue, and so dry it stayed clean and powdery. If you kicked it, it flew through the air in a stream of crystals and settled again like a fine layer of pure white gauze over mountains of other layers of pure white gauze. The layers were piled high and thick. Boots creaked against the deep powder and left deep dents.

On the streets the snow became packed down and condensed, and eventually the footsteps merged into narrow hard pathways and the pathways widened and finally the entire sidewalk was a clear layer of hard packed snow over a thick layer of ice.

When the walks were a thick, solid slab of ice, then sometimes old women with metal shovels chipped away the ice down to bare sidewalk. There were a few snowplows; they ran not on tires but on metal rollers such as army tanks move on. These plows ground along, shoving the snow into tall mountains at the sides of the streets. Occasionally they used a little sand cinder to cut the slickness of the ice; it was unheard of to use salt to crack the ice and melt the snow. It would surely take too much salt to do the job and of course leave a mess of salt residue to deal with in the spring. Instead, the ice remained and made for treacherous driving. Buses fishtailed, cars spun about, and collisions occurred at intersections as one vehicle slid irresistibly into another.

Once we saw an old woman using a shovel, its scoop made of plywood, to shovel the snow when it was still soft. I don't know why they didn't do more of this; the shoveling generally waited until the snow was hard-packed.

At the big Jewish bakery, twice a day, when the bread was baking, steam poured from the vents and wafted to the tall poplar trees that lined the street. Gradually, the dark bare branches were enfolded in layers of glistening ice.

The incredible cold of mid-December confined us. Just walking to the *rinok* to shop for dinner makings was traumatic. Cross-country skiing was out of the question, unless it warmed up, at least to zero or so. It was a half-hour walk to mail letters, our maximum in this weather. People warned us that it would grow worse as winter wore on.

There was plenty of time to study, to plan lessons, to have long aimless conversations, write our thoughts, and do all the little homely chores (scrub clothes, iron shirts, concoct winter stews).

The Peace Corps announced plans for a week of in-service training, in Vladivostok in January. John and I were asked to lead a couple of training workshops – he on classroom discipline and I on methods of language teaching.

The temperature continued to reach new personal lows for us: minus 39 F. one morning. When it rose to minus 20 F., it felt almost warm.

We watched the progress of construction on the city's ice sculpture, an annual event, on a wide field between the post office and the river.

Oleg, the young Russian man who taught Chinese at our college, stood around and translated between the Russian bosses and the Chinese workers who did the actual ice sculpting. He was the husband of Svetlana, who taught English in our department.

"The pay is very good, but next year he will not agree to do this," Svetlana told me later. "His feet are frozen. He will lose his health from standing on the cold ground for these weeks."

The field was flooded to provide a slick plane, like a huge skating rink, then blocks of ice were hauled from the river to the site and crafted into walls and platforms, fanciful carvings and massive statues. A three-story-tall wooden slide and a smaller version were built at the far end of the field, and the slides were flooded. The tall slide, especially, provided a thrilling ride.

One by one, day after day, children hurled themselves onto the slide – aboard pieces of cardboard or plastic – and rocketed down the long slick of ice and 30 yards more along the frozen ground, where they eventually stopped, picked themselves up, marched back to the ladder and climbed again to the top of the tall wooden structure. No rollercoaster could be more exhilarating.

Chores took a long time. Washing clothes, for example, meant scrubbing them in the bathtub, in harsh Russian detergent, rinsing them three times, wringing the water out, hanging them on the radiator to dry. Shopping meant going from vendor to vendor, daily, stopping when the backpack was full. To mail letters, we had to walk the half-mile to the post office, stand in line, buy stamped envelopes, and take a bus to another building to pick up any incoming mail that, for one reason or another, hadn't made it to our rented box at the post office.

Our college sponsored an academic conference, with invitations sent out to colleges around the Russian Far East, and some 50 papers accepted for publication. John, with his master's degree in English literature, was the "featured plenary speaker." But with no money to host the conference, only the teachers here at the college were able to attend. And only one paper was actually published – John's.

The lecture hall was high-ceilinged and cold. Metal straight-backed chairs, bolted together in rows, were on risers that rose steeply from the floor, a dozen rows to the back of the hall. The concrete-block building was scarcely heated, and the extreme cold outside had permeated the room. Two sparrows, trapped inside, flew back and forth between the floor on one side of the podium and the highest windows on the other side.

A longwinded bureaucrat in the Khabarovski Krai educational system was invited to speak and did so at tedious length.

He blamed American propaganda for the ruination of Russia's educational system, though he didn't detail his charge. He made no mention of the shortage of money from Moscow. He read aloud an article from a Khabarovsk newspaper. He spoke for an hour and when he finished, there was a scattering of polite applause.

John spoke next. His topic was "Figurative Speech in English." He spoke in English and Vera stood by his side and was his interpreter.

The man seated next to me, Dr. Boris Nikitin, who introduced himself as a scientist and a poet, kept turning to me and smiling, nodding his head, and saying in Russian, "Excellent!" and "Interesting!"

The figures of speech so common to every American and deeply embedded in our culture, were novel for the audience. The Russians have their own metaphors and similes, some of which coincide with ours, but Dr. Nikitin was fascinated by such Americanisms as "skulking like a sheep-killing dog" and "hard-hearted woman."

We had not seen our director, Anatoli Surnin, for several weeks. He gave the introductory speech, then slipped out of the room. He looked terrible. Knowing that he had cancer, I sometimes marveled at how dynamic he was, how energetic and forceful and domineering. Other times, like this one, I realized he was losing weight, his flashing dark eyes were ringed with deep gray circles, and he walked as though he was in pain.

We felt tired and sluggish in the extreme cold. The trip out to the main building for the conference, and later, just walking along Shalom Aleichem Street to the nearest stores, chilled us through.

We holed up in our apartment, cooked a lavish lunch of bacon and eggs and dark bread, snuggled under our heavy homemade Russian quilt stuffed with cotton, and read our books from home, hour after hour.

The afternoon sun slanted relentlessly white into the windows on the south side of the apartment, providing light but little heat. Beneath the window, two men and a woman, all wearing dirty raggedy clothes, trudged along the path in deep snow to the trash bin. They looked inside it, and walked on, without adding anything to their burlap sacks.

When we got home from our daily round of shopping, four children in tattered coats and torn knit caps were huddled just inside the outer door of our building, in the small dark alcove between the bitter cold outside and the barely heated hallway. The tallest boy, about ten years old, who had a newly blackened eye over older bruises and scars, grabbed my arm.

"Amerikee, hah? Amerikee! Hello!" he shouted, and the others also began shouting, "Hello! Hello!" and jumping around us.

Elvira, the old watchwoman, hurried to the doorway. She scolded the children and shooed them away.

As we went down the hall to our room, we could hear them calling out to us, "Hah! Amerikee! Hello! Hello!"

As Christmas approached, there was more merchandise in the stores than usual. Stores were crowded with holiday shoppers. Vendors gave me plastic bags with my purchases.

Russians endured winter.

"That is our mentality: We endure," our friend Pavel Nikolaievich Tolstogusov said proudly. "We Russians will always endure. We are strong. We can stand anything. We stood three hundred years of the Romanovs, followed by Lenin, followed by Stalin, and we are still here."

But their endurance was matched by a sort of paralysis of will, in the wake of decades of terrorism, preceded by centuries of serfdom.

Another reaction against constant frustration, on the street, in the social fabric, was alcoholism.

"We drink too much vodka. For three hundred years we have been cursed by our leaders and by our alcoholism," shrugged Vladimir, a retired accountant, who sold cigarettes and lottery tickets at the *rinok*.

Just as the seven decades of Communism severely disrupted Jewish culture and religion in the Jewish Autonomous Region, so did they disrupt Russia's Christmas traditions. The midwinter holidays went on for weeks; to us, they seemed vague, confused, temporal. Only the oldest people had any childhood memories of

110

Christmas songs and the religious aspect of Christmas was all but stamped out. Some secular traditions remained, but in a changed form: The Christmas tree had become the New Year's tree; Saint Nicholas had become *Dedi Moroz* (Grandfather Frost), who came on New Year's Eve with gifts for boys and girls; New Year's Eve, not Christmas, had become the time for gift-giving.

John and I walked along the river to the post office. The ice sculptures were taking shape. Children were skating on the big square, and lights were being frozen inside the large blocks of ice at the edge of the square. The shapes emerging were an ice castle, an ice frog, an ice Grandfather Frost, and something like a long ice snake or dragon.

Svetlana said her husband was suffering dreadfully from the cold.

"It is painful for Oleg to stand on the ice for hours and hours. His feet ache every night," she said. "I must bring him tubs of water, warm at first and later hot, to help him recover his circulation before he dares lie down to sleep."

We saw girls walking on the middle of the river now. The ice was so thick and blue, there was no danger of it breaking. Men were ice-fishing. They had big hand-cranked drills to keep the ice from crusting over the holes they had drilled.

John carried the camera under his down jacket so the workings wouldn't freeze shut, and clicked off photographs showing the bleak beauty of this scene.

Vera invited us to her new apartment for Christmas dinner. For weeks, she had been busy getting settled – with her friend Faina helping and coaching, she had spent every spare minute hanging wallpaper and curtains, buying furniture, and dealing with the persistent leak from the apartment above hers, whose owner she didn't want to offend, as he was a bureaucrat rather high up in the city administration.

The friendship flourished between Vera and Faina. They laughed easily together, and they had, after just a few months of knowing each other, a store of shared events, opinions and delights. Vera's father had died when she was seven. Faina had been raised in an orphanage.

"Somewhere in her genetic memory," Vera said, "there is the vast expanse of Asiatic Russia, the windswept grasslands and small wild horses; she dreams about them sometimes."

Faina, a year or two older than Vera, had a divorced daughter and a little granddaughter. Although Vera was a college professor with advanced degrees and very well read, and Faina had gone from an orphanage to a trade school, the two of them would talk for hours about poetry and life, politics and literature. Vera admired Faina for her wisdom and her curiosity and endurance through a difficult life. Faina seemed to take the dominant role, yet reveled in the joy of having a new best friend who was an intellectual and who delighted in her.

We arrived at Vera's apartment at six.

"Look!" I said to John as we approached. "The kitchen curtains are from the same funny fabric as ours!"

We looked through the new iron bars on Vera's first-floor window. There was no mistaking the pattern of those curtains: white, pink and black, with fat cartoon elephants. They were not what we or Vera would have chosen, but sturdy and practical, and the fabric was no doubt bought by the college in ample supply from the store in the corner of our building owned by Mr. Levin.

Vera proudly let us into the small foyer of her apartment, where we deposited our shoes and slipped into new slippers that she had bought for us, her "honored first guests," and she delighted in showing us all the improvements that had been made.

Faina called out *"Zdrastviytye!"* from the kitchen where she was putting the finishing touches on the feast we were about to share.

We had seen the apartment in its original state, and the before-and-after show dazzled us. The painting that Vera had admired at the Birobidjan art gallery, and that we now presented to her for Christmas, was perfect for the light, muted pastels of the living room. In the center of the room was a fine dining room table and chairs.

"The table and chairs are borrowed from the neighbor upstairs, for this special occasion," Vera said.

The table was set with new goblets, flatware, china, and tall white candles in elaborate silver candlesticks, which Vera proudly identified as family heirlooms. A Bach concerto wafted from a tape recorder in the corner of the room.

Outside, the December night descended, lit by a trillion stars glistening off white layers of snow, and we knew that later on we would have to enter the cold night, stand in it awhile to wait for a bus, and make our way back to our building, but for these evening hours we basked in the warmth of Vera's happiness and hospitality. We laughed, we ate, we gossiped, we ate again, and we sang Russian songs, relying on John to keep us on key. All the while, John and I struggled to stay in the Russian language, for Faina spoke not a word of English. We celebrated the excellent food prepared by Vera and Faina, the new apartment owned by Vera, our students, the holiday season, and, most of all, the joy of friendship.

Students of the English Language Department organized a Christmas party. In a corner of the cafeteria stood a spindly tall tree decorated with ornaments (no lights). The students dressed up. They danced disco style – sometimes in a large circle – and the girls were beautiful with their long legs, short dresses, ruffles, costume jewelry and artfully applied makeup.

My students Tanya Sherman and her boyfriend Sasha Lushchinsky starred in a skit based on a Shalom Aleichem tale, Denis Kopul appeared in a Dedi Moroz costume and handed out small gifts, and students bumbled through a few disorganized contests with great hilarity.

The raven-haired Svetlana Belokrinitskaya, stunning in a low-cut white gown, spent the evening silently dancing and holding hands with Boris, an emaciated young man from the fifth level class who wore a suit too large for his lean frame. Boris had nearly starved to death in early childhood and never regained vigorous health. Striking as they were as a couple, they neither smiled nor spoke.

Tatyana Makedon, the dean, sat as chaperone along the side. The pulsating disco light overhead sent streaks of color piercing into the crowd like lightning. During the slow dances, the boys pumped the girls' arms around in large circles as they swayed and dipped to old American songs like "Earth Angel" and "Love Is a Many Splendored Thing." Upstairs, in the classrooms, smaller groups of students, mostly boys, drank vodka and told jokes.

Before the party, John and I exchanged gifts in our apartment. I lit a couple of candles to mark the occasion. John opened my present, a photograph album and a Birobidjan map, and I opened his, a Mozart cassette tape and a red plastic colander for draining spaghetti.

Then we went to the dance. After awhile, John slipped upstairs to have a toast with the boys, absent-mindedly leaving me locked out of our apartment, so I sat with Tatyana for awhile, then he returned and we bade our farewells.

We boiled *pelmeni* for supper, and made a Russian winter salad of grated carrots, cabbage, onion, mayonnaise and dill.

We listened to Mozart, made love by candlelight to the distant strains of Whitney Houston's "I Will Always Love You," said "happy holiday" and "I love you" in Russian to each other, and went to sleep curled together like nesting spoons.

9

The Incident at the Bar

The dead of winter. Nighttime temperatures were down to minus 40F and days gusting up to about minus 5F. Layers of ice coated the streets. The soles of John's boots weren't made for Russian ice. He slipped and fell six times that first winter.

Our young translator Ellen came to say goodbye. She and her friend Alexandra would no longer be teaching in our department. That left only one teacher, Irina Alexandrovna, in Larisa's corner when she returned from America to find herself replaced by Vera as department chair. The college was sending Ellen and Alexandra to Moscow to continue their postgraduate studies. Having little money, they would take the trans-Siberian train, and be in Moscow in six days. We would not see Ellen again. She was leaving behind her the memories of her first boyfriend, who had committed suicide, and a more recent boyfriend who held out no hope of ever leaving his remote village.

"We are expected to return to Birobidjan in three years," she said. "But I hope that I will never return. I am sure my life will be happier in Moscow."

On the last day of the year, I awakened at six in the morning and went to the window. There was a three-quarter moon overhead, the constellation Orion off to the left, and bright snow, still clean, piling up on the dark branches of trees, rooftops, the windowsill and the ground below. A black-and-white vision, cold and brilliant.

Early on New Year's Eve, someone in a room below ours was singing an aimless tune. And our unencumbered life seemed just right, for the moment – no phone, no pressing problems, no connection to home except long letters that took weeks to get there.

The holidays continued. After the western Christmas on December 25th, which got a token nod, Russian Christmas would be celebrated January 7th, which corresponds to our Twelfth Night, and there are two New Year's celebrations, the main one on January 1st, and another on January 14th, *Stari Nove God*, Old New Year, based on the old Georgian calendar. In Birobidjan, people celebrated it all with fireworks and feasting, gatherings and gifts, and some of them got royally drunk for each event.

We went to mail letters home and found the post office closed and locked. Even the mailbox on the outside of the building had been unbolted from the wall. Until further notice. What happened to the letters we sent out last week, or any incoming letters? All letters to and from Russia were funneled through Moscow, probably a holdover from the Soviets' stranglehold on communication, and a remnant of the continuing strong centralized hierarchy of power. Maybe the letters just piled up in Moscow. Until further notice.

The ice palace was the center of city life in the dead of winter. The lights buried in the ice gave it a twinkling atmosphere in the evening, a giant New Year's tree had been installed, and there were the two slides which the children loved. Up and up the tall slide the children climbed, in long rowdy rows, pushing and shoving, and down they come, at an out-of-control speed, bouncing from one side of the slide to the other, ramming into each other, and sliding along the icy straightaway at the bottom for 30 yards or so. Then back up for another round. The second slide was shorter, and a little less steep, and the smaller children were there.

We went to the ice palace with Pavel and Lena Tolstogusov and their sons. We slipped around on the ice, admired the sculptures, listened to music over the loudspeakers, and said hello to people we knew in the crowd. The boys spent the entire time climbing up and hurtling down the slides – Kolya on the two-stories-tall slide and Vanya on the little one.

Even on the coldest days, the *rinok* was open, but only for a few hours at midday. Everything for sale was frozen solid – cans of tomato sauce, a few heads of cabbage, bulging plastic containers of cooking oil. One day we bought a frozen fish, and later when it thawed out and started to stink, we realized it was rotten to the spine.

The merchandise in the *rinok* was unpacked every morning, laid out on counters or hung on racks. Vendors huddled behind their racks or their long tin tables, their chins tucked into their collars. A few items were sold, and the rest was carefully folded and repacked into big bundles and carted away every evening – all the food, tools, clothing, cosmetics, herbs, blankets, electrical appliances, coffee, boxes of chocolate candy.

Sometimes snow covered the merchandise – sweaters, boots, pantyhose, and other displays. But since it never got warm enough to melt, the vendors just shook off the snow at quitting time. Ice cream vendors continued to sell their chocolate covered Popsicles and ice cream cups, popular treats even on the coldest days. And there was no need to plug in their freezers. The long extension cords that in summertime trailed from freezers to the nearest stores were put away for the season. We were living in a deep freeze.

Around the periphery of the *rinok* and along the sidewalk were kiosks the size of large tool sheds, made of tin or fiberboard; the side facing the customers had windows in which the merchandise was displayed. Bars shielded the goods from thieves. At night, tin shutters were pulled down over the windows and padlocked.

The vendors inside their kiosks opened the little window at elbow level to collect the money and pass through the vodka, wine, cigarettes, candy and other purchases to the customer. The bread kiosks, at which lines formed twice a day when the bread truck made its deliveries, dispensed hot loaves of heavy wheat bread for three rubles (about fifty cents) a loaf.

Bread kiosks attracted more beggars than alcohol and cigarette kiosks, though the beggars moved to these places too when they saw a likely donor. If a customer ignored a beggar, the poor wretch might tug at a sleeve and put on a tragic look to arouse sympathy. If he succeeded in extracting a donation, he slipped away quickly. Sometimes a customer would buy half a loaf of bread, and present it to a beggar, usually resulting in a sour look. The beggar would try to sell the bread to someone else in line.

Among the beggars were homeless children, small for their years, their faces weathered, their hair dull.

John and I often talked these days about questions of values, friendship, money, goals, what's important and what's not. When we left Los Angeles and moved to Beijing, China, seven years earlier (reducing our income by 90 percent), it had taken us several months to adjust. It was almost like recovering from an addiction, from the state of having money to spend for anything from a casual $100 restaurant dinner to a month's vacation in Greece. We were spoiled. Even the kinds of conversations we'd have with friends back in Los Angeles were consumer oriented – comparing restaurants, where to shop, remodeling projects, new movies, great vacations.

In Russia, along with the daily gossip, of course, we and our friends were more likely to talk about literature, philosophy, politics. We spent more time in conversation; there were fewer distractions.

Talking with Vera one afternoon, John mentioned Tolstoy's short story, "How Much Land Does a Man Need?" In the story, Bashkirs offer to give a man all the land he can walk around in one day. As the day goes on, greed sets in, and the man walks in an ever widening path to surround as much land as possible. Late in the day, he realizes how far he must go to complete his circle. He breaks into a run. He runs as fast as possible. Gasping and stumbling, he makes it back to the starting point by sundown, but as he reaches the finish line, he drops dead.

" 'Every man has a slave in his soul, and every day he should squeeze out this slave, drop by drop,' " Vera said. "That is from Chekhov."

After the holidays, when businesses opened and classes resumed, we went to the bank and took out six million rubles. Then we went to the exchange window and changed a little over four million rubles for seven hundred dollars and hid the money away in a book. The exchange rate went from 5,700 rubles for U.S. \$1 to 6,000. (This was months before three zeros were lopped off, and well before the "dark Thursday" of July, 1998, when the ruble all but collapsed.) We decided our money was safer hidden in our room than in a bank that might go bankrupt.

Tatyana Makedon, our dean, invited us to her apartment for dinner. The entire family was there.

Tatyana, a gentle soul, looked tired. She was a classically beautiful woman, with high cheekbones and delicate features. But she looked as though she was about to collapse under the weight of her responsibilities. Her son, Andrei, 16, was a tall, thin, nearsighted boy with thick glasses who was remarkably adept at the computer. He had taught himself to use one, from a book, before he ever got hold of a real computer, and we had often seen him at the college because every chance he got he spent time working on the antiquated computer in his mother's office.

Her second husband, Andrei's father, Leonid, a handsome man, was a genial host, taking our coats, pouring drinks for us, making conversation with us while Tatyana and her daughter, Masha, set out food on the table. Leonid showed us some of the columns he wrote for the local newspaper. He was often out in restaurants, meeting with people, a popular man, with plenty of time for his admiring public. But I don't think he made any money.

Masha, 22, a new English teacher at a secondary school, was married to Misha, a tough-looking stout man whom everyone considered beneath her.

People whispered that Masha married Misha on the rebound, that she had been in love with another man who left her for someone else. Misha had the unlikely job of selling Avon cosmetics from a booth at the local hotel.

Masha had made up her mind that she wanted to go to the United States, and she kept coming up with schemes to get Misha employed by an American company, somehow, though he had little education.

A few days after our dinner at the Makedons, Masha and Misha came to call on us, bringing lipstick and lotion samples, hoping that we could help them realize her dream. She told us her latest scheme: Misha should get a job on a ship, land in America, and then send for her. She asked us if we could give her information about American shipping companies. We were as clueless as she was.

We didn't tell Tatyana about their visit.

After they got to know us, our students and other Birobidjan people would talk to us about their history. Some were the children or grandchildren of Stalin-era political prisoners. Others had ancestors who came willingly from depressed areas of the country when the Jewish Autonomous Region was created.

Our friend Maria Grigorievna, who taught in a local elementary school, said her mother recalled the purges in the 1930s. But, she added, "There was a genocide all over Russia. Anyone over the age of 10 would know it. There was not a single place one could find refuge. The KGB would come nightly and take people away."

She whispered this as though the very utterance of such a history might get her into trouble sooner or later.

Two handymen from the college delivered a used telephone to our apartment. Even though it would only be an extension of the phone in the office downstairs, we were excited to have it.

As the two men were measuring the hallway, to determine the length of phone line they would need to install, Sergei, the foreign liaison officer, knocked on the door.

"Good morning," he said, with a formal bow. "Please to pay me three hundred dollars for telephone."

That came as a surprise. I said, "No thanks, Sergei. Just take the phone away."

"Where is John?" Sergei said.

The two men on their knees in the hallway stopped their work. I handed the phone to Sergei. He looked confused.

I said, "*Do svidaniya*" (goodbye) and closed the door.

When John came home, I told him Sergei wanted three hundred dollars to install a telephone. John called Anatoli Surnin.

"What's going on?" John said. "Your henchman is trying to collect three hundred dollars from us to install a telephone? I could have bought the wire for twenty dollars and hooked it up myself!"

"Tell Peace Corps to pay!" Anatoli Surnin yelled.

"Let's forget the phone," John told him.

"I wonder how much the college owes the phone company," I said.

John said, "Probably about three hundred dollars."

The next morning, one of the workers was back with a measuring tape, to check out the placement of the line.

I said, in Russian, that we would not pay the money.

The worker said, in Russian, "No problem! Director wants you to have phone!" Then he added, "Okay?"

So I said, "Okay!"

The man gave a deep, cigarette-growl of a laugh, took his measurements, and went away.

Later that day, Vera said that we had inadvertently done the right thing.

"It's best not to force any issue to a resolution, but to wait patiently," she said. "But it's also best not to raise your hopes up."

Another month went by. Still no telephone.

Vera said, "There's a Russian joke that goes this way: 'We pretend to work, and they pretend to pay us.'"

John said, "Maybe they're pretending to install a telephone, and our part is to pretend we'll pay for it."

The temperature stayed well below zero. Many towns in the Russian Far East suffered power outages; coal was in short supply. Birobidjan fared better than most. In Vladivostok, someone blew up the pipes that supplied heat to a hundred buildings. Political enemies of the mayor were suspected. Schools, apartments and hospitals quickly turned cold, water pipes froze, operating rooms were pitched into darkness. One woman was reported to have died in the middle of a caesarean section. Some elderly people were relocated to ramshackle old sanitoriums – leftover Communist health resorts – until the pipes could be repaired.

One of those same sanitoriums near Vladivostok was the scene of our January in-service training. The week-long event was for Peace Corps volunteers and our counterparts and sponsors. Vera accompanied us as our teaching counterpart, and city government official Vasili Nikolaievich Ivchenko, who had formerly worked under Larisa, came as our sponsor.

Neither the dining hall nor the meeting rooms were heated. We all sat around wearing our heavy boots and coats, hats and mittens indoors.

At least there was heat in the bedrooms. Unfortunately, our room was not only heated, it was full of the most awful odor I have smelled since walking through the musty cellar of an Indonesian jailhouse. I think it was a combination of sewage and mildew. Cockroaches thrived.

The highlight of the week was getting together again with the other volunteers, most of whom we hadn't seen since we were sworn in.

It was Vera's idea to invite Vasili Nikolaievich Ivchenko to the conference. We had heard that he was a bright, enthusiastic bureaucrat. He was one of the mayor's trusted advisers and he also happened to support having Americans in the city teaching English.

"He is a strong supporter of Peace Corps," she said. "It was he who saw to it that you got your visas and were registered with no problems."

Vasili Nikolaievich didn't look like a politician or a teacher. He looked like an actor. He had an expressive face, an actor's presence and sense of timing, a wry comedic manner, and a perpetual look of astonishment accentuated by horn-rimmed glasses.

Vasili was about forty, and he smoked incessantly. He liked nothing better than to be at the center of attention, telling an elaborate Russian *anekdot* or a long and convoluted story about someone's twisted life. He was very entertaining.

In Vasili's view, everyone he knew or knew about was worthy of being ground up in the gossip mill. Not the least of whom was "the dreaded Larisa," the former head of our department, although it was she who had first invited Peace Corps volunteers to come to Birobidjan.

"You know that I once worked in your very department," Vasili told us when Vera introduced us to him.

"He's got the goods on Larisa!" Vera said triumphantly. "I think Peace Corps should know what sort of woman they have been dealing with."

Vasili confirmed what we had heard already: that Larisa, the longtime girlfriend of the college's number-two man, the smiling Sergei Mikhailovich, used her influence to make life miserable for the teachers under her control. She knew how to manipulate people in high places, Vasili said. He told us about teachers she had fired, students she had flunked, lives she had tried to ruin. He listed seven teachers who had quit the department because of her, including himself.

Vera and Vasili spent hours together that week, talking and smoking in hallways and on porches. By the end of the week she had talked him into returning to his old position.

"I'm a teacher, not a bureaucrat," Vasili said. "And one never knows who will win the next election. The city pays me twice as much money as the college, but if the other side wins, they might well cast me out onto the street."

Lisa Cross came to the in-service training a day late and slept until dinnertime the second day. She had already made her reputation as a girl who loved to party. With her long brown hair, big brown eyes, and beautiful body, Lisa could have been a Hollywood starlet. Instead, there she was, in the Peace Corps, in the wild outback of Russia.

Ever since Thanksgiving, Vera had disapproved of Lisa, and at the conference she went out of her way to avoid her.

"That girl likes men too much," Vera said bitterly. "Especially men with money in their pocket and a bottle in their hand."

She managed to keep away from Lisa all week, which was not hard to do since Lisa spent most of her time elsewhere.

On the second night, Lisa and another volunteer, Daphne Early, a tall good-looking blonde, walked over to a small neighborhood bar near the sanitorium.

They spent the evening drinking with four Russian men. Taking turns, the men paid for each round of drinks, peeling ruble notes from the money clips they kept in their pockets.

The next morning, Peace Corps officials woke up to find the militia in the lobby and a problem to resolve involving Lisa, Daphne and four irate Russian men who claimed the American women owed them money. There were several versions of the problem.

Lisa said, "We didn't do anything wrong. The men were loaded. Why shouldn't they buy us drinks?"

Daphne said, in an interesting twist of logic, "As far as I was concerned, they were like paying for free English lessons."

Vasili Nikolaievich was also in the bar. Vasili had a young wife and stepdaughter at home, but he also enjoyed practicing English, especially with pretty women. Vasili's version of what happened was different from both Lisa's and Daphne's.

When the bartender said it was time to close, Daphne said she tried to get Lisa to leave, but Lisa didn't want to go back to the sanitorium. Vasili said he would stay with Lisa, so Daphne walked out of the bar alone.

Lisa's version: "The minute Daphne left the bar, the bartender suddenly locked the door!

"Vasili was talking away, in Russian, and I don't know what he was saying, but all of a sudden the four Russian creeps threw me to the floor and pinned me down.

"I'm sure they wanted to rape me. Well, at least the ones that weren't too drunk to do it. I was rolling around on the floor trying to get away. I tried to scream but one of them had his hand on my face. I could hardly breathe. I nearly fainted."

Lisa said the bartender must have changed his mind about what was going on, and he finally managed to pull the men away from her and shove her out the door.

Lisa said, "I thought everything was going along just fine, we were all having a good time, and then, I just don't know what Vasili said, but whatever he said, that's when the trouble started. I just thank God the bartender was a good man. I think he saved my life!"

Daphne's version: "Okay, I left the bar when the bartender said he wanted to close up. I tried to get Lisa to, like, leave with me, but no. *She* said, 'I'm not ready. I'm not going.' Well, fine, then. Vasili said he'd stay, too, so great, I get to walk home alone.

"I'm standing outside the door, like, trying to remember which way I'm supposed to go? Then I hear all this noise in there. It sounds like somebody's throwing chairs and breaking bottles. I try to open the door but it's locked. I hear a lot of grunting and yelling and furniture, like, scraping around."

Daphne said she pounded on the door and shouted, "Lisa! Vasili! Help, police! Call the police! Help!"

While she was shouting and crying outside the door, Daphne said, "All of a sudden, the door, like, flies open – I almost fall back inside – and here comes Lisa, all sobbing and hysterical. Well, like, drunk, too. She was pretty drunk. Anyway, she practically falls into my arms, and then here comes Vasili out the door, like he was pushed from behind, and then the door slams, and we get the hell out of there, and we're dragging Lisa away, through the snow. And get this – she still doesn't want to quit partying! She wants to, like, go to this other place, but we totally said: 'No way!'"

Vasili's version: "Lisa and Daphne wanted me to go to the bar with them and have a drink. I said 'no, thank you, girls,' because my wife knows exactly how much money I'm making and she would know if I started spending it in a bar. But the girls said they'd buy me a drink if I'd go with them, so, of course, I went.

"But I think American girls like to drink too much. They wanted to talk to these Russian men, and I told them not to do it. I said they

126

were Mafia. They didn't believe me, and then they thought it was funny, and they even told the Mafia men what I said. Those men were already drunk and they thought it was a very big joke.

"Soon all of us were talking and laughing together, and the Mafia men wanted to show off by buying drinks for the girls and me. I wanted to leave. But the girls didn't want to leave. And, to my mind, it would be a big mistake to leave them there alone with those men.

"But when the bartender said he wanted to close the bar, Daphne agreed to leave. Lisa did not agree. I said I would stay, too.

"After Daphne left, the bartender locked the door and started to collect the glasses from the tables. But then, two of the drunken Mafia men attacked Lisa.

" 'Hey! Ho!' I shouted. 'What are you doing?'

"And one of the men said, 'We are getting our money back!' He was sitting on top of Lisa and he started putting his hands in her pockets and searching for money.

" 'No!' I shouted. 'You will just have to forget about the money. You have made a big mistake, and you will pay for it.'

"Lisa was flopping like a fish, pinned to the floor by the two men. I turned to the other two, who were still sitting at the table drinking. I said, 'This is an American girl. If they harm her, you will all go to jail.' I persuaded the bartender and the two men to pull the drunken men away from Lisa and let her escape."

Vasili finished his story, then leaned closer and said confidentially: "To my mind, they let her go only because she is an American," he said. "If a Russian woman walks into a bar and asks men to buy her drinks, she is a prostitute."

The next night, Peace Corps volunteers organized a party at the sanitorium for the children in the neighborhood, with games and prizes and sing-alongs.

But again, Lisa slipped away early in the evening, this time with another young volunteer, Gina. Neither Vasili nor Daphne were interested in another outing with Lisa. The two women went to a luxury hotel nearby, and partied with a pair of U.S. Marines stationed at the consulate in Vladivostok.

They got back at 2 a.m., to find that the sanitorium door was locked. The temperature was 10 below zero.

Our room was on the second floor, right above the door.

John woke up suddenly, and sat up in bed. He said, "What was that noise?"

A snowball had hit the window. We looked out and saw Lisa and Gina standing on the snow below.

"It's Lisa," he said. "Wouldn't you know?"

We tried to turn on the lights but they weren't working.

We could hear the pair's muffled shouts, but our window was painted shut and they didn't notice us knocking on the window and gesturing to them in the dark.

John sighed.

"Daddy has to go help the children," he muttered.

He pulled on his jeans and I found the flashlight. We groped our way downstairs to try and awaken the night clerk. She had long since gone to bed in her room behind the counter.

When the clerk failed to respond to his knocking on her door, John looked in back of the counter and found a ring of keys. He began trying them, one by one, in the big front door as Lisa and Gina, stood outside, yelling and crying and pounding on the door.

"Please hurry!" Lisa wailed. "We're freezing to death!"

Finally, the commotion roused the clerk. She emerged sullenly from her room, wrapped in a big brown blanket and wearing thick felt boots. She wore the front door key on a string around her neck. She pulled the key out from under her blanket, opened the big door, and the two women stumbled in, relieved and annoyed at the same time.

"I can't believe this place!" Lisa cried. "I swear to God – if we get out of here alive – the Peace Corps should give us the Medal of Honor!"

10

'Voice of America'

In February, the temperatures edged upward, enough to turn the top layer of ice to a layer of slush, half an inch thick, which froze again at night. At this stage, workers began chipping and chopping in earnest at the ice covering the sidewalks. The city hired unemployed people and occasionally used soldiers to do this work. After chopping small squares down to bare concrete, they took the broken pieces of ice and tossed them into heaps at the edge of the road. Occasionally, trucks came and hauled the pieces of ice down to the riverbank and dumped them in.

Sometimes gentle snow, falling in the absence of wind, piled upon itself in precarious tall ledges on the thin outstretched branches of the poplar trees. In the deep, frigid quietness of winter, I never noticed the smallest peep out of the round little gray birds that foraged in our area. They seemed to be saving their strength for the severe tests of flying and finding food. When howling winds laid bare strips of earth here and there, and dirt blew into the snow enough to discolor it, soon there would be another snowstorm to add a layer of pure white.

Pavel and Lena and their sons came to our apartment for dinner. While we were sitting around the kitchen table talking, little Vanya – we thought – was quietly reading a book in the living room. But when Pavel looked in, he saw that Vanya was quietly playing with the computer. But it no longer worked.

Our librarian, Ludmila Anatolievna, said her husband, Sergei Buistrov, knew a lot about computers. We took ours to him. He said to come back in a week.

The temperature rose to 15 F. and the ice was slushy beneath our feet. We tried cross-country skiing. We could have used a lesson or two. We went to a big field near the college and walk-slid around a few times, and decided we'd rather walk, generally speaking. Seven children saw us and came running over. John slid on. The children surrounded me as I made my way around the field, asking me questions in Russian and beginner English and begging for my autograph.

Denis Kopul, one of my favorite students, practiced English at every opportunity. He would listen to "Voice of America" on the radio and come to class with a list of slang expressions he had heard and ask what they meant: "start from scratch," "check up on," "figure out," "back to go," and "never mind," to name a few.

"English is easy at the beginning, and it gets more difficult the more you learn," he concluded.

Denis had a charming crooked grin with a slight overbite, close-cropped reddish-brown hair, and an easy-going manner. But he was also ambitious.

He came to our apartment one evening and announced that he had applied for a scholarship to study at an American university for one year. The scholarship was offered by the Freedom Support Act Undergraduate Exchange Program to international students in their second or third year of college. He asked us to write letters of recommendation for him.

Not a single student from the Jewish Autonomous Region had ever won one of these scholarships; the few that were bestowed in

131

the Russian Far East went to students in Vladivostok and, occasionally, Khabarovsk.

John and I both knew Denis well, as we saw him every day and many evenings, so when we got our computer back, we both planned to write letters for him.

After a week had passed, we checked in at Sergei Buistrov's computer business late every afternoon. Day after day, we missed him. He was out of town, or away from the office, or unable to get his car started; one excuse after another.

Three weeks after we took our computer to his shop, when we had begun to despair of ever seeing it again, Sergei showed up at our apartment, plugged in the computer, turned it on, and showed us that once again it was working.

He refused to let us pay him.

Denis was in a room down the hall from our apartment, watching CNN on an old TV set that had been hooked up to a working satellite. We spent the evening writing the letters of recommendation for him. We mentioned that several times a week, after a heavy schedule of classes and homework, Denis would return to the college to watch CNN in order to improve his English. We knew when he came and how long he stayed because he had to come to our apartment to get the key to the television room. And even though he was only in his second year of college, Denis spoke better English than most of the other students.

Denis wrote in his application:

"I would like to study in the U.S.A., because it will give me a chance to study English more deeply and improve my skills in the language. Also it will give me a chance to study American culture and the way Americans live. During that visit I hope to learn more American methods and technology of teaching English.

"My mother is a teacher and when I was in the tenth grade I was sure I would become a teacher like my mother, though I didn't know exactly the subject I would teach. Then I met the Americans who came to our school. I could see that they were not like Russian people and I became curious about English language and American culture.

"During our meetings I tried to learn much about the language and the culture. I tried to develop my English by reading books and also by listening to different English programs on the radio.

"Besides English, my second favourite hobby is sport. I go in for sport because it helps me to stay in good shape and enjoy my life. I can swim, play volley-ball, ski and skate very well. Also I have been 'Body-building' for three years. I know that most Americans are fond of sport, so I think good skills in English and in sport will help me to get along well with Americans.

"Very early in my life I was in Germany, where my father was a Soviet military man. During our staying there I worked with my mother harvesting the fields, and we met many Germans. I had many German friends. Now I hope to learn about other cultures, including American."

I was also filling out application forms. We had acquired a used modem which could be attached to the old computer in the library downstairs. Now I was applying to the Peace Corps for a grant to get e-mail service, videos, VCR and television set, and postage to mail donated textbooks from the states. I asked for $5,000, and John and I lined up some possible book donors back home. We hadn't figured out how we'd get the books boxed, wrapped and mailed yet.

Seeking a grant was not only supposed to be a money-getting deal, but also a way of helping the Russians learn how to fill out such applications. They were intimidated by the amount of paperwork the grant required. So was I. Also, the college was supposed to figure out a way to pay for a portion of the project.

When I asked Anatoli Surnin what the college could do, he replied impatiently, "Whatever you want!"

"How about a room?" I asked. "How about some bookshelves? How about a telephone line so we can hook up to the Internet?"

"Whatever you say!" he shouted.

"This is a contract," I said. "I need your signature, and your promise to provide these things."

"Whatever you need!" he roared. "Leave the papers on my secretary's desk on your way out."

Somehow, it didn't seem that we were working together on this project.

John, Vera and I took the train to Khabarovsk for the weekend because Amy Dickerson was having a party and she invited us. Though it was only a three-hour trip, it was our first visit to Khabarovsk. Amy was a friendly young woman, and her apartment had become a social hub for Americans in Khabarovsk and the surrounding villages.

Khabarovsk had several universities, broad streets, a huge *rinok*, old trees towering over European-style buildings, and the wide Amur river running through it and providing a channel for the wind that chilled everything in its path.

I hadn't realized just how angry Vera was with Lisa for her slight at Thanksgiving. She wouldn't have gone to Khabarovsk with us if she had known Lisa would be there.

We checked into a three-bed room in Amy's dormitory – John, Vera and I. A few other volunteers were there; people had brought their sleeping bags and would sleep on the floor in Amy's room, and there was another three-bed room for the rest of the crowd.

Amy cooked a huge pot of chili, we opened beers, and made toasted cheese sandwiches. We ate, listened to music on Amy's tape player, and talked about everything from the stubbornness of village students to the passion of Russian lovers.

Daphne, an enthusiastic teacher to her village children, told how the Russian teachers in her school had slighted her. Although many of the teachers went from room to room, depending on the day's schedule, Daphne had demanded and won her own classroom. She had immediately set to work painting bright Roman alphabet characters on the walls, hanging up drawings and writings created by her students, and making the room a special place for English lessons. Her students yelled "Hello!" whenever they saw her around the village. They knew their English alphabet. They sang songs in English.

But Daphne was pointedly not invited to attend the local "Olympiad" in her village; this was a competition of students in speaking English. Winners got priority for scholarships abroad, and other advantages, and some of Daphne's own students were competing.

She found out about the event afterward because one of her students won the local competition, and would go on to compete in the regional Olympiad. When Daphne demanded to know why she hadn't been invited, or even asked to be a judge, she was told by her principal it was because her English "is not right." When she pressed for details, the woman told her that she "didn't understand prepositions." The principal referred to Daphne's "chronic and inappropriate use of the word 'like.' "

(Daphne, along with many Americans under the age of 25, had the slangy habit of using "like" in every other sentence: "I was, like, upset" and "He was, like, weird" and "We were, like, so hungry.")

Daphne was offended and hurt.

"I know the difference between 'like' and 'as!' " she said.

John pointed out that she did say "like" as a constant interjection in her conversations, and this probably confused the Russians.

Daphne didn't reply.

Late in the evening, there was a loud knock on the door and in walked Lisa. Vera froze, midway through a sentence.

"Hi, everyone!" Lisa called, sweeping the room with her dazzling smile. "It's time for champagne! Vera! Hi! It's so great to see you!" She dropped her backpack and tried to give Vera a hug.

"It is not so great to see you," Vera said icily.

Lisa stepped back as though she had been slapped.

"What?" she cried. "What's wrong?"

"Everything is wrong – with you!" Vera snapped.

"Vera, you must be joking!" Lisa was genuinely shocked at Vera's tone.

"I don't want to talk to you," Vera said, turning her face away and fishing nervously in her pocket for a cigarette. She lit it, her hand shaking.

"Vera, please," Lisa said, putting her hand on Vera's arm.

Vera jumped up from the couch and dashed to the doorway. "I will not talk to you!" she said. "If you persist, I will be forced to leave the room."

Lisa looked around for support. "What's going on here?" she said. "Does anybody know what I've done to her?"

"Tell your friend to recall what happened the last time we met in Birobidjan," Vera said to no one in particular. "Ask her if she remembers the incident at the Birobidjan modern art gallery." Then she took a drag on her cigarette and added, "But you may add that I do not wish to talk about it, as I previously stated."

But Lisa did want to talk about it. She wanted to clear the air. She wanted Vera to like her again.

"Oh, Vera, I'm so sorry! Whatever it is I've done, please forgive me. I didn't mean to hurt you. What did I do to hurt you? I would give anything . . . "

"You force me to leave the room!" Vera warned.

"Vera, please!"

Vera gave a short, exasperated sigh and whirled out of the room, slamming the door behind her.

I followed her to our room and found her crying. She refused to return to the party. It was nearly midnight anyway, so I decided to go to bed, too. It was after we had brushed our teeth and burrowed under the thick woolen blankets on our narrow cots, away from the partying crowd in Amy's room, that Vera told me how her friendship with Lisa had ended the day after Thanksgiving.

Vera had worked hard to get her new apartment ready for visitors, and Lisa was to be her first overnight guest. But instead, Lisa went off drinking with Boris from the art museum and Vera hadn't spoken to her since.

Her voice was shaky, and I tried to comfort her, but Vera said firmly, "I am crying because I am embarrassed, not because I care."

"I don't think Lisa realizes what's wrong," I ventured.

"I don't mind if she knows or not," Vera replied. We were quiet awhile, then she said, "Lisa drinks because she is looking for happiness."

Again, neither of us spoke for a few minutes, then Vera added, "I'm usually on guard for people who are looking for happiness forever; they are simpletons. Happiness is transitory and fleeting."

The room was cold, but our own body heat gradually warmed us, and Vera and I relaxed under the bright moonlight coming into the bare window, and had one of our best conversations ever. We talked about our childhoods, our mothers, our first lovers, our hopes and dreams.

"Why didn't you ever get married?" I asked.

"I nearly did once," she said. "But I had to send my lover packing. He loved me very much but he was too good-looking. He said I broke his heart, but I don't believe it. Men like that always recover from their broken hearts."

"Why did you send him packing?" I asked.

"I will tell you why. I understood that I could not have my life and at the same time be his wife," she said. "If I married him, I would always be sure that he would leave me one day. I would concern myself with his comings and his goings, and I would be jealous of women who tried to win his love. Everything in my life would be about him.

"But as it is, without him, I am completely myself, I am happy, I do as I please. I have energy for my studies, my students, my friends, and my own dear self."

John tiptoed into the room long after midnight. The moon was bright. I stirred, enough for him to realize I was still awake. He bent over and touched my face. I kissed the palm of his hand.

When we awoke early the next morning, Vera was gone. Neither of us had heard her leave. She had silently packed her bags and slipped out the door before the sun came up. She took the first train back to Birobidjan.

11

Fitting In

In spring semester, the college must have come into a little money. It published 100 copies of "Write It Like This," a composition textbook John had written for college freshmen and brought with him on a disk. The college kept seventy copies for the library and offered thirty for sale to the students in his writing classes. They, and other students, too, lined up and paid the librarian two dollars to get their own copy; several came and asked John for his autograph.

We had an average of about 10 students in each class. We both used John's textbook for our writing classes; it was their first exposure to organizing their writing into the essay format that Americans learn in their early years of school. We were used to getting papers from our Russian students that read like a stream of consciousness – from the first words that came into their minds about any given topic to the last words they could remember about it, everything their teacher had told them and no further analysis. I assigned my second-year students to write an essay based on a picture they liked.

Masha Voroshbit, the shy student who sat behind Lena Tsimbalyuk, wrote a well-organized essay based on the portrait of a mythical Russian female sitting on a balcony and gazing out at distant mountains. In her essay, Masha described the beauty of the scene and imagined a parallel despair in the woman's heart because the great world that existed beyond her balcony was not available to her.

We wondered on what day the Russians would declare it was permissible to go outdoors without wearing a fur hat. They had all started wearing them at once, and undoubtedly would all doff them at once, too. I began going out without my hat as soon as the weather warmed up, but I was often scolded by *babushkas* (grandmothers). Social approval was important to the Russians we met. Individualism was not admired – except on stage; our Russian friends loved their performers and they expected them to be nonconformist. John was also somewhat held to a different standard, because he was a foreign man, and an older one at that. Other than the *babushkas*, who could and did express their opinions whenever they had one, people usually avoided confronting him about his "strange" behavior or way of dressing. But I had the frequent advantage of unsolicited advice, especially from friends.

Some of the Peace Corps volunteers tried hard to fit in and "look Russian," while others consciously decided to be the Americans they were, and do things their own way. Either choice wasn't something they could simply unconsciously do, because there was always a reaction from people – whispers, stares, nudges, smiles, frowns. At worst, one would be shunned, and often not realize it for a time, and might not ever know why.

I went to an aerobics class at the local sports hall – same torture as back home, same mix of beautiful and not-so-beautiful bodies. Our leader was Nadya, a trim contortionist who could do the splits while sitting down and folding her body forward to touch her chin to the floor, while the rest of us did approximations, or while we at least nodded and swayed in the general direction of her fantastic gyrations. I supposed it was good for me, as long as I didn't dwell on the differences between her and me.

The clothes the women wore for working out were similar to ours: The pencil-shaped women wore body-hugging little outfits and the muffins wore big T-shirts.

Another pretty woman was Irina, the young wife of Vasili Nikolaievich Ivchenko. We invited them to dinner one night, along with Vera, to welcome Vasili back to the faculty. Irina had not been pleased about his decision, because of the cut in pay. She was several years younger than Vasili, her second husband.

With them came Irina's nine-year-old daughter, Olga. Both mother and daughter were dark-haired, slim, with large dark eyes and delicate narrow faces. Vasili was very proud of the little family he had acquired two years before.

Irina wore a blue cashmere dress and shiny high-heeled shoes. She brought the shoes with her in a little case, and changed into them when she took off her boots, rather than slip into a pair of slippers, which was the usual Russian custom. She showed little interest in us, none in Vera. She paid attention only to her watch. Vasili said later that Irina felt insecure and shy around academic people. Little Olga seemed closer to Vasili than to her mother; she would turn and whisper to him whenever she wanted anything.

The snow got slushier by the day, but in late March cars and trucks still drove across the ice to get to Khabarovsk on the other side of the river. In summer, cars crossed by ferry. A bridge for cars was under construction, but the project had been stalled for several years because there was no money to finish it. For a few weeks in April and May, when the ice softened, cars couldn't get across at all. The only crossing was a railroad bridge.

Under the heaving and melting and refreezing layers of ice, the river was treacherous in the early springtime.

Our students talked about the danger of "*polunia*," when the river begins to thaw and patches of water are covered by snow, and the moving water below is deep enough to fall into and be swept away under the ice.

"This happened to me when I was a child," my student Katya said. "We were having a picnic. I left the circle of my parents and their friends. I slipped under the ice. I was too shocked to cry for help, but my father saw me and he pulled me out."

Ludmila Vinnikova, whose Jewish husband was an important city official, told us that any registered Birobidjan resident who could prove some Jewish heritage was eligible for a free trip to Israel once every second year. There was also a brisk one-way emigration from the Jewish Autonomous Region to Israel; many people had already gotten out for good. People no longer tried to hide being Jewish; on the contrary, they went to a great deal of effort to prove that they were.

Irina, a voluptuous, flamboyant and decidedly unacademic student in my Yiddish class, whose family recently discovered Jewish ancestors, went with her mother to apply for a visa to Israel.

"The man refused me," Irina said. "He told me I looked like a prostitute, and Israel would not want me. What do you think of that?"

Since she asked me, I told Irina she would have a better chance if she wore a looser sweater, a longer skirt, lower heels, and a lot less makeup.

Many of the students found it difficult to formulate and express opinions; they were used to being told what to think. In most of their classes, the focus was on rote memory, not analysis and critical thinking. They found it exotic that we urged them to discuss their own ideas.

"How do you want me to answer?" Denis Kopul once asked, in confusion, when I asked him what he thought of a character in a story the class was reading.

We understood how foreign our questions were one evening when we heard Pavel, a generous and devoted father, say to Kolya, age 12, "Don't tell me what you think. You are not old enough to think!"

I kept remembering the words Milan Horak, our friend in Prague, said one day in frustration: "Our people have forgotten how to think!" He was speaking of Czech people, newly independent after 45 years of oppression under the Soviet system; here were the Russians after 75 years of Communism and, before that, the czar. They were people who had never been allowed to think for themselves, except in terms of trying to survive.

Our students, ages 17 to 23, were children in the last days of Communism. They started life singing praises to Lenin and Stalin, their older brothers and sisters belonged to the Young Pioneers, their parents had pledged allegiance to the powers that oppressed them, and they dared not speak of friends or relatives who had disappeared.

They learned in school that the world outside the Soviet Union was a hotbed of disease, corruption and poverty. It was a shock to them when they learned how behind the other developed countries they actually were. And they firmly believed in their own individual inability to make a difference, so they struggled just to cope and endure.

Eight inches of snow fell on Birobidjan the last day of March, but most of it melted within a week, and the ice on the river – although we saw a single hiker walking gingerly across – was treacherously thin. We took a two-hour walk through town, our jackets open, no hats or gloves – and felt euphoric. I asked my shyest student, Masha Voroshbit, when they would stop wearing their fur hats. The end of April, she assured me.

Trucks stopped driving across the ice to Khabarovsk in mid-March, and cars at the end of March, but there was still too much ice for the ferries to run. Pavel Tolstogusov, Ludmila Sergeievna

Tsimbalyuk, John and I took the train to Khabarovsk to lead some workshops at a Soros seminar for 65 teachers from towns and villages around the Jewish Autonomous Region. (George Soros, Hungarian millionaire philanthropist, has funded many educational events in formerly Communist countries.)

Boris Fineman, a college official, had apparently promised our presence at the conference, then showed up at our apartment to talk us into honoring his commitment. If there was money involved, he wasn't saying. He urged us to go "as a humanitarian gesture," but he seemed so anxious that we became suspicious. In any case, after much questioning, and concern about our students in the classes we would miss, we agreed to go. He was greatly relieved.

Once again, John and I were the first Americans most of these teachers had ever met. They treated us like movie stars. The teachers enthusiastically spent seven days of their own spring vacation at the spa to attend educational lectures and seminars for ten hours a day. Many of them hadn't been paid for months, but they considered the workshop a benefit.

"Were you sent to the Russian Far East to pay for your past sins?" one of the teachers asked John.

"Did you come to our region by choice or were you ordered to come here?" one of them asked me.

Young people were suspicious of our circumstances and older people questioned our motives. Some of our students were quite cynical and with good reason. It would be hard to be an idealistic youth in a corrupt society. Teachers and doctors went unpaid while the so-called "newly rich" threw money around and drove big foreign cars.

On the other hand, the Russians took for granted what I saw so clearly: the close connections they had with their friends, the pleasure they found in talking together for hours at a time, singing songs and playing games, their natural enthusiasm and generosity of spirit. When invited, I gladly joined them, and as we sang and laughed together, sometimes my heart ached with joy.

We were inspired by the Russian people's solidarity. Here were teachers and administrators, young and old, pretty and plain – four out of five were women – from isolated villages to Birobidjan itself, together night and day, arguing, laughing, sleeping, drinking, singing, relaxing. No privacy, packed schedule, no problem.

Boris Fineman grew very enthusiastic about his own presentations at the conference, having to do with the psychology of education, and one afternoon we came on the scene and surprised him in the middle of a raging argument with Ludmila Sergeievna over how much time we English teachers were taking. She apparently won the dispute and we saw Boris outside the conference hall later, walking off his anger, his "road-kill hat" bobbing up and down on his head.

Children who lived near the spa gave a performance at midweek – with elaborate costumes, no doubt made by their mothers. On the final night of the conference, the teachers themselves put on a performance of skits and songs. This was topped off by a long feast, with wine and vodka and cognac, fish and wild fern (a popular salad), meat and fruit and candy. Between courses, nearly everyone jumped up and danced – in pairs and lines and circles – then piled back to the tables for more toasts and the next course.

Sometimes all the teachers would start singing some soulful Russian song – and even the stout apron-clad serving women would stop, tray or dishpan in hand, and join in the singing. Then more toasts, more food, more dancing. We stumbled off to bed at midnight. Pavel said some people stayed up until four in the morning.

In what we by now considered typical Russian scheduling, we all had to get up at five in the morning to catch the bus into the city and be on the eight o'clock train.

In an unexpected meeting, Antonina Salinon, program manager on the Peace Corps staff, was waiting for us at the Khabarovsk train station. She unloaded on us eleven boxes of books from America.

Antonina, who had come to Khabarovsk to visit volunteers, was very happy to discover that we were there, too. She and her driver were trying to hire a helicopter to lift the heavy Peace Corps Land-rover over the river so they could drive to Birobidjan to visit our college. While the driver was calling around trying to find a helicopter, Antonina talked John and me into lugging the books to Birobidjan on the train.

"The books would be too much extra weight for the helicopter," Antonina said.

As it turned out, there was no helicopter available, so after unloading the books on us, Antonina and her driver ended up storing the Land-rover and taking a later train themselves.

With the usual five-minute stop in Birobidjan, it was a mad scramble getting the boxes off the train. Pavel Nikolaievich, Ludmila Sergeievna and some of the other teachers formed a line and moved the boxes along the corridor, out the door and onto the platform.

To our further annoyance, once we had gotten the boxes to our building and opened them, we realized that only three were for our college. The other eight boxes of books were the personal property of Antonina's friend Larisa Belichenko, the woman Vera had replaced.

Larisa, it seemed, had returned from her sabbatical.

Whenever we got out of town, we realized that Birobidjan was a good place to be. Streets were fairly clean, buildings were attractive, there were trees and birds and regular buses. The electricity didn't go out, there was hot and cold running water that didn't get turned off very often, and cars didn't swerve toward people in crosswalks.

Birobidjan's civic structure seemed to be more or less working. We asked our friends why this might be so. One said it was because the city administration was Jewish; another said it was because there was only one Mafia.

With the layers of snow reduced to patches in the lowlands and on the shady sides of buildings, people gathered for weekend picnics beside the river.

One evening as we ate supper in our kitchen, we smelled wood burning.

We looked out the window and saw that Valentina, the barrel-chested Kommandant, and her soldier husband Uri were in the yard below, having pulled a cafeteria table out the door and lined a circle in the dirt with gray bricks for a makeshift fire pit. They were barbecuing cubes of pork and drinking vodka.

"*Priatnova appetita*!" John yelled down at them. They laughed and hoisted their shot glasses in our direction.

12

Spring Cleaning

No sooner had the last of the frost melted off the windows than the first mosquito of spring found its way into our bedroom.

I cut a piece of screen into a rectangle, and drove skinny nails into the old wood of the window frame, installing a California screen on the bedroom window to keep out the mosquitoes. It was a time-consuming task. I tapped the big old Russian hammer gently, so as not to bend the cheap nails, then bent them over at the last quarter of an inch to hold the screen in place.

As I worked I could hear children playing and sometimes birds twittering, and the tunes of my past and present played aimlessly through my mind, lighting here and there like birds spying seeds, or like birds pulling invisible threads from clots of dirt to weave into their nests.

Below the window, a woman stooped over and pulled off the new leaves of dandelions and other weeds and added them to the greens in her basket.

The residents of Birobidjan took pride in their city, with its grand public buildings, city parks and statues, and wide tree-lined streets. Spring cleanup was a major event.

Birobidjan's 60th anniversary celebration was coming up in May. Why this year? The region's first Jewish collective farm began in 1928; the area's designation as the Jewish Autonomous Region was established in 1934. The 20th anniversary was observed in 1948, the 50th in 1984. At any rate, 60th anniversary signs were posted, potholes in the streets were repaired, buildings were painted, and flowers were planted along Shalom Aleichem Street, around the statue of Lenin, and in the parks.

Early spring in the Russian Far East was not altogether an aesthetic delight. I welcomed the eight inches of snow that fell at the end of March because it covered a blight of black ice and mud. Even the weeds, that pass for lawn in summertime, were dead and decayed. Icy puddles thawed to reveal frozen trash that had been embedded in snow since autumn. Only the most discerning observer could detect buds swelling on the willows and the poplar trees. A small gray bird chirped a monotone as if to clear its throat.

Nine days later, the daytime temperature was in the 50s, tall thin willow trees at the edge of the river bed were sprouting furry buds, and plants unfolded tentative swellings of pale yellow, orange and green.

We decided to go home to Santa Barbara for a vacation in the summer and, while we were there, round up some books and mail them back to Birobidjan ourselves. We bought our plane tickets: leaving Khabarovsk July 9, returning August 9.

John did most of the cooking. I specialized in such things as salad making, table setting, and cleanup. He did nearly everything else, and did it well, especially considering the limited setup – one cupboard, a cranky gas stove that sometimes leaked, no counter space. It took time. There were no fast foods, no mixes, no shortcuts.

Important kitchen tools were a fine Chinese cleaver, a bread knife from home, Swiss army knife, wooden spoons, and an iron frying pan.

Spring breathed new life into our hearts.

In the *rinok* the amount of fresh food for sale increased day by day as the weather warmed.

We also shopped in the big grocery store at the edge of the *rinok*, where the aisles were as crowded as Bus 21, with people squeezing by each other, the proximity as impersonal as pressed human flesh could possibly be.

In the late afternoon, we graded papers. We read. People came by. Hardly anyone had a telephone, and we had many visitors – students with a question, someone with a message for us, friends dropping by, the soldier temporarily staying next door (he came over to borrow a match; once he came to ask John to tie his necktie for him). Militia people came to check our visas; Kommandant Valentina found frequent needs to check up on one thing or another.

We took long walks. Down Lenin Street, through the park, across the square, then maybe along the river, maybe over the bridge. If we walked a long way, we would take a city bus home, which cost less than a dime.

We did little household chores. Elvira came in once a week to run the sweeper. When the old vacuum cleaner stopped working, she bent over and swept the carpets with a short-handled straw broom.

With no shelves or proper storage space, we muttered about our accumulation of paper, magazines, documents, file folders and books. Especially since eight boxes of books, stacked in a corner of our living room, belonged to Larisa Belichenko. Where was the woman? Why didn't she come to collect her belongings?

Dusk came around 9 p.m. that time of year. The comet Hale-Bobb splashed huge and bright across the late evening sky.

The Biro river flowed fast from the western hills, with big slabs of ice bumping into each other. But the Amur river, separating the region from Khabarovsk, was deeper and wider, and still unnavigable. The ice, though slushy and cracked, remained thick.

Our kitchen window was big, seven feet across and six feet high. But the panes of glass on each side were smaller than the window frames, so the frames had two panes of glass in them, overlapping. In the window that could be opened, which I had nailed a screen to, the larger piece of glass was cracked. Sometimes the wind blew this window open and it clattered against the cupboard.

Our building was ell-shaped. If we looked to the right, we could see into three classrooms; looking to the right and down on the first floor, we could see the windows of the clerk's office, and next to that, the cafeteria, which was often rented out for parties on the weekends. We could hear the bass throbbing of loud disco music and see the disco lights flash dimly on and off. Since the fight in our hallway, Kommandant Valentina took to locking the gate into our part of the building when there were parties. But as well as locking people out, this locked us in.

Being on the second floor meant that as we sat at our kitchen table, we looked out on the upper branches of the tall poplar trees in the courtyard. The yard below was a mess of dirt and broken concrete and scattered rocks, where children fought and played and threw empty bottles at the brick wall across the way to hear them crash and break.

A gaping trench was dug in the dirt below our window, and stayed open for several weeks while pipes were laid from our building to a new college building going up next door. When the trench was filled in, rocks were left scattered. Trees were spared, though some of their roots were damaged, and one or two of them stood teetering at the edge of the hole.

From the kitchen window, we could sometimes see our neighbor, the soldier, below in the yard trying to get his car started, or, failing that, hitching it to a friend's car and getting it towed away.

After that late snowstorm, one final layer of soft white snow to cover dirt and concrete chunks and garbage, winter was over. The snows melted; even the blackened piles of plowed snow at the edges of streets melted. In the yard, the ground was eventually laid bare. Long hard buds formed at the tips of the poplars, sprouting after some weeks into light green catkins which turned to fuzz and blew off, giving way to bright green leaves.

The Russians put away their fur hats. Buds swelled on the birch trees by the river. We went from winter coats to no coats in about two weeks' time.

Spring rains turned the limbs of the poplars and birches a slick dark gray; sunshine dried and bleached the bark to white, especially bright on the long narrow trunks where they faced the setting sun. Birds sang now, but not melodiously. They chattered and peeped. They grabbed hold of the bars on our windows, and flitted around below the eaves of the tin roof. We could sit and talk quietly about nothing of consequence, and notice the seasons passing through the poplar trees.

Denis stopped by with good news. Someone from the Freedom Support Act Undergraduate Exchange Program phoned him at the college Thursday afternoon and told him to be at the university in Khabarovsk at nine o'clock Saturday morning.

With his application and essay, he had passed the first level of the scholarship competition! Now there was a second hurdle: He needed to take a college aptitude test and a language test, and this weekend was the only time to do it.

Maybe Denis should have known about this possibility; maybe he didn't read the fine print in the application. We told ourselves that we should have worked more closely with him on the whole process.

Now it was a mad scramble. Denis had to find out exactly where to go at the university, buy his train ticket, and make sure he had everything ready that he would need to take to the test. He called relatives in Khabarovsk and arranged to stay at their apartment overnight. They found a friend with a car who agreed to drive him to the university Saturday morning.

Things worked out, at the last minute, as they tended to do, and Denis was back on Monday, eager to talk about the test.

"I met very intelligent people there," he said. "Every person except myself was from Khabarovsk. There was another group taking the test in Vladivostok. I didn't know so many Russians wanted to go to America. Thirty people took the test in Khabarovsk; probably more in Vladivostok."

In the evening, Denis came by to get the key to the television room so he could watch CNN, as he often did.

By then, he had given a lot of thought to the experience of taking the test, and he said, "I think that I did rather badly. I did not understand all the questions. Also, frankly speaking, I think I need eyeglasses. I have a case of the eye strain."

To get our Peace Corps grant money, we needed bids, in writing, on the local cost of a television set, video cassette recorder, e-mail service, and telephone line.

The television shop was unable to provide a bid, once because the boss wasn't there and the shop's official stamp was locked up, and later because the boss still hadn't authorized putting anything in writing. It would have been a simple matter to walk in and pay cash for a television set, but getting a bid was not simple. Maybe Russians feared such accountability. In those uncertain times and with the confiscatory tax laws, I would.

But the matter of getting e-mail service in the library was even more problematic. We finally found the e-mail provider in his office and told him we needed a written bid on providing the service, which he had told me on the phone would cost thirty dollars a month.

Now he said he was having a problem getting a local access number. Everyone was still waiting, he said. He got very excited about telling us he could provide Internet service but not e-mail access, though we couldn't understand how he could do the one but not the other. And he didn't want to put anything in writing either.

Then he phoned and said he would put a bid in writing. We rushed to his office, a small cubicle on the second floor of the post office. The bid: sixty dollars a month for e-mail only, plus two hundred dollars to set it up.

"He's fishing," John said, and we left his office without the piece of paper.

We still needed a phone line into the library, too. Anatoli Surnin's latest word was that it would be installed "as soon as the military releases some lines," whatever that meant.

Vera arranged to meet with Anatoli Surnin on our behalf and she asked him for an explanation about the phone line.

Anatoli got very upset at being questioned by Vera. He yelled at her and accused her of "interfering" with things that were none of her business.

Vera yelled back at him, saying she might be guilty of any number of things, but being a "nosy parker" wasn't one of them. (Vera got these great expressions from the 1930s and 1940s detective novels she loved to read.)

"You signed your name. You promised!" she reminded him, his signature having been an essential part of our grant application. Anatoli eventually calmed down and apologized.

"He realizes he has no choice," Vera said confidently.

Not that this meant we had the phone line yet.

The whole grant application process had started with a donated computer modem, which we thought would be a good first step in getting e-mail access in our department library. There was an old computer there; the modem would work on it.

But from the first moment, Anatoli tried to grab the modem for use in the main building. He actually told Vera to tell us that it would be impossible to get a phone line for our building. The message was: "Tell them anything; just get us that modem." It wasn't even a very good modem, just a castoff piece of equipment from a computer center.

We were being a lot less cooperative with Anatoli ourselves, now that we were learning how to negotiate Russian-style.

We refused to give up the modem, insisting that it must be used in our building. We reminded Anatoli that he had promised to provide a room for it, and we reminded him that a grant would help us get books and video equipment as well as e-mail service, provided he cooperated with us. We said we would even arrange for an expert to come in and lecture to the faculty on using e-mail.

"Good," Anatoli said. "But the lecture must be in the main building."

All of the teachers in our Foreign Languages Division – English, French, Yiddish, Chinese, and Russian as a foreign language – came to our building for a work day on Saturday. They had to clean up the teachers' room.

In the teachers' room were ten desks for a staff of about twenty. John, Vasili Ivchenko and Oleg, the Chinese teacher, were the only males. The teachers without desks had a couch to sit on between classes; there was a small mirror by the door, an extension phone, one filing cabinet, no privacy.

We cleaned the desks, swept down the walls, plucked the cotton batting out of the cracks around the window frames (stuffed there last fall), and washed the windows. Although the other teachers were required to do this work, John and I had to talk them into allowing us to help. We wondered if they would ever regard us as something other than privileged guests.

The indoor public swimming pool opened in the municipal sports hall. But a clerk there told us that we foreigners would need a medical examination and special permission to use it. We visited the pool. It was small and crowded with children. We gave up the idea of swimming there.

Slabs of ice floated down the middle of the river. Chunks of ice were trapped at the edge; they had partly thawed and refrozen so many times in the moving stream that they took the shape of thousands of straws bundled, like a honeycomb.

We watched an old woman – one long tooth hanging in the center of her mouth – picking the long green buds off the lower twigs of birch trees. We asked her what the buds were for. She grinned and said they were good for the health, and she massaged her joints and rubbed her stomach, describing her arthritis pains, her digestive problems.

"Do you brew it in tea?" I asked.

"*Nyet*!" she said with a cackling laugh. "Vodka!"

13

Orphans and Bureaucrats

The comet continued its spectacular domination of the evening sky.

A group of 16 high school students from Portland, Oregon, visited the college for an afternoon. They talked about their after-school jobs and asked the Russian students about theirs. I was touched that instead of expressing their usual frustrations about unemployment, vanishing paychecks and disappearing factories, our Russian students replied that they did some tutoring, they taught English, they gave guitar lessons, and so on.

"Do you have a minimum wage law?" one of the Americans asked.

"Yes," the Russians replied firmly, and changed the subject. Either they didn't understand the concept of a minimum wage, or they didn't want to start comparing the Russian pay scale to America's.

John and I visited the orphanage in Waldheim. At the Soros conference, we had met the English teacher who worked there, a thin, excitable and flamboyant woman named Tamara Anatolievna.

The orphanage was home to 186 boys and girls ages seven to sixteen. There was a staff of 67, many of whom had grown up in the orphanage themselves. They hadn't been paid since December, but where would they go if they quit their jobs?

As soon as we got out of the car, curious children approached, shyly at first, but soon bold and eager.

"Hello!" a few of them said in English. Then, in Russian, "How are you? What's your name? Where are you from?"

One boy bent his head closer as we walked along, the better to check out the watch on my wrist. Another skipped along backwards in front of me, smiling, catching my eye as often as possible. A boy who said he was twelve but who was very small for his age, kept practicing every English expression he knew, including a very long song that repeated itself in entirety with every added verse.

"My name is Ruslan," he said, several times.

The children fell away as we were ushered into the office of the orphanage director, Tamara Petrovna, a stout woman of about forty, blessed with a remarkably pleasant face.

She spoke Russian slowly and enunciated clearly, so we could understand much of what she said, and she took great pride in showing us around. The gathering of children shrank and grew as we passed from one part of the building into another. The dorms and classrooms, separated by a corridor, were old but clean, with tall ceilings and large sunny windows. The orphanage had been the central building of a communal farm in the 1930s.

Next door to this sprawling building was the village school. Although no fence separated the orphanage and the school, there was an invisible line that was not crossed. The children of the village and the children of the orphanage did not play together; the two groups of teen-agers did not mingle. We saw this for ourselves, but we also asked the question, to be sure, and Tamara Petrovna shrugged and said, "You can't blame the children."

"Oh, it is far better as it is. If they played together, the orphans would feel inferior!" said Tamara Anatolievna, the orphanage teacher whose own son went to the school next door. She brushed away the notion with a flick of her long red scarf.

Furnishings in the orphanage were Spartan and worn, but the general impression was of a well-ordered institution. Potted plants lined the stairways. Children's drawings were displayed in the classrooms.

Adolescent girls sat at black treadle sewing machines in one sunny room. One girl was stitching together a pair of cotton shorts; another was sewing a brown zipper that was too long into a black skirt that was too short.

In a room devoted to arts and crafts, a thin little girl with blond hair cut to various lengths thrust a drawing into my hand and waved me off when I tried to return it. Judging by her size and by the two large front teeth surrounded by baby teeth, I guessed she was about seven. Beyond her name, Irina, she had nothing to say, but she stared at my face and smiled broadly, her picture in my hand.

"Irina is ten years old," Tamara Petrovna said. "Some of the children are very slow in their growth." (We had heard of this condition: failure to thrive – a condition of simply not developing into the people they might otherwise have been, because of lack of attention, lack of nourishment, lack of love.) Whenever we visited, the younger children would clutch at my arm, hold my hand, peer into my eyes, and smile hard, showing their little gray teeth.

As we strolled, Ruslan reappeared and announced he was a writer. Tamara Petrovna confirmed that Ruslan wrote many stories, some rather fantastic, and some about ordinary children. Ruslan had small round ears that protruded directly out from his head. The look on his grave little face combined hope and despair, and his direct gaze seemed to express a frank incomprehension, and yet curiosity. His were the eyes of a child who understood he was not well loved, but who had not yet grown bitter or hardened by the knowledge.

One girl, Olga, said her thirteenth birthday would be the next day. Her clothes were ill-fitting and shabby, her shoes too small, and her heels bloody and blistered. She was a pretty girl, with dark hair and soft features.

John had brought the camera. He wasn't sure he would want to use it, but, seeing it, several of the children asked him to take their pictures. They piled into the lens' eye no matter how he tried to limit a frame to two or three faces. He snapped several shots; seven or eight faces or parts of faces, from a distance of three feet. They were disappointed when he ran out of film.

The children's bedrooms were fastidiously neat. Pillows were fluffed and stacked in eccentric triangular shapes. Corners of the blankets were tucked under mattresses, some so tightly as to pull the thin mattresses into oblongs that curved up from the corners. Each bedroom held six or seven beds. There was not much storage space; there was not much to store.

All of the work around the place was done by the children themselves, Tamara Petrovna proudly said. There was no money. Federal money had stopped coming in five years before. Sometimes people donated things. There were twelve computers, completely outdated, but still they existed – under lock and key. And there were tools – hammers and saws. And the children gardened.

Hothouses under the south-facing windows sheltered sprouting tomato vines, cucumbers and cabbages. Beyond the sheds, children were tilling the fields with shovels and hoes.

There was an auditorium and a room with mirrors where folk-dancing was taught. The dancing instructor apologized for the dozens of handprints on the mirrors. On May 9th, there would be a performance to mark Russia's Victory Day. We asked if we could attend.

Tamara Petrovna smiled pleasantly and said, "Oh, it will be far from perfect. We would be too embarrassed. You had probably better not."

She showed us small homemade items on display in her office – wooden trays, potted plants, bookmarks – and said they might be for sale. And if we wanted to make donations – money, clothing, books – anything would be gratefully accepted.

The children had no personal possessions. Their clothing was a hodgepodge of whatever was available, from a general supply arranged according to size. They may have had small boxes tucked away under their beds for their own things, but I didn't think so. They had each other. They clustered in pairs or small gangs, arms entwined, heads on each other's shoulders.

The most thrilling announcements that a few of them made were: "He's my brother!" and "She's my sister!"

Such a bond made those pairs special. In each case, it was said with pride, one child grabbing the one other person in the world who shared something of their particular heritage.

Technically, some of them were not orphans. They had parents living not far away. Did the parents ever visit?

"It's better if they don't," Tamara Petrovna said.

She left unsaid that some were too drunk, or disturbed, or too full of their own despair or rage or hatred. Some were indifferent, others impoverished or ill, still others whose whereabouts were unknown, but that didn't really matter in any legal sense; hardly anybody ever came here in search of a child to adopt.

The occasional Russians who wanted to adopt would go to the *detski dom*, the orphanage for babies and toddlers, to find a younger child than these, a child who was not considered too old, too abused, too disturbed.

Some orphans suffered the effects of the vodka their alcoholic mothers drank. Some had noticeable dents and scars on their heads and faces from having been beaten. A few of the children were physically beautiful. The younger boys and girls gazed at us with eyes full of longing for attention, willing us to be pleased, regretting in advance that we would not stay long.

Helen Wheeler, the Peace Corps country director, visited Birobidjan and decided this was a good place to train the next group of volunteers. Our college – and Vera – would be very helpful in making the arrangements.

Of course, everything depended on the Russian government, the issuing of visas, and other such details. Thirty-five new volunteers were coming to the Russian Far East. Their training would be under way when we returned from America.

John and I looked forward to having a whole tribe of Americans around for a couple of months. And the Jewish Autonomous Region was very friendly to the Peace Corps, now that the authorities realized we were not spies or religious proselytizers. Local officials had been uneasy about us at first; their minimal experience with Americans had been mostly with missionaries, and they were not pleased with them. "Russian Orthodox priests should go to Salt Lake City and try to convert the Mormons," a Russian political leader, Alexander Lebed, grumbled on national television. But as for Peace Corps, the schools around the Jewish Autonomous Region requested seven more volunteers.

Peace Corps officials approved our grant request. Happily, we rushed out and bought the college the television set and VCR from the local stores that had submitted bids to us. And we started looking again for an Internet provider.

Anatoli Surnin told Vera he wanted to reward us for getting the equipment.

"Please tell him that Peace Corps volunteers can't accept money," I said to Vera. "But remind him he must provide a room for this equipment. He signed a contract."

Vera promised she would deliver the message.

But Anatoli really didn't want to provide the room. He wanted to reward us. He ordered Vera to take us to a sanitorium in the village of Kuldur for a three-day holiday.

A few days after telling us that, Vera said there had been "a misunderstanding," and we should not count on going to Kuldur right away.

Vera said, in her formal way, "I cannot discuss the details until I have resolved the dilemma."

We had first heard about Kuldur from Vasili Ivchenko, who became familiar with it when he had his job in the city government. Traditionally, Russian bureaucrats and other privileged people were the ones who experienced such places. The village, surrounded by wilderness, was built around natural hot springs. It was east of Birobidjan, an hour down a narrow road from a station on the railroad tracks to Siberia. There were three sanitoriums in Kuldur: one new and luxurious, two old and very rundown.

Within a week, Vera told us why our outing had been delayed: Viktor, the potbellied maintenance chief, had been put in charge of arranging our trip. Viktor was the man who had organized our winter picnic. When Viktor heard that we planned to go to Kuldur, he tried to get Vera to invite him along.

"I put the stop to that idea," Vera said. "I told Viktor that you and John didn't want him to go."

It wasn't really a bad guess on Vera's part because Viktor truly was a party animal, and we hadn't heard a word from him since that picnic – when he got royally drunk.

But this rejection would not go unavenged.

As it turned out, Viktor had called the new sanitorium in Kuldur and discovered that it would be closed until the first week in June. However, he went ahead and made reservations in May for Vera and John and me at one of the old shabby places. Vera discovered this from some other source (which she refused to divulge to us).

Viktor thought we would get all the way to Kuldur and discover the situation when it was too late to change our plans.

John and I had been in Russia long enough that we could spend hours speculating about how such things happen. We thought of three possible explanations: By choosing one of the cheaper sanitoriums, Viktor may have planned to accompany us for the entire weekend, whether or not his presence was wanted. Or this secretive arrangement could have been Viktor's way of getting even with us for rejecting his idea of including himself in our plans. Or, maybe Viktor really thought that he was doing what we would want by booking us into one of the old rundown places.

It was a prototypical situation.

Whenever you tried to make arrangements through former Communist bureaucratic underlings:

First they would try to turn your situation, if at all possible, into some sort of advantage for themselves.

If this failed, they set to work figuring out some way of getting even with you for foiling their plan.

Finally, these machinations always included an escape hatch, so that if their attempt to sabotage you was revealed, they could put on an innocent expression and say they were only, with the very best intentions, doing what they thought you would want.

In fact, they could easily go so far as to work up a strong case of hurt feelings, that you would even question their good intentions.

There was no point in tearing your hair out over it or engaging in a confrontation; nothing would change anything. But we felt wiser for knowing such things do happen.

14

Spies, Heroes and Intellectuals

A tremendous explosion shook the earth on Orthodox Easter Sunday, and then reverberated in waves like echoes. We were on the way to the *rinok* and we stopped dead in our tracks. We wondered if there had been an earthquake.

"What was that?"

"I don't know."

A tall trail of smoke rose from the horizon in the windless clear air. We wondered if there had been a plane crash.

Everyone on the street was momentarily suspended, then animatedly turned to others with the same question. Slowly, people returned to the chores at hand.

It gradually became known that there had been an explosion at the military ammunition depot in Bira, 25 miles northwest of Birobidjan. All of the ammunition stored there had gone up in flames.

The residents of Bira, mostly a few military families stationed at the remote outpost, had run screaming from their apartments, their hands over their ears, their children wild with terror.

Women and children were rounded up and evacuated from Bira because of continuing minor explosions in the still smoldering dump. They were brought to the Vostok Hotel, next to the *rinok*, where they stayed for several days.

Initially, there was speculation that the cause of the explosion might be related to the war in Chechnya, as it happened on Easter, which also marked the anniversary of a hero's death.

But later the television news reported that the incident was a simple accident: A young soldier, guarding the ammunition dump, had carelessly tossed a cigarette onto the grass, and he didn't notice that it smoldered, then flared up, and finally ignited the stockpile – tens of thousands of pounds of explosives.

There were no deaths. No injuries. Not even the careless guard.

That was the story, and that was the end of it. No investigative reporters to ask hard questions. No further public announcements. Just a soldier, smoking.

"Blessed solitude, a gift beyond treasure, especially after the fearful loneliness of compulsory, unrelieved togetherness."
Eugenia Ginzburg, "Within the Whirlwind"

While we were reading Eugenia Ginzburg's remarkable books about her years in Stalin's Gulag system, John sank into a mild depression, and it gradually lifted only after we had finished. It wasn't only the depressing story, though. There were other problems: some unrewarding classes, too heavy a teaching load, uncertainty whether we were doing any good. John said he felt a sense of endlessness about our grand adventure.

There were times when I, too, felt a weight on my chest, like a shortage of air, a dullness of mind, a lack of color. I could not hope to lift his spirits when mine were nearly as low. I came to resent his attitude, his complaining.

"Why now?" I asked unreasonably, as he sat slumped in his chair. "Spring is here. The weather is warm. We can open the windows. Why can't you be happy?"

There were five married couples among the forty-five volunteers to the Russian Far East in our group, and not a single training session was held on the particular stresses of being Peace Corps married couples. We had sessions about drugs and alcohol, AIDS, homosexuality, how to put condoms on bananas, intimate relationships with Russian women or men, sexual harassment, and every other conceivable problem a single volunteer might face.

166

But I'm not sure what the Peace Corps would know about the problems of married couples anyway.

Gradually, an aspect of our life in Russia versus our life in America was becoming clear: The tapestry of our togetherness in Russia was so finely woven, there were no spaces, no escapes. No separate work lives. No jumping in the car to go shopping. No puttering in the garden. No retiring to another room to avoid conflict; there were no other rooms. Stay, be together, cope. "*Zhag za Zhagem*" (step by step). But what if we were pulling in different directions?

There were still those in Russia who were convinced we Peace Corps volunteers were spies. This view was especially prevalent in the old guard element of FSB (*Federalnaya Sluzhba Bezopasnosti*), a successor of the Soviets' notorious KGB.

An article appeared in the Russian tabloid *Dokumenti i Fakti* (Truth and Facts) about American spies disguised as Peace Corps volunteers. It named several names.

The most incriminating "evidence" that our ranks included spies was a photograph of Brian Keating, an environmentalist volunteer kneeling near a chain-link fence that enclosed a military installation in the former Communist stronghold of Komsomolski Krai.

The officials of Komsomolsk, a closed city until Perestroika, still resented the end of the old system; many would return to Communism in a minute if they could.

Brian had been arrested and taken to police headquarters where he was questioned for hours. The article never mentioned his reason for being near the fence: He was watering some new young trees that the Russians had permitted him to plant in a reforestation project.

Lena Tolstogusova and Ludmila Tsimbalyuk both supplemented their teachers' salaries by translating for Americans who came to adopt children from the orphanages around Birobidjan.

I asked Lena about the orphans, and the possibilities for adoption. There were three orphanages in our area: one for babies and preschool children, one for children with very serious mental, physical or emotional problems, and the one in Waldheim for children ages seven to sixteen. I knew Americans who had adopted children from China. Did people know there were many Russian children in orphanages who might also thrive in good homes?

International adoptions had become considerably more difficult in recent years, Lena told me. Such adoptions used to require only regional approval, but the law had changed, and now everything went through Moscow, and might or might not ever be finalized. Many foreigners had given up trying to adopt a Russian child, she said.

John and I were talking with Lena and Vera about relationships between old people and young, and how seldom we saw our grown children (John has four, I have three) and three grandchildren (John's two and my one) who live in other parts of the country.

Vera and Lena reminisced about their own relationships with their grandparents.

Vera said: "My father's mother wanted nothing to do with my mother or me after my father died. She never liked my mother and she didn't like me either, even though I looked more like my father than my mother."

Lena recalled how her mother loved her older son, Kolya, because she had cared for him for four months after he was born, while Lena was not well. But, Lena said, her mother does not love her younger son, Vanya, whom she had never had a chance to know well.

John asked me: "When did you last see your grandparents?"

I thought a moment, and replied, "When I was twenty."

My grandfather was very old by then, gaunt and weak, suffering from silicosis, a condition in which the lungs are scarred and breathing is difficult. He had been a glassblower in Corning, New York. When I was a child, my grandfather was a large man, massive, slow and strong. But during that final visit, I recalled, he was terribly frail and my grandmother was taking care of him. She was also bent and slow. I remember her old skin, white and soft, and her pale-blue eyes, deep-set in her wrinkled face.

"Were they important in your life?" John asked me.

It was strange that my husband of several years was just then asking these questions. I liked this about our living in Russia: We talked more, and thought more about our lives. There were so few distractions.

"Yes, they were important. I think they were more important in my life than I was in theirs," I said. I meant this in the way that old people who live nearby may be dominant in the family life of a child, but the child might just be another new person in a far-reaching web of parents and brothers and sisters and children and grandchildren in the life of a person who has lived for a long time.

May 9 is Victory Day in Russia, the celebration of the end of the Great Patriotic War (World War 2).

The orphanage invited us, after all, to attend their Victory Day concert the day before the big holiday. On the day itself there would be parades, singing and ceremonies in the town square, and everyone would go there for the occasion.

We arrived at the orphanage early. Tamara Petrovna was planting seeds in the freshly turned dirt in a small garden patch near the hallway window. I felt the children were fortunate to have her as their headmistress. She cared for them, though everything was under lock and key and she obviously managed the big operation with strict attention to detail. But she gave the air of being soft and warm. There was a frown line between her eyebrows, but her eyes were merry and she had a ready smile. The children clustered around her when there were visitors, but they also moved quickly away when she sent them a signal.

John and I sat on the hallway bench and were soon surrounded by children. Their shoes were old and cheaply made, canvas or vinyl, shapeless, and without sturdy heels. Their stockings sagged and their sweaters hung limply. They clustered together, touching each other, laying their heads on each other's shoulders, nudging and jostling for position.

We showed them the photographs John had taken of them on our last visit and we exchanged simple questions and answers in Russian and English. Soon Tamara Petrovna came indoors, washed her hands at the big sink by the back door, and took us into her office, where she summoned Tamara Anatolievna, the English teacher, to come and escort us to her class.

The dozen children in Tamara Anatolievna's class were eleven and twelve years old. A few of them were eager and responsive to her; four seemed to be learning disabled, two were unable to sit still or focus on the lesson, and two others were extremely shy.

One boy spent the entire class turned sideways in his chair, facing the wall away from us. Other students could hardly keep their eyes off us.

Tamara Anatolievna yelled, cheerfully and often, as she tried to keep the children focused on the lesson. She showed them pictures of flowers, shouting out their English names, then played a guessing game in which she chose a picture, put it behind the back of a student and coached that student in asking questions of the other students:

"Is the flower red?" "Is the flower big?" "Is it a wildflower or a garden flower?"

Then she led them in shouting out a poem: "April brings the primrose sweet; scatters daisies at our feet."

However, the textbook, poorly copied and much-used, called the flower "primerose" and the teacher and her students dutifully pronounced the long "i."

I will always remember "the primerose sweet" and think of Tamara Anatolievna and her incredible energy.

One boy had his head turned toward his friend and away from the teacher, yet it was his friend, Vanya, that Tamara continually scolded for talking; Vanya was the one whose face she could see. Or maybe she scolded Vanya because she recognized the intelligence in his serious face, and she knew it was pointless to try and correct his friend. Vanya, like many of the children in the orphanage, was small for his age. If not for the mature, even aged, look in his sad eyes, he could be taken for a much younger boy.

Ruslan, who had gotten our attention during our first visit, sought us out as soon as he heard we were there. He wanted to walk alongside us and try to make conversation, never smiling, but eager to speak English to us.

We also met Yana, a baby-faced girl, age ten, who smiled at me incessantly, clutched my hand, gazed into my face, and was determined to stay by my side as long as possible. Her short blond hair was pulled into a stubby tail and tied like a bundle of straw on top of her head, held there by a bright blue polyester bow. Yana had wide front teeth, crooked and jagged, maybe worn down by too much sugar.

Two other girls who stayed in my mind were Oxana, fourteen, a serious girl, also short for her age, and pretty, and her friend, Natalia. As we were leaving, they stood quietly by while we waited for the bus, looking from one of us to the other, not saying anything, but listening intently. Prompted by her teacher, Oxana told us she had parents who lived in Khabarovsk. Natalia, a round-faced girl with black hair and dark skin, shrugged when the teacher asked her where her parents were. She said she was nearly sixteen and would leave the orphanage at the end of the next school year.

"Then what will you do?" I asked her.

Natalia shrugged.

"Technical college, or pedagogical college, maybe," her teacher said, although chances of that seemed slim. We had not met a single college student who had been raised in an orphanage, though there probably were a few. In such difficult times, it was more likely that Natalia would join the vast force of the unemployed.

The orphanage concert was performed in honor of veterans of the Great Patriotic War. Two rows of old veterans attended the performance, eighteen in all, including three women. Some of the men wore their military uniforms from fifty years ago and all of them proudly wore rows of ribbons and medals.

A dark-haired adolescent girl cited the first eight lines of a poem, then stopped. She repeated the last line she could remember, then froze, and finally she ran off the stage, red-faced.

The show ended with the smallest children marching in a circle, each carrying a little red flag, and singing about brave comrades and Mother Russia. When they came to the last verse, the veterans stood and joined in the singing. Several of the old men had red faces and their eyes were filled with tears.

Tamara Petrovna introduced us as "the Americans who came to be our friends."

John, in Russian, thanked the veterans for their friendship and their heroism during the war.

Then all of the old veterans and John and I were taken to a sunny room on the second floor and treated to tea and cakes at tables set for the occasion. The three women, round and wrinkled, wore handmade sweaters and old soft scarves. The oldest veteran, seated at the head table, was a baldheaded man with rigidly erect posture, who had the most medals of all. Displayed in rows across the left side of his military jacket, they numbered nineteen.

Tamara Antolievna whispered to me that these veterans had all grown up in that very orphanage. They had gone off to serve in the war, and returned to live out their lives in Birobidjan. Every year, for Victory Day, she said, they came back to the orphanage to be honored.

"We will wait for you impatiently," Pavel said. He and Lena had stopped by to invite us to join them and their friends in the afternoon for a Victory Day picnic. They instructed us to go first to the town square at 10 a.m. for the parade and ceremony.

Lena said she wanted to take the boys, too.

"No, you must stay home and prepare the picnic!" Pavel said.

We offered to come by and get the boys and take them to the square with us, but Lena told us, "No, they will be sleeping."

There was no use questioning them. The plans would sort themselves out, on their terms. We were glad to be included.

I was to bring a blanket for us to sit on, and, in case it rained, umbrellas.

The parade, consisting of a brass band, a choir, small units of young soldiers, and old soldiers who proudly wore long rows of medals and ribbons, marched into the town square where crowds were gathered. The young soldiers of the last unit wore long ponchos, like shrouds, and round helmets. To the slow throbbing of a single drum, this unit, twenty rows of five men, marched slowly up the steps of the Monument to Dead Heroes, to the top, over the top, and down the other side, personifying the many who marched off to battle and disappeared from life. The drumbeat segued into martial music from the brass band, then turned into a dirge, then into a sort of rhythmic hymn. Eight girls in loose-sleeved white gowns, waving blue flags, ascended to the platform at the top of the steps and danced around like angels.

To our right, a soldier in dress uniform, carrying a rifle, stood guard over the flame that had been lit to open the ceremony. Children, in sweaters and knit caps against the wind that chilled the sunny morning, ran and danced along the inner circle of the crowd. Two little boys took turns showing each other how to march, doing the straight-kneed parade march that we call the goose step, typical of German troops and those of Eastern Europe.

John took a picture of a tall, handsome old Kazakh in full uniform, his chest covered with medals and ribbons. He was proud to pose and gave me his name and address; we promised to give him a copy of the photograph. It turned out that he lived in an apartment on Lenin Street, just around the corner from our building.

When the ceremony ended, we walked to the edge of the park and watched a photographer at work. We had seen him before, and had talked with him occasionally. He had told us that his grandparents were among the early Jewish settlers of Birobidjan. Sometimes he stood in the park for hours without a single customer. But on this holiday, children stood in line to have their pictures taken with one of the three large stuffed animals he used as props – Sylvester the Cat, a panda and, of course, Mickey Mouse.

The photographer's wife and son stood nearby. She kept glancing at us, and finally she spoke.

"Are you the Americans?" she asked, not smiling, but anxious, as though we might mind her asking.

"Yes," I said, with a big American smile.

"Americans saved our son's life," she said. "When I saw you were the Americans I wanted to thank you."

Her son was born with a serious heart problem, and somehow she had found a humanitarian group that was able to arrange for her to take him to America and receive the care he desperately needed.

"I want Americans to know that our son is fine now. He is well and happy. For this, every day we thank you."

We and the woman and her little boy smiled at each other, and I promised to deliver her message.

When the crowd began to drift away, we went home and got our picnic supplies, and a big bowl of potato salad I had made the night before, then boarded a breathlessly crowded Bus 21. At the end of the line, we got off in front of the big apartment complex at the edge of town where Pavel and Lena lived.

I thought I had dressed warmly enough, but Lena insisted that I wear her yellow woolen sweater under my jacket because the day was still chilly. It bothered me less all the time that my Russian friends constantly corrected me, that I seemed to require their better judgment, that apparently without their regular intervention I might not make it through the day.

From their apartment, we hiked for half an hour along the river to their favorite picnic spot, where there were already logs rolled into place, forming a square around a depression in the ground. This dent served as our food area, sort of a sunken table, and the jars of pickles and preserved tomatoes and bottles of orange drink rolled to a stop in the center. We positioned bottles and bowls carefully to minimize spills.

In our group were Pavel and Lena; their sons Kolya and Vanya; John and me; Tanya and Oleg, history professors, and their dog Dali (the most relaxed poodle I've ever been around); Sasha, Pavel's best friend, a driver for the college, and Sasha's cheerful, chubby wife, Luba, a professor of elementary education, and their teen-age son, Igor.

Pavel and Sasha were like boys together, and in fact they had been friends for many years. Pavel said he preferred Sasha's company to that of his fellow teachers.

"I don't trust intellectuals," he said.

Usually Vera joined us when we were with Pavel and Lena, but this time she was absent. I wondered about this, but I didn't ask or dwell on it.

We all gathered twigs and logs to keep a fire going. There was no shortage of these. Although the forest was not dense, there was an abundance of scrub and broken limbs from the spindly trees. The trees that had survived the winter were sprouting light green leaves. In the clearings there were wildflowers – light purple flowers that opened like long bells and little white flowers with flat petals – and small leafy plants that looked like wild marijuana.

Tanya and Lena picked bouquets of wildflowers and put them in jars of water to take home. On the other side of our clearing, a broad expanse of rocky land led to the branch of the river that circled past this area.

Sasha opened the first pint bottle of Stolichnaya vodka and proposed the first of many toasts: "to victory."

We clinked glasses and the men downed their vodka in the typical Russian manner – that is to say, in one gulp.

Pavel said formally, pouring a second round of vodka and raising his glass, "I congratulate you on our mutual holiday."

"Yes," John said, raising his glass. "We were allies."

We drank to friendship, we drank to victory, and we drank to our countries having fought against the common enemy in the Great Patriotic War. We women watered down our drinks with mineral water or orange drink, and John sipped his vodka sparingly, trying to pace himself, while Oleg avoided too many refills by being on the other side of the inverted "table."

But Sasha and Pavel were drinking to get drunk, and so they did. Happily, loudly, singing as they progressed to their goal, they lorded it over the afternoon events by sheer volume.

We ate, on and off, for six hours. When the campfire of sticks and logs burned to glowing embers, chunks of beef, marinated in peppery sour milk, and pork, marinated in wine, were jammed onto six skewers of tempered metal (*champeurs* in Russian), handmade by Lena's father, and six birch-branch skewers skinned and sharpened on the spot by Sasha.

The first round of meat cooked nicely over the wood coals, slipping occasionally into the ashes, soaked with another tablespoonful of milk, set back on the coals to sizzle, and pronounced done when crisp on the outside. We gnawed at these morsels, a little tough, but delicious, along with olives, pickles and tomatoes.

Later came the salads, passed around in bowls and jars: wild garlic in a milky sauce, our American-style potato salad, Russian carrot salad, some other mixtures heavily doused with mayonnaise or oil, and a bowlful of raw radishes and cucumbers. There were hunks of dark and weighty Birobidjan bread, slathered with red caviar or cheese or butter.

Suddenly Pavel sprang to his feet and announced it was time for a break from eating and drinking.

We all rushed to the nearby clearing and kicked a soccer ball up and down the uneven expanse of grass, the goals being a pair of trees at one end and a couple of posts at the other. Tanya played with aggression equal to that of the men, more determined than they to score, less determined to collide and roar. We women won, because Tanya was on our side. Lena and I were mainly determined to stay out of the way and avoid getting hurt.

Later, Pavel and Igor played some sort of game, tossing a hoop back and forth between long sticks. The sticks were made of thin green birch branches, skinned of bark, and the hoop was an even thinner twig bent into a circle and tied into shape with a flexible band of the shaved bark.

Ever drunker as the afternoon wore on, Pavel and Sasha belted out song after song, ranging from patriotic to sentimental, then drank more toasts and pulled the women's heads toward them and kissed them long and loudly, one after another, myself included, willing or not.

In a sudden move, Pavel yanked Oleg backward off a log and wrestled with him briefly, losing interest when he proved to his own satisfaction that his will to fight was superior to Oleg's.

Several times, Lena warned Pavel not to drink too much, but mostly she ignored his shenanigans. More wood was collected, the fire stirred again, and – digging into her picnic satchel – Lena pulled out a bag of chicken pieces and started skewering them.

Pavel leapt up to help. He stirred the fire, sparks flying, added more wood, and started to rearrange the stones that encircled the fire pit. But the stones were hot, and he burned the palm of his hand. He yelled and jumped around for a minute, clutching his right hand by the wrist, then went back to his work, pushing the rocks into place with the sides of his shoes. I don't know whether the burn was superficial or he was too drunk to notice. At such times, I had trouble remembering that Pavel was a distinguished professor of Russian literature.

We ate chicken, more salad, and then later, cookies, chocolate candy and cake. Oleg produced a big thermos of strong, sweet lemon tea, deliciously thirst-quenching.

A round of jokes were told by the men, each one producing hearty laughs. Kolya and Igor told jokes, as well as their fathers. Sasha's joke had to do with several rounds of increasing amounts of vodka being served, each being inadequate to the need, including the punch line: an oceanful of vodka was still not enough. And Kolya's joke was about a teacher asking increasingly difficult questions and a student giving increasingly ridiculous answers.

"Okay," Pavel said. "Here is best joke. Doctor is saying to very sick man: 'Do you have problem with alcohol?' Man is saying: 'No! Kiosk near my building sells vodka twenty-four hours a day. No problem!'" That drew much laughter from the drunken men.

Suddenly Pavel, who had been pacing back and forth, sat down on the hard ground and put his head on Sasha's wife's lap. Luba indulgently stroked his thick tousled hair and he fell asleep so soundly that he began snoring. Kolya crept up and put the video camera near his father's face to record the noise. We all laughed and talked, disturbing him not in the least.

Before long, Kolya lay down next to his sleeping father and napped, too. And Oleg curled up beneath a nearby tree. Tanya pushed him to wake him up, insisting that he put a blanket beneath him. Tanya picked a tick off her leg. (Tick-borne encephalitis was one of the diseases the Peace Corps inoculated us against.) Then she pulled a book from her pack and began to read. Luba rolled over, wrapped herself around the sleeping Pavel, and went to sleep, too. John propped himself against a tree and tried to sleep as well.

Lena, Vanya and I went for a walk and picked more wildflowers. Vanya tried throwing stones at the little gray birds who darted among the trees, but his aim was wild and the birds hardly noticed.

When we got back to the picnic site, I practiced my halting Russian on Sasha, who was still alert, even though he was quite drunk. I asked him if he was born in Birobidjan and if he liked it here.

Tears welled up in his dark brown eyes and spilled down his face as he spoke passionately of his childhood home, Ussuriisk, where the weather was fine and the sky was blue and the birds sang and his friends still missed him.

At six in the evening, we awakened Pavel and the others, and gathered up the remains of our long party, the empty bottles and cans, leftover food and dishes, cups and blankets, and packed everything in satchels and bags. The men kicked ashes over the campfire until it smoldered and sank under the weight. Then we paraded back to the apartment buildings, singing as we went, little Vanya dawdling behind, reluctant to end the day.

Lena apologized for the men's drinking. "Last time, they only took one bottle of vodka," she said. "To my mind, it was much better. This time they took three."

Along the way, other groups of holiday celebrants sat on the banks of the river. As we approached each group, Sasha sang louder, and the people we passed joined in. Pavel begged us to come in and have tea, or vodka, and celebrate awhile longer.

"You must stay," Kolya whispered. "You must watch the video of Papa snoring. It will be very funny."

"No, no," we both insisted. "Thank you. We had a wonderful time. Good night."

We trudged, exhausted, to the bus stop. We boarded a crowded Bus 21 home.

"That is the last time I will ever go on a Russian picnic," John said.

15

Unfriendly Feuds

I liked hearing the children play outside. It reminded me of my New England childhood, as did many things in Birobidjan. People were outside, sitting on benches talking, sometimes singing or listening to someone play a violin or an accordion, or playing soccer in the empty field near our apartment.

There was a covered walkway across the yard from our window, a discreet place, where couples sometimes stood, whispering, kissing. One evening, under our window, a drunken girl stumbled around, her boyfriend trying to hold her up. She wore a bright green dress; he was wearing a suit. A dance in the cafeteria, too much to drink. Friends came and helped them back inside. This was the passing scene, live and up close.

One cool, sunny day, we strolled along a country road south of town, stopping at the cemetery. Grave markers were of painted wood and some graves were surrounded by tall fences. Two artificial red roses lay crossed the mound of one grave. The mound was covered with moss, and a stone rested on top, along with the roses.

I recalled the stones that people laid on the graves of Paris and Prague, in cemeteries so densely packed that the headstones seemed piled on each other, like fallen dominoes, with crosses at a jaunty angle, obelisks leaning like the tower of Pisa, and stars of David all but buried by the swell of the next plot.

The cemetery near Birobidjan reminded me, as well, of one outside Skagway, Alaska: graves looked as if they had the staying power of a generation or two at most, scattered over an untended acre or so, in springtime cool and delicately shaded by tall, crooked trees, and encompassed not by manicured lawns but by earth that heaved and fell as the seasons turned from bitter cold to swampy hot. The lumpy dirt nourished patches of weeds, delicate yellow and purple wildflowers, ubiquitous dandelions.

We spent the rest of the day reading, talking, cooking and eating, staring out the window at the brilliant yellow-green leaves of the poplar trees, the late evening sun slanting in from the right, Schumann's heroic classics on the tape player (only because we couldn't always play Mozart and Chopin, though I was tempted to do just that; complicated, happy melodies were my current favorites).

John pulled a muscle in his right leg and he limped around for days. There was a small dinner-dance in the cafeteria, and in his exuberant way, buoyed by a couple of shots of vodka, he had tried Russian squat-leap folk-dancing.

"I pulled whatever's attached to the kneecap," he said. "And it hurts like hell. *Mnoga stari rezat gorchitsa seichas!* Too old to cut the mustard now."

We found a shop that sold popcorn, but they popped it in a big air-popper, doused it with sugar, and sold it by the bag. I tried to get the clerk to sell me a half-kilo of unpopped corn from a giant bag near the popper, and after several days she agreed. Calculating the money she made from popped and sugared popcorn, she decided to charge me 180,000 rubles, about thirty-five dollars. No sale.

Vera no longer seemed close to Pavel and Lena. One day, she summed up Pavel's character this way:

"He is quite communicative and tractable. On the other hand, he says himself that he can be secretive and thrifty, and well, if he doesn't mind saying this, then I don't mind telling you."

As for history professors Tanya and Oleg, Vera said they had "a compatible and stable intimate relationship," although at times

Oleg "strives to give the impression of being wiser and more mature than he is."

We hadn't realized it, but Tanya was 12 years older than Oleg. And, as Vera explained, "he knows that she has more life experience than he does."

In another interesting marriage among our faculty, there was Svetlana, the head of the Russian department, who had a doctor's degree in Russian language and literature, and her husband, a common laborer.

"When she gets up to speak in front of the faculty, all the men shudder," Vera said, "because she will be sure to tell them in very precise and pointed language exactly what they do not want to hear."

But the inequality between Svetlana and her husband created an unholy alliance in their home life, or so everyone believed.

As for our director, Anatoli Surnin, who controlled the college by sheer energy and shouting, he was married for the second time – each wife being several years younger than he and each having already had a child – and people said he was severely henpecked, also for the second time. At work, he was terribly dynamic and energetic, running things like a whirling dervish, hardly listening to anyone, ready at any moment to lash out, make promises, level accusations, move mountains to get what he needed. Yet someone else had to carry through on any decision Anatoli made, because whatever he promised was easier forgotten than accomplished. We began to realize how much he valued Vera, as evidenced by the apartment of her own that she happily occupied.

For sheer volume of gossip they inspired, the most interesting couple at the college was Larisa Belichenko and Sergei Mikhailovich Turbin. By now, the removal of Larisa from her chair was official, and she had returned to Birobidjan to find Vera efficiently running the department.

However, Larisa's sabbatical would not come to an end until September. She was working at home, writing up her research. No one quite knew whether she would try to regain her power or what would happen if she did.

My student Oxana had bleached her long brown hair, but the dark roots were beginning to show. She and her friend Katya, both with remarkably long and shapely legs, wore new mini-skirts to class.

Oxana's mini-skirt was a white vinyl – spectacular, with her bare white legs and white stiletto heels. She wore a fuzzy pink sweater that was so short it left three inches of body exposed.

Katya topped her dark gray miniskirt with a sheer magenta-colored blouse, of such flimsy fabric that the lacy edging on her narrow black bra could be traced in detail. She wore mesh stockings, also black and lacy, with seams up the back. Her hair was purplish-red, and part of it was tied in a topknot that spilled down over her ears and face.

Not to be outdone, Vika, with a perfect profile and dimpled smile, came to class in a hot chartreuse blouse and forest-green vinyl miniskirt, separated by a wide, black, shiny-buckled plastic belt that cinched her tiny waist.

The Russian boys showed no reaction.

Walking around town, John discovered that in fact there was a second e-mail provider in town. He promised to bid substantially lower than sixty dollars a month.

Then I discovered that Anatoli Surnin had already re-installed e-mail service in the main building. This explained why he wanted the e-mail lecture to be held there. But had he forgotten his promise to provide e-mail access in our building, too? It was necessary not only for our grant project, but also for the upcoming Peace Corps training.

Vera reminded him – again. Surnin agreed – again.

The Vinnikovs were among the few families in Birobidjan who owned a car. They invited John and me to go with them to their family *dacha* in the countryside. The *dacha*, beyond the Waldheim orphanage, was in a cluster of *dachas*, on acreage divided into plots of land each about 60 by 100 feet. Most of the plots had little houses or shacks on them and large gardens that were tended mainly on weekends. The Vinnikovs' *dacha* had a two-room cabin, a greenhouse, a tool shed, an outhouse and a barbecue area. They grew strawberries and cabbage, carrots and potatoes, beans, tomatoes, onions, and several kinds of flowers. They also had a berry patch and a couple of fruit trees.

We all worked for hours, weeding and tending the garden under a cold gray sky. Petite blonde Ludmila Borisovna, who looked so delicate and dressed so fashionably for school, hauled pails of water from the pump, turned the soil, planted cabbages. Next weekend, she said, they would plant potatoes.

On a dark and rainy afternoon, John and I visited the old Kazakh we met on Victory Day. John had taken Vladimir Andreievich's photograph in his army uniform, and we called on him to take him some copies.

He was a strong old man of seventy-two, very stern and military when he wore his uniform. Now he looked kind and grandfatherly in his heavy sweater, rumpled pants and floppy slippers.

He was happy to get the photos. Tears came to his eyes as he looked at them. His wife was in the countryside, he said, tending the garden at their *dacha*.

Vladimir Andreievich offered us tea, though we could hardly communicate, so of course we decided to stay. He went to the kitchen and puttered around awhile, putting water on to boil, dropping several cubes of sugar into tall glasses. I called out to him in Russian, "Without sugar, please." He came to the doorway, glass in hand, and stared at me as though I had lost my mind. I smiled apologetically and repeated my astonishing request. Finally, he shrugged and fished the sugar cubes out of my glass, incredulous that anyone would drink tea without sugar.

I gazed around his apartment while we waited. There were boxes of books and dolls and a child-size chair in the corner, so there were grandchildren around. Yes, he said proudly. Ten. There was a light fixture over the table with three sockets, but only one bulb lit the room. The furniture was old and plain. The straight-backed couch was covered with a faded blanket. A curtain hung in the doorway between the main room and the bedroom.

The three of us sat around the wooden table, pleased with ourselves, we for being welcomed guests and he for our presence. We drank our tea and talked, slowly, usually understanding each other. He apologized for having no cookies; he wasn't expecting guests.

He wanted to show us something. He went into the bedroom and brought out the ceremonial whip Kazakhs wore into battle – a braided leather thong with four nails pounded into the tip, with the other end encased in a coil of tooled copper and attached to a wooden handle molded to fit the user's grip.

Vladimir Andreievich brought out his other treasures, handed down from his grandfather – a pair of shockingly heavy swords, polished and sharpened to a lethal edge, and kept in thick leather scabbards. His grandfather was in one of the Kazakh units that guarded the border between the Russian Far East and China, between Birobidjan and Lake Baikal, a long and winding border down the center of the Amur River, still disputed.

After we had admired them, he put the whip and swords away and showed us his equally treasured collection of family photographs. These were kept in two packages, one for the generation of his children, and one for the generation of grandchildren. Each small stack of photos was carefully wrapped in a piece of newspaper.

I felt an impulse to rush out and buy him an album, a door for his bedroom doorway and two more light bulbs for his lamp. But it was enough to overcome that we had casually given him seven or eight photographs.

"*Podarok*" (gift), we said, when he rubbed his thumb and two fingers together with the question, "*Dengi?*" (money). He was pleased.

But later, as we sat and drank tea, he wanted to know how many rooms we had in our California house, how many cars we owned, how many cars other people had in California, how much money we made. We hedged, lied a little, pretended we didn't quite understand.

Next week, after the parade for Birobidjan's 60th anniversary, he wanted us to come back to his apartment and meet his wife and drink a toast to celebrate the occasion. He flicked the side of his neck to indicate that he'd have vodka on hand. (That gesture, a flick of the finger to the side of the neck, means alcohol; often it's used to mean someone is drunk.) Today, his wife wasn't expected home until late in the evening. He wished we could stay and meet her.

The rain lasted all day, and the wind blew furiously from time to time. Outside the window of his fifth-floor apartment, we could watch the tops of the tall poplar trees whipping about, their new yellow-green leaves flapping from side to side. On the window sill was a clay pot with a red geranium in bloom.

Antonina Salinon called from the Peace Corps office to ask again if we had a phone line and e-mail access yet. I told her the promises were getting stronger. The latest word was: "next week."

Even if that happened, there would be no guarantee of smooth and efficient communication. The phone lines in Birobidjan were often busy, sometimes calls were cut off in mid-conversation, e-mail at any given moment might or might not exist. There was a fax machine in the main building, a mile away, but it wasn't turned on unless you phoned first – if you could get through. And the copy machine was broken. We were confident the trainers could adjust to these inconveniences.

Many people in the Russian Far East have tragic stories in their family histories, having been pulled up by the ancestral roots and transplanted in this primeval territory. Their stories are of political prisoners, of adventurers, of poverty-stricken people, intellectuals and common crooks, from western Russia, Ukraine, the Baltic states, the Steppes, and central Russia. Here they ended up, and here their descendants call home.

Over coffee late one afternoon, Vera told us that she knew of three brothers of her grandmother who were killed by the Reds in 1917. Her grandmother, a teen-ager, fled their village, deep in east-central Russia, and hid out in the town of Ussuriisk. When her grandmother was twenty, she returned to the village by the trans-Siberian train. In some places, she and the other passengers were taken across trestles that had been destroyed to a train on the other side. When she got to her village, she found the small children of her slain brothers in an orphanage and she was able to rescue them and take them back to Ussuriisk, where she raised them herself.

When Vera applied to go to the university in 1976, she said, "I knew this and I said nothing."

That troubled her still, even though to say anything would have jeopardized her own academic future.

"I was born during the thaw," Vera said, a period of time in the 1950s when there was a loosening of the rigid controls of Communism. But then the circles of control closed in again. Vera said this "glimpse of spring" gave children of her generation a primary taste of freedom that they then had to stifle, as school began, as the Communist Youth Party opened its arms, as patriotic songs were committed to memory and sung, and sung again.

Not only were Vera's grandmother's three brothers killed, her husband in Ussuriisk was taken away from home when Vera's father was a boy of eleven.

Vera's grandfather was thrown into a labor camp. Three years later, when Vera's father was fourteen, his father was released and returned home, half starving, his health ruined.

He had been the chief accountant at the main Ussuriisk department store, a position that could have been connected with corruption, but he was scrupulously honest. Maybe, at that time, in 1937, honesty was not the best policy. When he died, broken in spirit and in body, he left nothing, and Vera's grandmother became a charwoman to support herself and her son.

Vera's father, an artist, died was Vera was seven years old. His heart gave out, she said.

As she talked, a huge bumblebee flew in and buzzed around our living room. Vera trapped it against the window with a jar, slipped a piece of paper over the top of the jar, and took the creature downstairs and to the great outdoors.

"My father said never harm anything if you can possibly avoid doing so," she said. "The bee has the right to live, just as you do."

I looked into the teacher's room after classes one afternoon. Irina Alexandrovna was having a little birthday party. One table was set up in the corner of the room, in contrast to the usual large table in the center for such occasions, and Irina sat there with Ludmila Borisovna and Veronika, the secretary. Since I had stumbled upon the party, they insisted that I join them. There was Moldovan wine (Irina said she is Moldovan herself), and tea, sliced apples and a chocolate roll cake from the bakery.

Svetlana was sitting at her desk across the room, and I impulsively asked her to join us, but she blushed and said she had work to do.

One of the other teachers came into the room, sat for a few minutes near the window, then left. She also refused the offer to pull up a chair and have a drink of wine, a cup of tea or a piece of cake.

The four of us chatted. Both Irina and Veronika had small sons; Irina's Mark (a Moldovan name) was five and Veronika's son Denis was three. Irina said she turned 28 that day and Veronika was 25; they both said they dreaded turning 30. Ludmila Borisovna avoided mentioning her age, though she had a teen-age daughter and a son in college. She was glamorous, as always (except at the *dacha*), with her fair hair and artfully applied makeup. Besides her delicate beauty and her endurance for rugged work, Ludmila was remarkable for her truly sweet temperament.

Irina was one of the three teachers who had once been students of Larisa, and who supported Larisa when the other teachers joined battle to remove her from the department chair; the other two Larisa supporters, Ellen and Alexandra, were now in Moscow. I wondered if the loyalty to Larisa meant Irina would be forever shunned by the other teachers.

The three of us who had joined Irina at her party were all new to the department that year, so we weren't in on the split between Larisa's friends and her enemies. I wondered if Ludmila and Veronika were even aware of it. For the other teachers, apparently, to sit with Irina and help her celebrate would be tantamount to coming out in favor of Larisa's return to the department and, therefore, Vera's departure.

Later, I asked Vera what she thought about the possibility of recommending Irina Alexandrovna to be one of the Russian language teachers for the upcoming Peace Corps training.

Vera said, "Oh, no. I would not be interested. You know, she is a spy for Larisa."

16

I Love a Parade

Vera called in sick one morning. Even to manage that, she had to go upstairs to a neighbor who had a telephone.

"I dare not work today," she told Veronika, the secretary. "I have the grippe. If I come to work, everyone will get the grippe. And besides, I can hardly move. My backbone and all of my extremities are nearly paralyzed."

On that same day, Sergei Mikhailovich Turbin arranged with another secretary to send a message to Vera. He knew that she was sick in bed with the flu and that she lived at the other end of town from our building.

The call went to Vera's neighbor who then had to go downstairs to get Vera. The message was that Sergei Mikhailovich ordered Vera to rush to the director's office to deal with "the Americans." The secretary didn't specify who the Americans were, though we were the only ones around, and Vera naturally assumed there was some problem involving us.

Vera threw on her clothes, beside herself with fever and concern, and dashed off to Anatoli Surnin's office. She interrupted the director, who was in the middle of a conference with Mr. Levin. Surnin was very displeased with her and refused to listen to her excuses.

"They are your Americans. They are not my Americans," he said sharply. "Whatever the problem is, I expect you to solve it without my interference. And," he said as an afterthought, "I would appreciate it very much if you would leave me to deal with my concerns, without *your* interference!"

Vera rushed to our building, tapped on John's classroom door, then mine, and finally realized that neither John nor I had any immediate problems that she needed to solve.

I never saw Vera more upset. Not only was she feverishly hot, she was pale with exhaustion and quaking with anger at the same time. It was all she could do to make her way down the hall to our apartment and fall on the bed in a heap. But before classes ended for the day, she had managed to crawl out of bed and make her way back home to her apartment. Her illness lasted for the rest of the week.

When Vera recovered, she marched into Sergei Mikhailovich's office and confronted him.

"I have evidence," she said, eyes flashing, "that John and Sharon did not call for me, and I have further evidence that you are the perpetrator of the scheme to lure me to the office of the director under false pretenses! I have caught you out red-handed."

Sergei Mikhailovich denied nothing. He grinned malevolently and said, "You didn't die, did you?"

The Russians conducted their battles out in the open and face to face.

Americans may be more inclined to whisper behind a person's back or say damaging things about them privately, but we think it's civilized behavior to act with a certain amount of carefully contrived politeness, preferably with a tinge of cool distance.

When John and I worked at the Los Angeles Times, the newspaper offered a seminar to employees that included a session entitled "How to Distance Yourself From a Failing Supervisor Without Appearing Disloyal." Many Americans can readily justify the need for such instruction. It isn't easy to walk the tightrope between nastiness and phoniness, displaying just the right small smile, being just cordial enough, being beyond reproach by either camp, those on the same cheering squad and those on the other side. It's part of our competitive system, that is in some ways a complicated game, and the aim is to come out on top.

The Russians played elaborate games, too, but the rules were different. Their way was more like slugging it out bare-fisted. (As I understand it, boxing gloves protect not the faces of those receiving the blows, but the knuckles of those delivering them.) If a social dispute, or misunderstanding, came up among the Russians, everyone took sides, and everyone knew who was on which side. If people had to work together, they managed to do so, but they saw no need to pretend they liked each other when they didn't.

When Vera met Larisa Belichenko for the first time, it was in the hallway outside our apartment, where Larisa had come to meet us and to check up on the books we had lugged home from Khabarovsk for her and stored behind our door for so many weeks. Larisa, tall and handsome, with long hair wrapped into a huge bun at her neck, gave us a broad smile.

I invited her in, she looked at the boxes, counted them, introduced herself to us, complimented John on his height and obvious strength, and mused about how she might get the books from our apartment to hers. She chatted cordially for awhile; my first impression was that she was intelligent and charming, just as we had heard from Peace Corps officials. Since John wasn't offering his strength as a solution, Larisa decided she would ask Sergei Mikhailovich to come and fetch the boxes for her.

Just as Larisa was leaving, Vera knocked on the door. Larisa, standing nearest to the door, opened it. They stared at each other, then Larisa smiled.

"Hello," she said. "You must be Vera Borisovna. I've heard so much about you."

Vera said the briefest "Hello," turned quickly and strode off down the hallway. Whatever she wanted was quickly forgotten. Not for Vera the social chitchat that an American would find mandatory.

Larisa kept saying, "What's wrong with her? I can't imagine what's wrong with her!"

But I seriously doubt that she was bewildered. This was just the way it was done here. Gloves off.

I love a parade. The day dawned bright and sunny after several days of chilly overcast and rain. It was a great day for the celebration of Birobidjan's 60th anniversary.

The parade ambled up Shalom Aleichem Street, children and teachers, dressed in bright, elaborate costumes – small bears and cats, princesses, turbaned fortune telling children, miniature soldiers, dancing girls, tall-hatted boys, drummers, gypsies, flower girls, and an assortment of elves and other fairy tale creatures.

They glittered and glistened in sequins and tinsel, they grinned behind their mascaraed eyes and painted-on freckles, their hair braided or elaborately curled. They scanned both sides of the street, looking for familiar faces.

So many people were in the parade, there were only a few of us standing along the curb to watch.

It wasn't the teams of marching youths, bands, and floats that mark parades of our experience. It was a curb-to-curb crowd of paraders strolling past, each school's entire population of children and teachers taking up the whole street and moving along in a crowd with no discernible order, balloons flying overhead sometimes, tall contraptions held aloft by tall children sometimes, marking the school number, and teachers somewhat shepherding the procession along.

The children's parents strolled alongside, aiming cameras into the center of their child's group. Children who recognized us waved to us, sometimes stopping to whisper to each other, and then many would look our way and grin broadly. We waved and smiled until our cheeks hurt.

On a big wooden stage set up in front of the Palace of Culture, throughout the afternoon, dancing children and singing adults and

194

speech-making politicians performed for the crowds that ebbed and flowed.

Across a couple of wide boulevards, in the big park near the river, behind the Children's Cultural Center, rides that looked rusty and abandoned all winter came to life, newly painted, oiled, and movable – tall rotating wheels, high swings, a merry-go-round. On that stage, children from the parade lined up to have their costumes judged.

The outdoor market was busy; crowds moved between carnival sites, stopping to shop. Everyone in town must have been on the streets most of the day, strolling, performing, watching, enjoying, until eleven o'clock, an hour after sunset.

One could not be pessimistic on such a day, with so many children excited and happy about being dressed up and parading around in the Birobidjan carnival.

The dismally low Russian income, with teachers and doctors and many others stretching money as far as possible, didn't dominate the occasion. It wasn't money that mattered, on a day like this, or lack of money; what mattered was being with friends, having a good time, stepping proudly up onto the stage and doing the dance one had worked so hard to perfect.

I nailed two pieces of wood against the bottom of the wall behind the refrigerator, where the wall doesn't meet the floor. I sealed the remaining gap with duct tape. A dusty, dreary job, but the gap was a mouse freeway. I wanted to shut them out. I was tired of having them run for cover when I appeared in the kitchen, tired of clapping my hands to frighten them before they frightened me.

A nail fell into the gap between the wall and the floor. It looked as though I could reach it. I felt around and came across something like a wood chip. Balancing it between my fingers, I lifted it out. It was the Saint George medal the Siberian sailor had given John. It had been lost for months. I took the discovery as a sign of good fortune.

At last, the extension telephone line was installed, both in the library and in our apartment as well, *and* an e-mail account was set up. We were connected to the world again.

We were still at the mercy of the front desk. The first night, Elvira shut off our line at five o'clock because she wanted to keep the office line open. The second night she was on the phone all evening.

Kommandant Valentina hosted a party to celebrate her 45th birthday. She and Uri had just returned from Moscow, where Uri underwent an "alcoholism cure" and Valentina went shopping. At her birthday party Saturday night in the cafeteria, she wore a white crocheted tunic over her off-the-shoulder dress. She tossed aside the tunic late in the evening, after working up a sweat dancing, exposing her large round shoulders and deep cleavage.

(Valentina had put on a good 30 pounds since we met her. Stress, she said. But we noticed that she kept a stash of calories – cake, cookies, cheese – in the refrigerator in her office and occasionally the excess landed in the refrigerator of the empty apartment down the hall from ours. There were four kilos of butter in there.)

Valentina and Uri traveled on a military plane. He was in the army, and he didn't get paid regularly, but once a year he got a free trip to Moscow. This year, Uri "got coded" – a treatment to enable him to control his drinking.

"Every other day, he gets drunk, and abusive," Valentina said, although Uri was several years younger and many pounds lighter than Valentina.

But on her birthday, Valentina herself was pouring vodka in Uri's glass as well as into her own, and they toasted each other several times and gave each other smacking wet kisses.

One of her toasts was this:

"There's only one thing in my house that is really valuable, and that is my dear husband."

Viktor showed up. Viktor, the potbellied, vodka-drinking party animal we had last socialized with at the winter picnic at the *dacha* (and who wanted to tag along with us to the spa at Kuldur). And there was Galina, a fat Russian *babushka* who was a friend of Uri's late mother. John asked Galina to dance, but she said she was too old (she was probably in her fifties).

The rest of us danced – John and I, Victor and Vera, Natasha, the tall cook, and Irina, the short cook, everyone except Irina's chubby dark-haired daughter, who pouted most of the evening.

John recognized before I did that Irina's daughter, sitting there pouting, was the very same person as the lean little blonde bride we hid in our apartment six months before. That bright-eyed girl, Oxana, with the slim waist, in the white satin wedding dress and beaded crown, had already turned into a sullen, double-chinned, plump little housewife, her hair returned to its natural color, and so round that we hadn't recognized her. Her skinny young husband was not at the party.

Natasha the cook had had a sad life, a philandering husband, no children, the most menial of jobs. Every day, she hacked meat off huge carcasses, ground it, made meat patties, cooked masses of vegetables, stirred borsch, washed dishes, and kept the steam trays filled in the cafeteria.

I looked at her hands. The skin was tough and worn, her fingers meaty and strong, with big knuckles, cracked fingernails, broad grayish hands and thick wrists.

But on the dance floor, Natasha was graceful. She glided around, moving her body and her hands in sensuous ways, to any kind of music.

John invited her to dance with him.

Vera turned to me and whispered, "She will remember this all her life, the night she danced with the American man."

Elvira the night watchwoman, sold me a jar of strawberry jam, which was delicious, and gave me a bunch of salad greens. There were green onions, some broad-leafed grass, and a bitter but tasty little leaf that might have been dandelion. These combined with green pepper and tomatoes, and tossed with a spoonful of oil and vinegar, made a delicious salad.

We'd had no hot water for a week, and no gas for the stove, but fortunately Valentina allowed us to cook in the empty apartment down the hall. Uri, her husband, promised to deliver a new supply of propane gas. Very soon, probably.

17

From No to Yes

Denis Kopul stopped by our apartment with a sad look on his face.

"I didn't win the scholarship," he said.

After we commiserated with him about this huge disappointment, John and I both urged him to try again next year.

"I don't think I can," he said.

"Yes, you can," I said with great eagerness. "The competition is open to second- *and* third-year students. Now that they have met you, they will remember you when you apply again."

"But they already said no," he said firmly. "It would not be polite to try again."

I tried another tactic. "Denis, remember what you said about wanting to learn about American culture? Here's an adage that every American knows: 'If at first you don't succeed, try, try again.'"

He looked at John, as if he didn't quite believe me.

"That's right," John said. "And when we go back to the states next month, we'll bring back some books so you can practice taking those tests. You'll be ready next time."

"I don't know," Denis said. "I will think about it."

After three weeks of having no hot water, we found out that the problem was minor: A plumber had closed a valve to make a repair, then forgot to open it back up.

Elvira, the clerk, finally got around to telling us there was hot water elsewhere in the building, and so she started to wonder why we didn't have it in our apartment. She opened the valve, and the problem was solved.

Meanwhile, we decided to tell ourselves, it had been good discipline. It gave me the opportunity to adjust to a cold shampoo, and gave John the pleasure of having a wife willing to pour warm water from a pan for him to rinse his soapy head. The alternative to our cold-water sponge baths was a public banya, some distance away, or a swim in the river, much too cold.

Two Peace Corps volunteers, Deirdre Keating and Robert Greenan, at the end of their second year in Russia, were in Birobidjan all week to plan the training for the new volunteers. Deirdre had lived for two years in a village with her husband, Brian, the ecology volunteer who was accused of being a spy. Deirdre had the basic Peace Corps experience – pumping water from a well and heating it over a wood stove using logs they split themselves. So our adjustment-to-Russia stories were not too impressive to her.

Deirdre said her worst frustration was caused not by primitive village life or cold winters, but by the Peace Corps staff itself. She needed to take prescription medicine, and someone on the Peace Corps staff told her she had to travel to Khabarovsk to pick it up.

"But that's ten hours by train," she said.

"It's Peace Corps policy not to send prescription medicines through the mail," she was told.

So in November, Deirdre and Brian took the train to Khabarovsk to get the medicine. Winter came early. The wind blew in from Siberia with a vengeance while they were away, and the temperature plummeted to 40 below zero. The fire in their stove went out, and some pipes that circulate water to heat the cabin burst, resulting in about $1,000 in damage. The cabin they lived in was owned by the village school.

The Peace Corps tried to reimburse the school for the cost, but the proud villagers repaired the cabin themselves and refused to accept the money. Thereafter, the Peace Corps sent such prescriptions by mail, with no further mention of "policy."

At the end of the semester, we took the train down to Vladivostok for some Peace Corps meetings, including a three-hour interview with an investigator from the Peace Corps Inspector General's office whose job it was to check on Peace Corps posts around the world and be sure things were going as they should.

On the way back to Birobidjan, we rode in a second-class open-sleeping car instead of the usual first-class compartment. The tickets were only half the usual fare, but some of the sleeper-seats had collapsed, the bedding was extremely tacky, and the toilet was horrendous. There was one advantage – the Russians around us were eager to make our acquaintance.

From the time we were awakened by their quiet murmuring, at 6:30 a.m., until we arrived home, at 7:30 p.m., we practiced our Russian.

Our most eager conversation partner was a huge fat woman who sold Herbal Life products. She said she had lost ten kilos (22 pounds) since she discovered Herbal Life (which she pronounced Gurbal Life). She and her sales companions, six women in all, asked us everything from how old we were to whether we believed in God. They wanted to know if my hair was naturally curly, were my teeth real, how many rooms there were in our house and how many cars did we have, why were we in Russia, and what did we think of Russian people.

For John's birthday, I had bought him a used guitar in Vladivostok from a volunteer who was leaving Russia. John got it out from under the seat and started playing it. He taught two Russian children some American folk songs. Nearly everyone in our car gathered around to listen to us sing, and it was great fun, though John's fingers were sore from playing after so many months without his guitar.

In Birobidjan it rained steadily for four days; people started to worry about their gardens. They hoped the sun would come out before the rain washed out everything they worked so hard planting and tending.

John and I each flunked two students who seldom came to class and who never did their assignments.

The Russian system registered shock at such accountability. The four students we flunked were stunned when we refused to sign their little class books so they could move up to the next level. We were not sure how the administration would handle it, but some of our fellow teachers said they were willing to support us in drawing the line where we did.

Antonina Salinon wanted me to check out the hotel situation in Birobidjan. The Peace Corps trainees were coming soon and they would need a place to stay before they moved in with their host families. Vera and I went to the Vostok Hotel to see the manager. We thought he might give the Peace Corps a discount, since we wanted to reserve rooms for 30 people twice during the summer, for the first few days of the new group's training in June and for our own group's mid-service training in August. After telling Vera on the phone to show up in 20 minutes, the manager, Viktor Krivenko, was nowhere to be found when we arrived at the hotel.

We went upstairs to talk to Faina, the contractor who had remodeled Vera's apartment and was now her best friend. Faina worked part-time at the hotel as a maid. Half an hour later, Krivenko showed up and nodded at us. A former Army colonel about 35 years old, Krivenko walked with the casual saunter of man without much to do, and wore horn-rimmed glasses and a deadpan expression.

With a halfhearted twist of his wrist, he motioned for us to follow him. Vera and I trotted down the hall a few paces behind him, he went through the door to his office and let it swing shut in our faces.

Maybe that's when we should have walked away. But it wouldn't have mattered in any case.

Vera pushed open the door and we walked in. He motioned us to a chair, as though both of us could sit on one chair. Vera told me to sit down and she pulled another chair forward.

Negotiations began.

No discounts for large groups. No discounts for any reason, Krivenko said. The hotel was state-regulated. Yes, Antonina Salinon had visited the hotel, looked at a room, and left. No deals were made. He would have told her the same thing if she had asked, which she didn't.

The four floors of the hotel were mostly empty most of the time. The top two floors, in fact, were closed and locked and had had no paying guests for at least a year, according to Faina.

"Viktor makes his money elsewhere," she said mysteriously.

As we rose to leave, Krivenko opened the drawer of his large desk and pulled out a slick white business card.

"Call if you decide you want the rooms," he said, not bothering to show us out.

"*Do svidaniya*, Viktor Krivenko."

I told Vera I hoped we could find another suitable place. But Krivenko's complacency was based on the fact that his was the only decent hotel in town.

The meeting with Krivenko was Faina's idea, but she and Vera had a good laugh at his boorish behavior and shrugged off the incident as a nice try.

"It could have worked," Faina said.

There was another hotel, the Nadezhda (which means "hope"), a smaller place two bus stops north on Shalom Aleichem Street. A striking middle-aged woman greeted us warmly there, but ultimately gave a tragic smile to let us know how deeply sorry she was that she would not have rooms available on our August dates. Construction crews were coming in and would fill the hotel by then, she said. There were only eleven rooms anyway.

The manager herself looked like a character from a cowboy movie. She wore a purple velveteen dress, softly draped to expose her ample cleavage, and her hair, twisted into a high roll, was held in place with hair spray and barrettes. Glistening lipstick traced the edges of her lips, cheating a little to give them an impression of being even fuller than they were. She had a nervous habit of rubbing her hands together, though her voice was controlled and throaty and her smile the essence of relaxed splendor. I thought of Hollywood's Old West bordello scenes, where the madam gives the grubby gunslingers what they want as long as they behave themselves. The manager of the Nadezhda would have made a great madam.

Antonina Salinon wanted Peace Corps volunteers to stay in the dormitory of the Teachers' Retraining Institute on Lenin Street.

"Have you *seen* that place?" Vera asked me. "I can't imagine you would want any of your American friends to stay there."

Vera took me to check out the dormitory. The rooms were adequate, though Spartan, but the toilets and showers were an abomination. They stank horribly, the cement walls were cracked and glistening with seepage, and the floors were unmentionably dirty, scabby and worn, with cracked linoleum that didn't quite meet the walls.

Antonina telephoned and asked me what I thought about those accommodations. She was not pleased when I said it wasn't a good place to stay, no matter how much money the Peace Corps might save.

"Then you find a place," Antonina said.

That was why Vera and I were making these rounds. And the Peace Corps had officially hired Vera to be the administrative assistant for the training.

Our next step was to check out Pronkina, a spa in the countryside, a few miles beyond the orphanage.

A still, hot day. The catkins – long, cottony seed pods on the poplar trees – were in full fuzz. The least breath of air sent the fluff flying into the air, into eyes and noses, and swirling along the streets. It piled up in the gutters.

Just as John and I approached our door, hot and thirsty after a long walk, Vera rushed toward us.

"Sharon, you must come immediately!" she commanded. "Gubienka is waiting!"

Viktor Gubienka, one of the top administrators of the Jewish Autonomous Region's education department, was the man responsible for booking rooms in Pronkina.

We had been trying for days to see Gubienka, hoping to head off Antonina's plan to book rooms in that shabby dormitory on Lenin Street.

I wanted to run upstairs, have a tall drink of water and change from my T-shirt and jeans into a cotton skirt and blouse, but Vera wouldn't hear of it.

"You look great! We have no time to delay!" she said breathlessly.

Vera and I raced down Shalom Aleichem Street and over to the big square administration building that blocks the massive Lenin statue's view of the Bira River. We said Gubienka's name and the guard wrote our names on a slip of paper and allowed us into the building. We got to his office at precisely one minute to four, only to find that he had been called into a meeting and left word for us to wait.

Forty-five long, hot minutes later we were ushered into the big man's office. I'm sure he cast a disapproving glance at my clothing before negotiations opened. However, the prospect of two Peace Corps conferences pleased him immensely. He penciled us in on the Pronkina spa calendar. The price seemed reasonable – 170,000 rubles per person per day (about twenty-four dollars), with meals and full use of the spa. I hoped it wasn't just another promise that, when it came to signing a contract, would double or triple in price.

Pronkina, the so-called spa, turned out to be as unacceptable as the dormitory. John and I learned this first-hand by spending a night there, fortunately for our fellow volunteers (not for us).

The worst problems were mosquitoes and isolation. Gubienka had told us that the place was twenty minutes from town by bus, but it was more like forty-five minutes, and there was not a shop or a kiosk in sight, meaning no chance for a volunteer to buy a soft drink or anything else. Gubienka had also said that each room had its own bath, which turned out to be toilet and sink only; there were a few shower stalls, but they were in the basement, and they were out of order. There were no screens on the windows and the mosquitoes were huge in both number and size out there in the heart of the swampland; worse than in Birobidjan.

We stood in the main conference room at Pronkina, Vera and I, Antonina Salinon, and Michael O'Donoghue, Antonina's boss. Intensely bright sunshine streamed through the tall windows.

"All volunteers will have mosquito net," Antonina said.

"Forget it," Michael said.

"All volunteers will have bug spray," she continued.

"Yes, they'll need mosquito nets," Michael said. "And yes, they'll need bug spray. But no, they don't need Pronkina."

We were relieved, because we agreed that Pronkina was woefully inadequate. So Peace Corps would have to use the Vostok

Hotel after all. Viktor Krivenko, the manager, had correctly predicted that we'd be back.

18

Power to the People

Our long-delayed visit to the grand spa at Kuldur, the Sanus Sanitorium, came about in June. By Russian standards, the place was luxurious.

The owner was a Korean man who used to keep the books for one of the old government sanitoriums, where Viktor tried to book us when we didn't invite him along.

We walked by those two places during our stay. They had both become derelict-looking – drab stucco walls, cracked and unpainted, lawns overgrown with weeds, broken benches – but they were still in use. They catered to unions who booked coal miners and other underpaid – or unpaid – workers for vacation weeks. Several of these workers, lounging in their undershirts on the front steps of one place, stared at us wide-eyed and open-mouthed as we passed by.

The former accountant, on the other hand, had not only survived Perestroika, but had thrived on it. His luxury spa was the nicest place we'd seen in the Russian Far East, outside Vladivostok.

Our room was prettily decorated, with curlicue plaster forms around the wall lamps, and a massive black lacquer dresser, with matching end tables and bedstead. Our window opened onto the front lawn, where guests strolled near the flower beds and sat in white gazebos.

Vera's window opened onto a passing stream with a dock built out over it where large women in tiny bikinis turned ever redder under the hot afternoon sun. On one side of the hotel there was another place for sunbathers – a bed of raked sand on which people laid out large straw mats and spread themselves to bake.

We took long hikes, read for hours, practiced our Russian, and sweated in the sauna. We showered under sprays of salty mineral water, and we ate three big Russian meals a day, promptly at nine, two and seven. Most of the guests at the other nine tables dressed up for meals, especially the women.

The large middle-aged blonde at the table next to us wore cute casual clothes at breakfast, dressy daytime outfits at lunch, and elegant costumes at dinner. Her stout husband gazed at her with admiration and affection, except for one noon when they were not speaking to each other.

On our second evening there, while waiting for Vera in the bar, John and I introduced ourselves to this couple and chatted with them in Russian. Just as Vera approached us, the husband gave John his business card.

Vera eagerly grabbed it away.

"I knew it!" Vera said in English, her voice triumphant. "He is a big cheese." ("Big cheese" was an idiom John had taught her, and she always enjoyed trying out new English expressions.)

She continued to enlighten us, in a loud, excited voice. "This man is responsible for the hot water in Vladivostok! Excuse me, I should say – the *lack* of hot water!"

Then she sat down at our table, her back to the couple, and lowered her voice a notch, her expression one of righteous indignation.

She said, "At this very time, the bureaucrats from Moscow are in Vladivostok to check on things. And where is our big cheese? He is hiding out in Kuldur!"

She glared at him, and concluded her speech: "He *knows* how to stay out of the way!"

The chubby executive didn't understand a word of English, but Vera's disapproval transcended language.

"What are you telling the Americans?" he demanded.

Vera kept her back to him and refused to say another word. She crossed her right leg over the left, and her right foot jittered with the excitement of having crossed a "big cheese," but her face stayed resolutely grim.

As much as the Vladivostok official might have wanted to continue talking with us, the force of Vera's personality, and her obvious distaste for him, cut short the conversation. They gulped down their drinks and left the bar.

Americans tend to try and keep the political and social spheres somewhat separate, especially in casual encounters, but not the Russians. Not since Perestroika allowed the public airing of their inner feelings.

Resentments and attitudes were everywhere on the surface, and our Russian friends saw no point in pretending to feel something different than what they felt in their hearts.

On the way back to Birobidjan we had to take a train that left the nearest station at one in the morning. We asked Vera why we couldn't take a daytime train. There was no direct connection, she said. We would have to board a noon train going in the wrong direction and stop over at a more distant village to wait for an eastbound train.

"How long a wait?" we asked.

"Nobody knows," Vera said. "We'd better take the night train."

So we left Kuldur before midnight, in the spa's big four-wheel-drive van, sat in a cavernous train station for an hour, and then boarded our train. At five in the morning, we stumbled onto the platform at Birobidjan, and went home to sleep.

June 22 is a national day of mourning, marking the bombing of Russia by Germany in 1941, and Russia's entry into "The Great Patriotic War."

And since Perestroika, Russians had learned they must also adjust to long-secret and newly revealed information about their once-revered leader Josef Stalin – who, for example, planted bombs in Stalingrad (now Volgograd) instead of food supplies, greatly contributing to the starvation of one million Russians in that city during the Germans' siege.

Birobidjan's outdoor marketplace was lively at noon, but by midafternoon the streets were eerily devoid of traffic. And there were no children playing in the amusement park by the river although it was Sunday. Kiosks and shops were closed and locked.

I gave little Vanya a glassful of grape juice and he downed it gulp after gulp, as fast as his throat could open and he could pour it in. The same way Russian men drink vodka – a hearty toast, then open the throat and swallow.

Besides the favorite drink, vodka, there was the "medicinal" drink of the Russian Far East – Ussuriiski balsam (45 percent alcohol). The brand name on a bottle Vera gave us when she returned from visiting her mother in Ussuriisk was Russian Island Balsam.

The label, in English, read: "Russian Island Balsam is made of extracts from more than 30 herbs from the ecologically pure regions of the Primorye in Russia. Russian Island in tea, coffee or juice increases the body's resistance to depression and reduces alcohol dependence."

Vera and I sat in the kitchen for two hours, drinking tea and talking over problems. We had our own problems, but we sometimes avoided talking about them even in these intimate kitchen talks. Instead, we solved the problems of the world.

Vera suddenly remembered that this day was June 27, the one-year anniversary of the day she first set foot in America and changed the course of her life.

While Vera noted the anniversary of her first visit to the United States, we marked the end of our first year in the Peace Corps.

Knowing we were going home for a visit soon, she asked, "Do you ever think that two years in Russia might be too long? Might one year be better?"

"Vera, we are coming back," I promised.

Ludmila Borisovna Vinnikova came to say farewell; the Peace Corps had hired her to be a language teacher for the new volunteers, and she was on her way to Vladivostok for three weeks of training.

Lena Tolstogusova and her two boys said goodbye, too. They were going to central Russia for the summer to visit her parents, leaving Pavel Nikolaievich in Birobidjan to work on his post-doctoral research paper.

And we were heading for America.

I wondered if we would notice what the Russians said was their first impression: that Americans are very loud. Did John and I talk more quietly now? What would our impressions be?

A Birobidjan official – we never found out which one – made vaguely threatening innuendos regarding "the problem of getting too close to Americans." Because of this – and no one would be more specific with us – three families were intimidated enough to back out of their agreement to host the new Peace Corps volunteers in training. Ludmila Borisovna was warned about teaching them, too, but she was still planning to teach, and Vera still planned to be the logistics coordinator for the training. And a few of our students' parents, including the Kopuls and the Voroshbits, still wanted to be host families. Having Americans in their households all summer would be tremendously beneficial for their study of the English language.

As welcomed as we Americans were by some of the local officials, there was no denying that resistance to our presence continued to exist in the hearts and minds of others. The old system would take years to die out, and it would be years more before old attitudes might change.

"People have it in their genes," Vera said: the fear of punishment, the survival instinct that keeps them from challenging authority, the possibility of future retribution for stepping out of line even though currently stepping out of line was not dangerous.

Under this kind of intimidation, how bold one must be to stand up and assume a sense of being in control of one's life.

Vera shrugged and said defiantly, "I have nothing to lose; I am sick of the way things were!"

This struck me as extraordinarily brave.

19

Home Is Where the Heart Is

We left Khabarovsk July 5, but flew across the dateline which made it July 4 again. At 11:30 p.m., about half an hour out from the airport at Anchorage, Alaska, the flight attendants on the Alaska Airlines plane put on tall Uncle Sam hats, started playing patriotic songs over the loudspeaker, and marched up and down the aisle with whistles and noisemakers.

They played the military theme songs, for Army, Navy, Marines and Air Force. Veterans stood in the aisle saluting an American flag that was suddenly unfurled and waving at the front of the plane. The few Russians aboard were amazed. So were we.

As the plane descended into Anchorage, the city's Fourth of July fireworks show got under way. "America, the Beautiful" was playing over the loudspeaker in the cabin. Fireworks burst into the sky below us, and the thrill of the music, the fireworks, and the people's excitement around us brought sudden tears to my eyes.

What an exuberant welcome home after a year in Birobidjan, the remote outpost that had also become our home.

We visited my father and other relatives in Indiana and Tennessee, then came home to Santa Barbara by way of Los Angeles International on a late evening flight.

By the time we got our rental car onto the Los Angeles freeway system, it was 2 a.m.

A few miles from the airport, the car started to shimmy and shudder, and just before the intersection of the 405 Freeway and the Santa Monica Freeway, the engine overheated and the needle spun to maximum red.

John coasted the car to a callbox just beyond the looping on-ramp, but before he could steer it off the road it died, in the right-hand lane of traffic. He left the lights on and we jumped out of the car and headed for the callbox – number 10-49.

We felt nervous and vulnerable, standing there as cars sped past, one small truck nearly hitting the car we had left there. As I yelled out information to the California Highway Patrol operator over the emergency phone, John ran back to the car and pushed it to the shoulder of the road.

The CHP operator called the 24-hour Budget Rental Car 800 emergency number and reached a recording that said the office opened at 6 a.m. She tried another number. I kept repeating the information about the car, the problem, the contract number, the license, my name, to one person after another on the call-box phone, while standing there in the middle of the night, frightened that any of the cars speeding by could contain a drunk driver or a murderer with a gun, or that some creep could crawl up the hill out of the bushes next to where we were standing, and do God knows what awful thing.

My mind, so recently filled with the solitude and everyday quiet of life in "back of beyond" Russia, now filled with stories of freeway killers and cold-blooded thugs who would just as soon murder someone as rob them; I asked the operator if she could send a California Highway Patrol officer to us while we waited for a tow truck to arrive. After a long twenty minutes, while I waited, the phone pressed to my ear, she assured me that help was on the way but the tow truck would take forty-five minutes to get there.

The officers arrived, two men in their 20s who were polite and sympathetic. It was a relief to have them there, their heavily armed presence and their big black-and-white car between us and the oncoming traffic.

"Can you take us someplace safer than this to wait for help?" John asked.

I kept thinking how long everything was taking; late night was turning into early morning. At least we were strong and healthy, not bleeding and dying.

"Yeah, you'll get chilled if you stand out here for very long," one of them said.

It seemed we had already stood out there for a long time.

But before they would let us in their car, one of the patrolmen said, as though reading a memorized script, "First we have to search you, to be sure you aren't carrying anything that could be dangerous to us or to yourselves."

As I stood there at the edge of the freeway with his hands patting the insides of my legs and around my back and sides, I felt a wave of despair about America, as deep as the euphoria I'd felt a week earlier when the fireworks burst into the sky in Anchorage.

The officer put my purse and John's Swiss Army knife in the trunk of the patrol car and left our suitcases in the stalled car.

As they drove us off the freeway, I asked one of them if he thought the problem of crime was better or worse than ten years ago.

"I think we sink a little lower every year," he said. "Nobody takes any responsibility for their behavior. They kill someone and they blame it on their lousy childhood or their messed up families or their hard life. Nothing's anybody's fault."

His view of life was through the lens of patrolling the freeways of Los Angeles, from picking up frightened travelers to scraping dead bodies off the wreckage of their cars, from the adrenaline rush they experience as they approach a car they've stopped, wondering if the driver will shoot them in the face, to collecting evidence in the aftermath of a freeway shooting.

They dropped us off at a service station at a nearby intersection, where a large black man was mopping the floor. He let us come in and buy a Coke, but he said the place was closed and we would have to go outside to wait for the tow truck.

We spent another hour in the cool night air, watching the empty street.

One carload of people came in, three men and a girl. They slid a credit card into the slot on the gas tank, pumped in some gas and left. The man finished his mopping. He closed and locked the door behind us and rode off on his bicycle. The place was empty.

Finally, around 4 a.m., a tow truck appeared, towing a better car than the one we had rented. The driver detached the car and gave us the keys. We got in it and followed him back to the freeway.

We got our luggage out of the disabled car, thanked him, and drove away.

Exhausted, we made it to Kanan Road, about halfway home, beckoned by a 24-hour sign at a restaurant, where we were welcomed by a jolly waitress, and we relaxed over eggs and toast and coffee. Then we drove home, tired but feeling better. Happy to be alive.

Later that morning, there was a call for us on the telephone in one of the rooms we had rented out to tenants during our stay in Russia.

"We are confirming your order of twelve hundred dollars worth of ski equipment on your Visa charge card," the cheerful voice began.

"Wha-a-a-t?" John said. He assured the Visa clerk, with extreme firmness, that we had not ordered ski equipment.

Our next call was to the police.

We both had our charge cards. Who could have gotten our charge card number? And who could have both that number and the phone number of our tenant?

There was only one possibility: the same person at the rental car company who rented us the broken-down heap of junk that we left on the Los Angeles freeway!

A policeman came to our house and took the report. He told us other stories about similar cases, and worse cases than those. He thought we were eccentric to want to spend two years in the wild Russian Far East.

It occurred to us that we had not felt as frightened or as victimized in our entire year in Russia as we had in the past twenty-four hours.

Near the end of our stay in the states, we had a good swim in the ocean. A swell came in and we were afraid of getting scraped on the rocks. But it felt beautiful to be in the ocean again. I mentioned to John that the water was quite warm, warmer than the usual Santa Barbara surf in early August.

"Maybe too warm for gaining in clarity," John said. "And too rough."

Later, we sat on our deck watching the bamboo at the edge of the yard tilt and dip in the early evening breeze.

"I feel like congratulating us," John said.

"What are you congratulating us for?" I asked.

"I don't know," he said. "But I always have the feeling that some sort of congratulations are in order. Maybe only because we survived another day and I am grateful and happy about that."

"Yes," I said, grabbing his hand. "I agree."

We spoke about Russia to the Rotary Club in Ventura, and people were interested; they asked many questions. They donated two boxes of books.

We rented a video camera and shot some scenes around Santa Barbara to take back to Birobidjan. We could show it to our students on the VCR we had bought with the grant money. They were very interested in Santa Barbara because of the television soap opera set there, which was still popular in Russia.

We collected about eight hundred books, from my brother's church in Indiana, from our own bookshelves, from friends, and from schools in Santa Barbara. We boxed them all up and mailed them to our college in Birobidjan. It was easy. Everyone had English language books to spare. School officials were glad to contribute, including two boxes of psychology and biology textbooks that Boris Fineman had begged us to try and find for his department.

"They'll be in English," I reminded him.

"I will have them translated!" Boris said. "Anything is better than nothing!"

"We throw books away," said John Richards, Santa Barbara High School principal. "Taxpayers don't like to see perfectly good textbooks out there on the shelves of used bookstores."

And what Santa Barbara schools threw away, our college in Birobidjan would treasure.

We got a small package in the mail from a woman in Kentucky who wanted us to take it with us and give it to her son, Peace Corps volunteer Harry Anderson. When he heard we were going to the states, Harry had asked us if we would bring back a package from his mother, but he had been coy about what might be in it.

We decided to call the phone number on the note that came with the package. It was Harry's mother.

"May we ask you what's in the package?" John said.

"Just some little old bottles of stuff," his mother said.

John gave up trying to wrest the secret from her.

"Little bottles of *what*!" he muttered after he hung up.

Drugs, we imagined. Maybe even bullets. Or money. No, probably illegal drugs. We talked ourselves into justifying our curiosity, on grounds that airlines people often ask, "Did you pack everything yourself?" and "Has this luggage been out of your hands?"

Unable to resist, I opened the box.

John grabbed a bottle and started laughing.

"Hair restoring cream," he said. "Six bottles of hair restoring cream!"

He decided that if Harry asked if we had opened the package, he would play dumb. "I'll just say I assumed he had some loathsome social disease that was of no concern to me."

I tried to remember whether Harry's hair was thinning. Maybe it was, a little. Not noticeably. He must have been hoping to arrest the process before it was too late.

We did not talk about the possibility of staying in Santa Barbara. We had round-trip tickets. John was not as enthusiastic as I was about going back to Russia. I was silently grateful for his willingness to return, and he silently resisted any tendency he might have had to blame me for going back.

On the Alaska Airlines flight back to Russia, we recrossed the dateline. Over the water between the two countries, a middle-aged Russian man, quite drunk, decided he needed a cigarette, so he went into the toilet and smoked one.

A flight attendant smelled the smoke and knocked on the door. She scolded him when he came out. He shrugged, mumbled something, and sat down.

Half an hour later he got up again and, gesturing with an unlit cigarette, tried to bargain with a flight attendant:

"This cigarette, or more vodka."

"No," she said firmly.

He made an obscene gesture and sat down again. After she walked away, he got up, went to the toilet and locked the door. Soon we smelled smoke.

The scene was repeated, this time with two flight attendants, and louder words, then he stumbled back to his seat and got quiet. Soon he was snoring.

Two hours later, the plane landed in Magadan for refueling.

The man was told to get off the plane. He appeared shocked, and refused to move from his seat. A huge uniformed man from Magadan boarded the plane and repeated the order.

Finally, the man, cigarette in hand, headed slowly down the aisle, resigned to his fate but still angry. When he got to the door, he turned and yelled at the flight attendants in heavily accented English: "Goodbye. Sank you," and then in Russian, "*Vui ni prava*!" (You are not right!)

He would have to wait in Magadan for the next available Russian plane to continue his journey.

Three of our Peace Corps friends showed up to meet us at the small Khabarovsk airport. They helped us get the tons of luggage we returned with onto the bus into town, and later, onto the train to Birobidjan.

On the bus, we watched a man about fifty years old progress in a matter of minutes from being lugubriously talkative, to dead-eyed sleepy, to barely hanging on to a stanchion, to collapsing on the floor, dead drunk. Another man tried to help him up, but he was a dead weight, and finally the man just left him on the floor. We stepped over him on our way out. The bus driver paid no attention.

"Welcome back to Russia," John said.

Vera appeared at our apartment door within an hour of our return, carrying a bottle of wine and a box of chocolates to welcome us back. Three boxes of our books had already arrived at the Birobidjan post office. Peace Corps trainees were settled in around town. And there was lots of news to catch up on.

20

The New Volunteers

Training for the new volunteers was concluding its second week. They had moved from the Vostok Hotel to host families, including the families of Denis Kopul and Masha Voroshbit. Masha and Lena Tsimbalyuk became good friends that summer. By the summer's end, all three students had improved their English remarkably, thanks to the presence of an American "brother" and "sister" in the two families.

It rained almost constantly the first week we were back, a dreary, dismal gray curtain. The laundry, hanging in the kitchen, wouldn't dry. Fungus oozed from the cracks between the windows and the walls. There was so much summer rain that tomato crops were ruined; Russians complained about having to buy more fresh vegetables from China than usual. We heard such complaints:

"Chinese tomatoes aren't as good as ours." "Their watermelons aren't as sweet." "Their green peppers have less flavor."

I speculated that the mice and cockroaches would be happy to have us back. But they were not lonesome in our month of absence. We discovered that our apartment was used to house visiting Americans and Russian teachers while we were in the states. Not that anyone asked us about it, or suggested that we put any of our things away.

We brought back with us two small American mousetraps and a can of bug spray, so we were armed against the vermin.

Vera caught us up on the events of summer. She was working with the Peace Corps, as the logistics coordinator for training, but mostly her duties were to assist Kathy, a woman who came from a

Peace Corps post in Africa to direct the training. Kathy's office was in the formerly vacant apartment down the hall from our apartment. Not speaking Russian, she wanted Vera to stay by her side in case something came up, so we saw little of Vera, except after six in the evening.

The first day on the job, Kathy made Vera go back home and put on a dress instead of the slacks and blouse she was wearing. Vera, who was used to running her own department, was deeply offended.

"She has only worked in Africa, never in Russia," Vera fumed. "She thinks she can treat me like a slave."

But Vera wouldn't complain to Kathy. She did as she was ordered, then later she would sit at our kitchen table, tapping her foot vigorously as she described the various insults she had suffered during the day.

Rain, rain, rain.

A stout vendor shouted in Russian, "*Kashde dyen, doscht*!" (Every day, rain!) and I replied, "*Da! Ploha*!" (Yes! bad!)

Bad for the *dacha*. Our friends, Ludmila and Sasha Vinnikov, had planted cabbages, not once, but twice, during the spring; the first young plants were devoured by bugs. And now they feared the second crop would mildew and rot in the swampy soil.

Potatoes, at the beginning of harvest, came to the market coated with mud. Carrots were big, but spongy and tasteless. Tomatoes hung on the vines, refusing to redden and ripen under the relentlessly soggy skies. Raspberries, plump and sweet when they were picked at dawn, mildewed by noon.

The fungus on the walls took the form of black and slimy puddles with a puffy gray mass in the middle like a cancer. The cockroaches scuttled boldly across the table, scampering when I made a move to crush them under a cup. The mice thought they could nibble the cheese right off the new mousetrap John had

223

carefully set, as they had done from the big steel Russian mousetrap. But with the two flimsy little American mousetraps, John immediately caught three tiny mice and the rest stayed away for weeks.

The training suffered from the gloomy weather, too. The new volunteers were all living with host families, and there were petty disagreements and disputes to be resolved.

Sandy, the new Peace Corps medical officer, left training to go to Khabarovsk at the beginning of the week and hadn't been heard from since.

One of the trainees complained of fever and diarrhea. Another was offended because her host mother told her to keep the tattoo on her lower back covered up.

Several host mothers were furious because their children weren't being allowed into the English-language classes the trainees were teaching.

Kathy was upset because she thought it was "a sign of Russian corruption" for the host mothers to expect special treatment; she had set up the classes on a first-come, first-served basis.

"Why weren't they here? Why weren't they in line?" she complained.

"They didn't think *they* would have to stand in line," Vera explained.

"Why didn't anybody *tell* me this *before*?" Kathy wailed.

There were many headaches. Yet, in a way, Vera seemed to be thriving on the chaos. Vera would tell us something "outrageous" that Kathy had done, but when we protested or made a suggestion, she would reply: "Let it be. Let her be as she is. She will be gone soon enough."

Vera herself, however, would never "let something be." Every action got a reaction. We had long since learned not to mention something to Vera unless we wanted her to do something about it. Because she inevitably would.

One afternoon, for example, John went next door to where the new building was under construction and found some cinder blocks and two pieces of old gray board with rusty nails sticking out. He used these materials to fashion a bookshelf to put next to his chair in the living room.

The next day, propped against our door were two new boards, the same size, with a note from Vera attached:

"Will they do for a shelf?"

She claimed she obtained them for free, though I suspect she bought them herself.

Having the new volunteers training in our building reminded us continually of where we were a year ago. They were stressed out from struggling with the language, living with host families, and adjusting to Russia. We felt comparatively wise and serene.

Bill, one of the young men, demanded a change of housing; he said his 35-year-old host mother, a pretty redheaded divorcee, had tried to give him a massage. Another trainee, Josh, was having a great time – especially at parties, drinking way too much vodka.

We heard that Phil and Linda Huelsbeck, a young married couple from Wisconsin, would be assigned to stay in Birobidjan, living down the hall from us in the apartment that was Kathy's office during training. Four others would be sent to nearby villages, for a total of eight volunteers in the Jewish Autonomous Region. Adrienne Stone, from a wealthy Santa Barbara family, would serve her two years in a remote, poverty-stricken village north of Khabarovsk. And Allison Reid, a loud but endearing young woman, would finally settle in a village near Birobidjan, but within months would have a traumatic experience that would send her back to Washington for counseling.

Seeing volunteers from our group again was one of the best aspects of the summertime in-service training. But we were also surprised to discover that several had already quit the Peace Corps and gone home. Others would leave, as well, one by one, until our group arrived right at the Peace Corps average: for various reasons, about a third of all volunteers leave before their two years are up.

At last, the rain ended. We assessed the damage. Our apartment had sprung some leaks. Water ran down behind the cloth that covered the living room wall and soaked the desk. Fortunately, the computer had been put away. Water had dripped into the light fixtures and mushrooms grew around the edges of the kitchen window. The building wasn't constructed with flashing or roofing tar, so the water ran into cracks and the roof leaked in spite of its tin surface.

A new Peace Corps medical officer, Anna Krumpe, came to Birobidjan during the training.

At three o'clock one morning, Anna got a phone call from Daphne Early, who had been taken from her home in a village near Khabarovsk. Daphne was hysterical, but she managed to say that she was being held against her will in a Khabarovsk hospital. Anna woke her driver, and they rushed to the hospital.

We suspected the worst, because of the incident last winter when Daphne and Lisa had been trapped in a bar by some Russian drunks. But this time, it wasn't a barroom brawl. Daphne had been seized by a sudden illness, and the mayor of her village called in the militia to deal with the problem.

Daphne speculated that she may have had food poisoning.

She told us later, "I got to school, and suddenly I was, like, vomiting! My blood pressure dropped off the charts! I got so dizzy, I fell and bumped my head against the blackboard!"

The children in her classroom ran to get the mayor.

The mayor decided Daphne might have had a concussion from bumping her head, and so he called for a helicopter from the nearby militia outpost to take her to the hospital.

The helicopter picked up Daphne and the mayor at the school, buzzed into the air, over the forest and across the river, and landed on the hospital roof. Daphne was rushed inside. A hypodermic needle was plunged into her arm, and, half-dazed, she was put into a small dark room where X-rays were taken of her head, her chest and her stomach.

Next, Daphne said, "They ordered me to stand naked – I am serious: Naked! – in front of a panel of medical experts while they started asking me questions in Russian!"

Daphne spoke enough Russian to understand what they were saying about her.

"Okay, get this: They were – no kidding! – discussing whether they should operate on me! They wanted to do, like, brain surgery! I totally freaked out!"

Daphne kept insisting that she had the right to call the Peace Corps. She was ordered to stay in the hospital overnight, and told that it might be as long as two weeks before she could leave. She became hysterical and began crying loudly, "I must call the Peace Corps! I must call the Peace Corps!"

Hospital workers helped her into a cotton gown and put her to bed in a room with five other women. She continued crying and yelling about making her phone call. The other women in the room tried to get her to be quiet and sleep. But she was afraid to sleep. Finally, a worker helped her make the call.

Anna arrived and signed Daphne out of the hospital, against the advice of the Russian doctors. She brought her back to our apartment around noon.

Daphne hugged me. "I'm so glad to be here!" she cried. "What's to eat? I'm starving!"

John had just taken a pot of soup off the stove for lunch, and there was a loaf of dark bread and slices of Edam cheese.

Daphne savored the first food she'd had in a day and a half. She stayed in town for a couple of days; her health seemed fine, and she took the train back to her village. Maybe she had the flu. Maybe a touch of food poisoning. Definitely not a candidate for brain surgery.

Within a week, the village mayor sent the Peace Corps an itemized bill for Daphne's care. The cost – for the helicopter ride, the hospital, the doctors, the X-rays, and the telephone call – was three hundred dollars.

21

Attitude Adjustments

In September, school began. With the Peace Corps training going on, our college classes were moved to a building around the corner. I went over there, met the old woman who was the janitor (the all-important dispenser of keys to the rooms) and moved our new television set and VCR to its temporary classroom.

The weather, at last, was glorious: early autumn, crisp cool air, bright blue sky, leaves rustling dryly and losing their rich green sheen of summer.

We visited the Buistrovs, Ludmila Anatolievna and her husband Sergei, and their little daughters Nastya and Olya. Sergei, a computer whiz, had restored our laptop to usefulness after it crashed. Ludmila Anatolievna, our department's librarian, was home on maternity leave. The baby, Olya, was four months old and Nastya, four. Olya was placid and pink, and had fat cheeks that make her look like a chipmunk. And Nastya had turned from an adorable little princess into a devastated and jealous older sister. She had not been told there was a baby on the way, and she was surprised and outraged by its arrival. She took every opportunity to pinch the baby's cheeks until she cried or hug her until she gasped for air.

Larisa Belichenko was not back at work when the school year began, in our department or any other. She had been having severe headaches and back pains for months. Finally, she went to the hospital. Cancer, the doctors said. A clerk at the college announced the news to us.

"I do not wish her dead, but I do not wish her to return either," the clerk whispered.

The trainers were on edge. The Russian language teachers claimed Kathy took a box of candy out of Robert's desk drawer and presented it to them as a gift from herself and the other Americans on the staff. Robert was not pleased to have his candy stolen and the Russians felt insulted by being given a "tainted" gift. The language teachers from Vladivostok wanted to retaliate by playing a practical joke on Kathy, but the Birobidjan teachers didn't want to participate. So everyone was sullen.

The language teachers said Kathy monitored the use of supplies so closely that they had started using their own money to buy what they needed. They said she kept the paper locked in a cabinet in her office so no one could get it without her consent.

Kathy came to our apartment (down the hall from her office) and questioned us about the cost of a train ticket to Vladivostok, because she suspected Robert of cheating on his expense account. He hadn't.

The language teachers surprised Vera with a party on her birthday. After presenting her with flowers, toasting her with champagne, and dining on apples, cake and chocolate candy, they stood up and sang a long song they had created about Vera. There was lots of laughing and singing, all in Russian. Kathy was upset because she couldn't understand what they were saying and no one took the time to translate for her. Then the teachers played Russian folk music on the tape recorder and some of them took turns dancing around the room, while the rest of us watched and applauded.

At the next staff meeting, Kathy said to the Russian teachers: "Now that I know you are so talented, I want you to dance for the trainees. They deserve to see you dance as much as Vera does."

The first week of the semester was a flurry of confusion. My first class was supposed to meet second period, the students were told, but the schedule given to me said third period. So I missed them. My fourth class was attended by only three students, and one of them should not have been there because I flunked her last year.

On the second day, seven students in the Yiddish group showed up for first period. The flamboyant Irina wasn't with them. She and her mother had emigrated to Israel during the summer.

"Irina scrubbed off her eye shadow and lipstick, and she dressed herself in a gray suit belonging to her mother, and she got the visa," her friend Vika announced.

My second-period class was sent to another classroom to meet with two Peace Corps trainees doing their practice teaching. I didn't mind, except that no one had told me, so I sat waiting for my students, not knowing where they were.

I was having trouble maintaining my enthusiasm. With her Peace Corps duties, teaching, and running the department, Vera was too busy to visit us, even for my Russian lessons. I began to have doubts about teaching English, and doubts about learning Russian. I harbored bleak thoughts about age, a bad haircut, vague ambitions and unsettled purpose.

Two volunteers in our group, Alice Hengesbach and Kristy Baughman, led a good exercise during our mid-service training: They told us all to write a paragraph about something that depressed us.

"Just write it down. Don't worry, nobody's going to read it," Alice said.

When everyone was finished, Kristy said, "Now, crumple the paper it's written on, stomp on it, tear it up, and toss it into the garbage."

That was the Alice and Kristy method of dealing with a dark mood. I wished it were that easy.

Vera's former friend Lisa Cross came late to the mid-service training, having just returned to Russia from a month's vacation in Australia. The last time we saw her was at a party; she was upside-down, laughing, her long hair dragging the floor, her legs being held in the air by a large Russian youth.

Before winter set in, Lisa realized she was in love with a cowboy she had met in Australia. She packed up her belongings, said goodbye to her Russian village, quit the Peace Corps, and headed once more for Down Under.

On the way home from class, I stopped at the Nadezhda Department Store, an all-purpose general store, with clothes and shoes for men, women and children; household goods and appliances; dishes and tools; cosmetics and jewelry.

One side had been cleared out, completely, down to the concrete walls and floor, and the other side has been reduced to one counter displaying odds and ends (buttons, glasses, wallpaper, a few blouses) and a back wall of kitchen supplies and spare automobile parts. I found two bottles of Bingo, a serviceable dishwashing liquid, and bought one of them. I considered buying both, because they were hard to find, but it seemed somehow decadent and ostentatious.

My spirits were lifted when Ludmila Borisovna's thirteen-year-old daughter Masha, once so shy and reticent, saw me shopping and rushed over to hug me and give me a soft kiss on the cheek. It meant that she, as well as I, treasured the time we spent working together at her family's *dacha* and socializing at long Russian dinners. Masha's English was admirable and she blushed and smiled endearingly. Her friends looked on with interest as she chatted with me in English.

The gas went out on the stove again. We found a hot plate for heating coffee water and boiling eggs, and we bought a little toaster-oven.

We took a long walk, with the camera, but the sun disappeared behind a layer of high clouds. On our way home, the sun reappeared momentarily and seven soldiers strode toward us on Lenin Street. I rushed up to them with the camera, stifling the Peace Corps' admonition "not to take pictures of military installations and personnel," and they gladly stopped and posed for a group photo, their arms draped over each other's shoulders.

The day was beautiful – golden, cool, a slight breeze, and the clouds drifted away in late afternoon, leaving bright sunshine on the *rinok*.

John wanted to go to dinner at seven, just as I had settled in the television room with Anna, the medical officer, to watch a show on CNN about Princess Di, who had just died. John insisted on his timetable, and further, he said he couldn't in his wildest imagination understand how anyone could want to watch a show about "a royal blonde bulimic." He must have been really hungry. So we went to supper. Immediately. But I was resentful.

Then Mother Teresa died, too, and our Russian friends start asking: "Who'll be number three? Don't they always come in threes?"

It's strange: the rapt and fleeting attention of the mass audience.

"On the sixth day after the death of the princess, the people are still mourning," intoned the CNN newscaster.

How trivializing the media can be. And the people, sobbing. The public outpouring of mass grief. Mesmerizing, temporary. Tears not shed in some past personal grief, saved for when everyone was stricken, everyone could share.

Then the cameras moved on, people turned their attention back to the pursuits of their private lives, and some other event occupied the broadcast news.

A local tragedy can stay on the front page, and the top of the news, for about a week, a journalism professor of mine once said;

a national or international tragedy has staying power of about three weeks (unless it is sustained by continuing unfolding aspects), and then the public is tired of hearing about it, and the news moves on.

Dan Wallis, one of the older Peace Corps trainees, had just finished a day of practice teaching. All of his anxieties about Russia came together at the end of that day, in a frightening encounter that left his thin legs wobbly with exhaustion.

Dan had finished his classes and was walking to the school where his wife was teaching.

He heard a motor behind him, and he turned around to see a black van heading toward him. The van passed him in a cloud of dust, then swerved and stopped suddenly, in front of him. A heavyset man got out, slammed the door, and looked in his direction. The man was wearing a black suit with a black turtleneck jersey and black sunglasses.

"I thought of every Mafia movie I had ever seen," Dan said.

The man walked slowly over to him, stopped directly in front of him, looked at a paper in his hand, looked down at Dan, and said, "Dan Wallis."

Dan nodded.

"I felt my knees turn to jelly," he said.

"Come!" the man in black said. He grabbed Dan's sleeve. The man spoke little English, but he tugged on the sleeve and motioned with his head for Dan to get into the van.

Dan said, "I didn't know who he was. I didn't know what he wanted. But I knew one thing. I wasn't getting in that van. He'd have to kill me right there."

Dan yelled, "No!" yanked his arm away, and marched along the road to the school, as fast as he could go without breaking into a run.

Dan wasn't sure why he didn't run. Maybe in the movies, running is when the shooting starts, he guessed. Maybe he was afraid he'd fall. Maybe it was something about dignity.

His heart was thudding wildly in his chest and he dared not look around.

When he turned the corner into the schoolyard, he allowed himself a glance back. The man was walking behind him, trying to keep up, maybe gaining on him.

Dan raced into the building and headed for room 32 where he knew his wife and her friend, Tanya, were waiting for him.

The man in black followed close behind.

Dan said, "I figured if I made it into the room, at least there'd be a witness to my death."

Breathlessly, he told the women what was happening, then the man in black burst into the room.

Dan froze.

Tanya said, in Russian, "*Zdrastvuitia! Kak vas zavut?*" ("Hello! Who are you?") to the man in black. He had stopped right next to Dan. Both of them were breathing hard.

The man, catching his breath, explained. He was sent by the school where Dan was working, and he needed Dan's passport to get him registered.

By late September, I put the heavy Russian quilt back on the bed against the chill of cold and rainy nights. It would be four more weeks before the city turned on the heat.

Our friend Pavel Tolstogusov wasn't allowed to leave town without permission from a judge. He was under supervision for punching a man in the nose.

We had not seen Pavel and Lena all summer, but after school started we had them to dinner again. They told us about the incident that got him in trouble with the law.

It happened when Lena and their sons Kolya and Vanya were visiting her parents in central Russia.

Pavel and his friend Sasha had gone to the public sauna at the edge of town. Pavel had hung his gold chain and his keys on a hook, along with his clothes, while he was inside basking naked in the dry heat. Later, after he had sweated and swatted himself with oak branches and jumped in the cold water and toweled himself dry, he went to put on his clothes and go home.

"Where is my stuff?" he asked Sasha who was dressing nearby.

"Ha! I thought something was strange about that guy!" Sasha said. He told Pavel that a man, someone Sasha knew slightly, had lifted Pavel's chain and keys off the hook and put them in his pocket.

"I gave him a suspicious look," Sasha told Pavel. "I even asked him, 'Hey, is that yours?' and the man said, 'It is now.' "

Sasha and Pavel asked around, and tracked down the thief's telephone number. Pavel went home and called him.

"I know who you are and I know that you have my gold chain and my keys, and I want you to return them to me this evening," he said. He gave the man his address. The man said he couldn't come that evening but he would be there the next night and return the stolen things.

The next evening, there was a knock on the door. The thief and two of his large friends stood outside Pavel's apartment door. The man handed Pavel his chain and his keys, then Pavel punched him in the nose.

The man's two friends threw Pavel to the concrete floor of the dark hallway and shouted at him, demanding that he apologize. Their friend the thief stood with his back to the wall, crying and holding a handkerchief to his nose. Blood was streaming through the cloth and dripping onto the floor.

Pavel, held to the floor by the two men, yelled at them, "You can kill me right now, but I will never apologize, and you should not have a thief for a friend!"

"Can you imagine this?" Lena said. "I am glad the boys were not there to see their father in such a fight!"

Neighbors opened their doors and some of them crept out onto the stairway to see what was happening.

Suddenly, the men let go of Pavel, grabbed their friend and stamped down the stairs, yelling as they shoved open the outside door, "You'll pay for this!"

Two weeks later, Pavel was summoned before a judge. The court had received an application from the alleged victim. He complained that Pavel was a menace to society and applied to have him punished for punching a man in the face without provocation.

"But Pasha, why *did* you hit him after he returned your things?" Lena asked him after he had finished telling the story. She was still genuinely puzzled, trying to understand her thin, brave husband, about whom she had once told us, "He is not a man; he is an intellectual."

"Of course," Pavel answered, putting a tone of great patience into his voice, "I did not dare to hit him before he returned my things. Or I never would have gotten them back. I had to wait until I got them back. And then, I was so mad – I was so mad that someone would steal something that belonged to me – that I had to teach him a lesson."

Furthermore, Pavel is writing his own letter of application to have the thief punished by the judge as well.

"If that's the way he's going to be, it's good enough for him," he said.

John caught a terrible cold, the weather was colder by the day, the hot water was off again, and the petty quarrels continued among the Peace Corps training staff down the hall.

One of the trainees, Allison Reid, complained that during her visit to the village where she would be teaching, the Russian teacher who was to be her counterpart couldn't keep her hands off her. I

237

told her that I'd noticed many Russian women tended to touch other women when they were talking to them. I'd had my collar straightened, my hair patted, my sweater buttoned, all in the course of a casual conversation. But Allison said she felt smothered, and she was sure the woman was a lesbian.

The swearing-in ceremony for the new volunteers was set for October 3, then training would end and they would leave for their villages and towns. Josh was supposed to go to a village and be housed with Allison. After Josh and Allison visited their site, they said they needed a wall built in their apartment so they could have separate bedrooms. A reasonable request.

Vera came out of the training director's office and walked to the front door with us, so tense, she was shaking.

As we got to the front door of the building, she said: "Kathy was chanting, 'I hate Russia. I hate Russia. I hate Russia' – as if I were a piece of furniture or the wall, as if I were not Russian."

Vera was on her way to a host family to ask them questions about a missing one-hundred-dollar bill.

"A cousin of the family is the prime suspect," she said.

Later, over coffee, Vera told me about an elderly Birobidjan woman who had rented her vacant apartment to the Peace Corps to house one of the trainers. The old woman telephoned the director's office, demanding an extra nine dollars because her electric bill was higher than expected. Vera handled the call, because the woman spoke no English, but Kathy told Vera to have the old woman come into the office and justify the increase before she would pay her.

"I went to her apartment and paid her out of my own pocket," Vera said. "I did not want her to think badly of Americans."

Most of the leaves had fallen from the trees. John wore his heavy flannel shirt, long johns and thick socks. I had my old quilted silk Chinese jacket, long johns, and a small alpaca blanket, so we kept warm. I stuffed cotton batting back in around the edges of the windows to keep out the draft.

For a week, janitors were in our building, tightening loose pipes, scraping them out, and forcing high-pressure sprays of water through them, in what we were told was an annual purging that culminates in turning on the citywide heating system. We never knew when or on what pipes they would be working. In fact, we thought they might have finished.

I started a load of laundry, mostly underwear and white socks. I put detergent in the bathtub, started running the water, and began soaking the clothes. When the tub was about half full, the water suddenly turned a rich, murky, rusty brown. The white clothes lay under the deluge, their fibers soaking up the silt.

I turned off the hot water immediately and turned on the cold, sighing in relief as the cold water poured in a clear stream from the faucet. But this only lasted for a few seconds. Then the cold water too turned a deep brown. There was nothing to be done but wait. An hour later, the water was again fairly clear, and I set about rinsing the worst of the rust out of the now beige socks and underwear. The sky was dark all day, and by late afternoon it was raining again.

The next day dawned bright and the sun warmed the windows. When I opened the kitchen window, the air felt delightful – warm in the sun and cool in the shade. I looked forward to a walk after my last class, around 4:30.

But around 2 o'clock in the afternoon, the classroom suddenly turned cold and dark. I looked out the window. Huge clouds had moved in and spread a quilted layer of gray over the sky above, leaving the bright blue only at the horizon, like an edge of colorful lace sewn onto a drab blanket. I felt chilled.

When class was over, I headed back to the apartment and pulled on my quilted silk jacket. Alone, I felt unbearably sad and tears welled up in my eyes. I turned on the computer and sat facing the screen. There were so many times when I would start writing, only to be interrupted. By a chore. Or by John. Or by a knock at the door.

The Russian poet Anna Akhmatova knew from girlhood she was destined to write great poetry and so she did. In the back of my mind, I thought that I would write something important, or I should, or I should have. Or, like Tillie Olsen's short story, would I just "Stand Here Ironing"?

Peace Corps decided at the last minute to move Allison from the "problem site" where she would have to share an apartment with Josh and where she thought her Russian counterpart was a lesbian. Her new site was a village close to Birobidjan.

On the afternoon of the swearing-in ceremony, Antonina Salinon went to Allison's host family's apartment and told Allison to come with her immediately to visit her new village. Allison wanted to change out of her jeans and sweatshirt, but Antonina said there was no time.

On the way back to Birobidjan, their car stalled, and it took several hours for the driver to get it running again. Allison and Antonina arrived back at our building with just enough time to get to the concert hall for the ceremony.

Allison charged into the building, Antonina right behind her. Allison raced up the stairs to our apartment and pounded on the door. We were getting ready to go. When I opened the door, she burst into tears. Alarmed, I put my arms around her and tried to comfort her. "What's wrong?" I cried.

"Antonina hates me!" she sobbed.

"Try to be more specific," John ordered.

"I have to change clothes," she wailed. "Everyone will be dressed up. I can't swear in like this."

"There is no time," Antonina said.

"Look at me! She won't let me go home and change clothes!" Allison bawled, a huge childish cry that sounded like a two-year-old being pulled down off a kitchen cabinet.

Antonina jabbed at her watch. "Allison! You must not be late!" she scolded, and Allison started yelling again.

"Here," I said, pulling a black pleated skirt and a white sweater out of my tall wooden wardrobe. "These clothes might fit you." I found a pair of tights she could wear as well. She wouldn't win prizes for best-dressed, but at least she wouldn't be in jeans and a sweatshirt. The clothes fit, Allison was wild with gratitude, and we all rushed off to the concert hall.

As the new volunteers raised their right hands to swear in, Allison stood in the back row so no one could see that she still had on her hiking shoes.

The training staff packed up and left, the new volunteers moved to their sites, and Phil and Linda moved into the apartment down the hall. Peace returned to our building.

22

If, at First, You Don't Succeed

Vera, John and I took a week off and visited Blagoveshensk, which now claimed from Birobidjan the distinction of being the farthest Peace Corps site from the Vladivostok headquarters. We helped the two new volunteers settle in.

Blagoveshensk has grand old buildings and wide tree-lined boulevards in the downtown area. But its outlying areas were littered with piles of dirt and ugly concrete high-rises. A river divides the city from a modern-looking city on the Chinese side, Heihe. Shopping was better in Blagoveshensk than in Birobidjan; we enjoyed checking out the stores and the fashions. Every afternoon during the week we visited, a strong wind lifted off the river and chilled us to the bone.

Blagoveshensk was off the trans-Siberian railroad route, on a short turn south that ended there at the China border. Though the border was strictly guarded, there were ferries that transported Chinese workers back and forth to their jobs in Russia. Still, gazing across the river at the high-rise buildings, smoking factory chimneys and other signs of industrial activity, Heihe seemed the more prosperous place. Both cities were entities unto themselves, reflecting each other's presence, each complete with shops and restaurants, public buildings and universities, yet seeming isolated and remote from every other place on the planet.

One of the Blagoveshensk volunteers spent her entire settling-in allowance on a huge boom-box, and had no money left to furnish her room. The other, a Stanford University graduate, didn't know how to boil eggs. John, helping her prepare breakfast, slipped six eggs into a saucepan of boiling water.

"How do you know when they're done?" she asked. "Do they change color or something?"

We arrived back in Birobidjan after an overnight ride on the slow train and found that our apartment was still unheated, although the first snow of winter had fallen two days before. More importantly, the rest of the building was warm enough, so we knew at least that the town's central coal-fired furnaces had been lit and the heat should reach our rooms soon.

We unpacked, and I washed a load of white clothes and hung them on the radiator and on the clothes rack in the kitchen to dry overnight.

John cooked a light supper – thin slices of fried beef with boiled potatoes and beets – and we opened a bottle of Moldovan red wine. At seven o'clock, we were sitting down at the kitchen table to eat when Valentina's husband Uri knocked on the door.

Uri, a small man with a twinkle in his eye and a nearly uncontrollable lust for vodka, came in wearing his camouflage-design army fatigues and carrying a handful of tools. He gestured toward the radiator, mumbling about fixing it so we could have heat. We nodded and continued eating while he went to work on the radiator.

Uri gripped his wrench with two hands and twisted something on the end of the pipe. We heard a hissing sound. To our horror, as Uri stood in the corner of the kitchen, brown water began to spray in his face, all over his clothes, and all over the refrigerator and the wall behind him. Uri stared at us, his eyes wide with – what? – terror, surprise, remorse? His eyes were like white spots in the mud on his face. We didn't know if the muddy stream was scalding hot or ice cold. The water coursed from the radiator in a forceful stream, then began to spin and spray.

Seemingly in slow motion, Uri turned around and tried to tighten down the bolt he had loosened and stop the spray. Mud spewed onto the ceiling, over the white laundry, onto the windows. It flowed down the wall and across the floor.

"Where is the valve?" John yelled.

Uri stared at him.

"Is it hot?" I yelled. "Is it burning you?"

Uri had no words. Only the look of wide-eyed horror and the hands fidgeting with little tools. I was afraid he was being scalded to death. Then the stream of water gyrated as Uri got a handle on the valve and gave it a twist. It shot in my direction.

Warm. The water was only warm. Thank God.

John grabbed the English-Russian dictionary and ran down the hallway and down the stairs to get someone to help, yelling, in Russian, "Water! Help! Turn it off!"

Mud flooded out of the kitchen into the hallway, making its way to the living room. John looked up the word "mop" as he neared the classrooms. Students from a night class piled into the corridor to watch and whisper.

"Where is a mop?" he asked, holding the dictionary out toward them.

Suddenly Valentina appeared, in her best black dress. She had been hosting a party in the cafeteria. She shooed the students back to their classroom and followed John to our apartment. By then, Uri had managed to tighten the valve and stop the flow.

The muddy water was warm, chocolate brown and slimy. Mud dripped from everything and lay in rivers on the kitchen floor, in the entryway and just under the edge of the thin living room carpet.

Valentina stomped away in her high-heeled black shoes and came back wearing old work shoes, carrying rags and buckets, and followed by her teenage son, Igor. She took off her big watch, three rings and a set of keys and handed them to me, and directed me to sit in a chair out in the hallway. That was fine. I wasn't ready yet to

244

face the mess. The three of them went to work silently. Uri and his stepson swabbed the floors, handed muddy rags to Valentina and she rinsed them in the bathtub, wrung them out and handed them back.

After a half hour of sopping up the mud, Valentina determined that the worst was over and she could go back to her party. She recovered her jewelry and keys and said that painters would be here "on Monday, maybe Tuesday" to paint the walls.

As soon as she was out of sight, Uri and the boy handed us their rags and left.

The refrigerator, the radio, the canisters on the shelf, the radiator itself, the stove, the table, the laundry, and all other surfaces and objects in the kitchen were left for us to clean up. John went down the hall to show Phil and Linda.

"Do you want to see the worst kitchen catastrophe you've ever seen short of an earthquake or a fire?" he asked them.

"Sure, I'm always up for catastrophes," Phil said cheerfully.

I put the muddy laundry back in the tub to start over.

Linda and Philip came over, surveyed the damage, and kept saying, "I don't believe it. Look at this. This is incredible."

They took a stack of dishes and all the knives, forks and spoons to their apartment to clean for us. They were such good neighbors.

One thing worked out right. The radiator in the kitchen began to put out some heat. The bedroom was barely heated and the living room radiators weren't working at all.

Uri left his tools here. We thought maybe we should hide them.

Vasili Nikolaievich Ivchenko was in the teachers' room grading papers after school one day and Olga, his little stepdaughter, sat quietly drawing.

"She has been very naughty," Vasili said, emphasizing the words for dramatic impact. "Her teacher called and I had to pick her up from school." He furrowed his brows and said in an exaggerated voice, "She knows that if this ever happens again, I will beat her with a stick and stand her in a closet!"

Olga gave him a charming smile, secure that she needn't take his threat seriously. "I'm very sorry, Daddy," she said sweetly.

"It's not your fault you are exactly like your mother!" Vasili said, patting her shoulder. "It's difficult for other women to tolerate you. You should try to be twice as nice as the homely little girls."

Olga smiled and turned back to her drawing.

"How is Irina?" I asked.

"I will tell you a secret," Vasili said. "Well, it's not really a secret. Everyone knows. But you must swear not to tell anyone. You see, I want to tell the secret myself!"

"My lips are sealed."

"All right. I will tell you then." He turned to Olga. "Shall I tell her?"

"Tell her! Tell her!" Olga cried.

"Irina's pregnant!" he whispered, swelling with pride. "I'm going to be a father!" He glanced at Olga and added, "Again."

"That's wonderful!" I said. "Congratulations! When is the baby due?"

"April. Until then, I will do everything, the cleaning, the cooking, the laundry, and looking after Olga. Irina is a fragile woman and I do not want her to have a single worry."

"I will help, too," Olga said fervently.

"Yes," Vasili said. "You and I will work together."

The temperature was 25F. The autumn leaves were gone. A young man with a thin scar from his left eyebrow to the side of his mouth came and checked out the living room radiator. There was still no heat from it. I covered the computer with a towel, just in case there was a repeat performance of the calamity in the kitchen, but it wasn't necessary. The young man was supposed to come back at five and check the radiator again. But he didn't show up.

After our week off to go to Blagoveshensk, we expected to begin teaching again on Monday. As of Sunday afternoon, our names weren't on the schedule, so we didn't teach Monday. They weren't on the schedule the next day either. Finally our names were posted; we had classes on Wednesday.

Scheduling was generally very casual. Each week, the complete schedule was posted outside the teachers' office on Friday, sometimes as late as Saturday. And it was subject to change on a daily, sometimes hourly, basis. But we had learned to be flexible.

"There's no reason to take things too seriously," John said. "The schedule is just a suggestion."

Kommandant Valentina stood in our kitchen, on a stool, on top of the table, whitewashing the mud-splattered kitchen ceiling with a rag. She looked like a balloon on a stand, one of those kind that wobbles from side to side, but won't tip over when you bat at it.

She worked with a thick gauze bandage on her left hand because she had cut it on a razor blade just before beginning the job. She said she had wadded up a scrap of paper to throw in the wastebasket, and it had a razor blade inside it. Her blood was on the stairway.

I had students' papers to read. John went for a walk.

"I don't want to be here if she falls," he said.

It was nerve-wracking to think about the times a stool has simply collapsed under the weight of a student sitting on it, and see big Valentina standing on one, on top of the table, in the middle of our kitchen. Valentina muttered and wobbled, slapped the whitewash back and forth across the ceiling, climbed down, shoved the table this way and that, climbed back up, went at it again. Finally, she finished and left, exhausted and splattered with whitewash herself, but still in one piece.

In my conversation class, the students and I talked about American and Russian adages. They came up with a list of Russian adages, then translated them into English. We noted that many of the American adages I had listed for them were similar to these common Russian adages:

A friend appears during trouble.

Time is the best doctor.

All roads lead to Moscow.

One is not a soldier alone in the field.

Morning is wiser than night.

To know how much food a wolf will eat, look in the direction the wolf looks.

There is one law for rich, another for poor.

It's better over there where there is no us.

All that glitters is not gold.

There are a lot of devils in a quiet pond.

The walls have ears.

A titmouse in the hand is better than a crane in the sky.

One of the students, Igor, didn't attend classes and hadn't learned anything, but his parents threatened to sue if the college flunked him out. His mother was a local judge.

Anatoli Surnin insisted that the teachers retest Igor, and retest him again, until he passed his tests. The fact that he refused to study was irrelevant. Regarding his absences, the director declared that the teachers must be more firm in insisting that students attend class. They must track them down and force them to comply. If that failed, he said, the teachers were to blame.

Vera steered a collision course against Anatoli's order. She flunked Igor. "Let the director put the scoundrel in another program," she said defiantly. "He has no place in our department."

It was not only our college that changed its schedule daily. Linda Huelsbeck, who had started working at another school, was supposed to teach a first-period class. She found this out when she checked the schedule at five in the afternoon the day before. She got to school early in the morning, only to find that someone had rescheduled her class for later in the day.

Phil's classes at the college were canceled for the rest of the week when he mentioned that he and Linda were thinking about going to the nearby village of Bekinskaya to visit a teacher there. But the same secretary who canceled Phil's classes told him that he couldn't go to Bekinskaya until he got his visa, which was supposed to be ready at two that afternoon but still wasn't ready when the visa office closed at five.

Phil came down the hall to ask us whether we thought he could go to Bekinskaya without his visa. And he asked if we thought his classes would be rescheduled. We didn't have the answers, but we tried to assure him that uncertainty was bearable, and he would get used to it.

The morning sky was pink and red in the east, a sign of rough weather, and the day turned colder as it went by, then there was a little rain, and snow was predicted.

Denis Kopul decided he would apply, for the second time, for the scholarship offered by the Freedom Support Act Undergraduate Exchange Program. Lena Tsimbalyuk and Masha Voroshbit also entered the competition. John, Phil and I wanted to recommend every one of them.

Vera wanted us to choose only one.

"Denis has the best chance of winning," she said. "I am quite certain that if you support all three students, none of them will win."

The last time we were in Vladivostok, I had met Dennis Boyle, a former Peace Corps volunteer who was now representing the scholarship program. I telephoned him and told him about our three exceptionally talented students.

"We want to support all of them," I said. "But we don't want to hurt anyone's chances. Each one of them deserves the scholarship. But Dennis, please be completely candid. Is there any chance that our recommendations would cancel each other out?"

"Absolutely not," he said. "Each candidate is judged on his or her own merits. If you think any one of them would have a good chance to succeed, then you should feel free to pull out all the stops."

John, Phil and I each wrote three letters of recommendation.

Then began the test-taking training of our three scholarship applicants. The practice scholastic tests, so routinely used in America, were unheard of in Birobidjan. Besides, Russian students weren't used to taking tests the way Americans take them. They were used to standing alone in front of a professor and talking their way through a semester's or a year's worth of knowledge, an incredible feat of memory. Many Russians could recite entire poems, entire plays, entire theories, background, bibliographies, with not a single written reference.

But a booklet of questions, five possible choices labeled A, B, C, D and E, and an answer form with small circles to fill in, were testing devices they had never seen. Added to this would be the stress of getting the instructions that time was limited for each section of the test, and they probably wouldn't have time to answer all the questions. Seat them in a room near other test takers and admonish them not to look around or whisper, and the foreignness of the experience can be overwhelming.

Now we knew this, and we could make a difference. We were prepared with sets of practice tests, language and scholastic, for the three to take.

Once a week, after classes, Denis, Masha and Lena practiced taking the tests. Their progress was measurable; their scores improved. They already knew the information, and now they were learning how to take the test, American-style.

Linda and Phil were in their apartment down the hall from us when they heard someone jiggling a key in their door.

They had the bolt locked from inside, but Phil quickly opened the door and surprised the intruder. The man ran into a classroom and jumped out the window, ran across the roof near Kommandant Valentina's office, dropped to the street below, and got away. When the militia arrived, Valentina told them she saw the man on the roof clutching a ring full of keys. Now all the locks had to be changed.

Phil's and Linda's apartment had been the Peace Corps office during training, and Valentina said the trainers often left their keys hanging by the door. She figured the would-be thief had somehow gotten hold of the keys, and made copies of them.

Vera was quite agitated about this breach of security, especially about Valentina's strong suspicion that someone in the building might have slipped the intruder some keys. In the fine phrasing of one of those old American detective stories she loves, Vera said with great excitement, "There may be an inside finger man on the premises!"

Kommandant Valentina fired Elvira from her job as janitor. We ran into Elvira at the *rinok*.

"Don't worry about me," she said. "I am much happier now." She said Valentina accused her of stealing, and even though Anatoli Surnin believed she was innocent, he supported Valentina's rule of the building.

A missionary named Mike lived in Irkutsk, near Lake Baikal. We learned he was there because we got his mail.

Two boxes of books – two mutilated boxes – were stuffed in a big canvas mailbag and tied up with a rope attached to a mailing label addressed to us. There had been other packages delivered to us over the year, when we were the only Americans in town; apparently, when the postal workers saw a package labeled in the unfamiliar Roman alphabet, they just tossed it our way. Usually, we noticed in time if it was not for us, and simply refused to accept it.

But this mailbag label had our name and address on it and we had been waiting for books from home, so we signed for it, hoisted it into a taxi and took it back to our apartment.

There we opened the bag and regarded the boxes inside. They were addressed to the missionary in Irkutsk. We checked out the contents: The titles of the books included "Living as a Missionary Family," "Saving Your Marriage Before It Starts," "The Physician's Medical Guide" (a 20-pounder), the autobiography of Winston Churchill's wife, a few bestsellers and a few more Christian self-help books. And a funny little potholder that looked like a fat French chef.

One of the boxes with Mike's name also included his e-mail address. We e-mailed Mike to ask him what he wanted us to do with his books, and of course he replied right away: He wanted us to mail them to him.

We went back to the post office and asked whether we could put the books back in the bag and return them because they had been sent to us by mistake.

The answer was no. We had opened the package, and therefore it was our problem.

We asked if we could send the books to Irkutsk C.O.D. (cash on delivery).

The answer was yes, there was cash-on-delivery postal service in Russia. But it worked this way: We would pay the postage, then

Mike would pay the postage when he collected the books, then the post office would reimburse us.

And we couldn't just stuff the books back in the mailbag and send them. The post office confiscated the mailbag from us, on grounds that it was postal property, and not ours to use. We had to find new boxes and repack the books, then sew canvas or burlap bags around the boxes. I shopped for strong string to use, but I couldn't find any. But I had an inspiration: dental floss. We found boxes, repacked the books, and I spent several hours sewing the boxes into burlap bags with dental floss. Then we hired another taxi, took the packages back to the post office, and sent them on their way.

We assumed the dental floss held and the boxes arrived at their destination, because two months later, the post office paid us back our money.

Someone telephoned the college and said that a bomb was planted in our building and would soon explode. That took a couple of hours out of the heart of the day. Everyone in the building – students, teachers and residents – was ordered to get out and stay out for two hours.

Kommandant Valentina ran down our hallway yelling, "Lock your doors! Lock your doors!"

We had just started cooking lunch. Potatoes were frying, bread was sliced for toast, eggs ready to boil. We turned off the stove, grabbed our coats, locked our door as ordered and hurried outside. The militia made a thorough search. No bomb was found.

Vera said later she was glad she didn't have to apologize, bomb scares not being strictly a Russian phenomenon. (Vera often apologized for Russian this, Russian that. We didn't complain too much anymore about anything to Vera, because she expressed a sort of universal guilt for every specific problem.)

As department chair, Vera was questioned by the militia. They asked her who might have a grudge against the school.

She told them that a grudge was held "by the local female judge whose son, Igor, has just flunked his way out of school."

But John and I wondered whether the bomb scare might have been called in by the cook's helper who had just been fired. That young man had been accused of being "the inside finger man" who helped an accomplice in the recent robbery attempt by making duplicate keys to the Americans' apartments.

It was a problem trying to cope with having new locks installed. We refused to let the carpenter pound any more holes into the concrete wall next to the door frame. The bolt hole couldn't be put into the wooden frame itself because the door hung crookedly, due to the fighting couple who crashed into it the year before.

There were other problems in the building, too. The cafeteria workers were no longer able to cater private parties here because the tax men came along and demanded so much money that they couldn't make a profit. So that was the end of the general populace coming in to book their weddings, wakes and birthdays on these premises.

The sky was still dark at 8 in the morning although we had turned the clocks back to Standard Time, and there were two months to go before winter Solstice. Long nights, short days. But the skies were clear, and midday was bright and sunny. Each day was a little colder.

Our students had a Halloween party. Halloween is not a holiday celebrated in Russia, but the college put it on as part of the English-language program. I bought a pumpkin at the *rinok*, removed the pulp, and Vera enthusiastically carved it into her first Jack-o-lantern. I lit a candle in it and set it on the cafeteria windowsill for the party.

Tanya Sapunova, a first-year student who had spent a year as an exchange student at a high school in Ohio, decided to present an "American Halloween tradition." Under her guidance, her friends threw long trails of toilet paper high into the thin poplar trees that lined the front of our building. (The streams of Russian toilet paper, tough fibrous tissue, clung to the bare branches throughout the long and windy winter.)

The students enjoyed putting on skits, so several of them dressed up in costumes and provided entertainment. After the performance, they turned up the volume on the sound system and danced for hours to a reverberating, thumping roar with a universal disco beat and no discernible melody.

Peace Corps headquarters in Vladivostok reported that several boxes of books addressed to us were held up in customs. We had already received the first eight boxes from our summer mailing. Of the eight boxes, three contained children's books. We took a third of them to the elementary school teachers of English and a third to the orphanage in Waldheim. The rest stayed in the college library, because some of our students tutored children in English, and they could use them.

When we arrived at the orphanage with our treasured books, the children welcomed us, as they always did, with an intensity of eagerness that was heartbreaking. They didn't hide behind a facade of toughness. They were exposed, raw, like a new wound. I felt the desire to embrace each child and the despair of their overwhelming need.

The semester settled into a reasonable routine. We both had several classes, which kept us fairly busy.

John and I took long walks on the weekends, by the river, past the post office, and beyond the *Dom Buila* (White House) department store to the edge of town. There were strollers, children, picnickers on the bank of the river even though ice laced the water's edge.

Ludmila Sergeievna Tsimbalyuk called one evening, to say hello and ask how we were doing. She appreciated our work with her daughter, Lena. And, by the way, could she borrow our home video about Santa Barbara? And would we mind too much if she asked us to make cassette tapes of English-language folk songs? "The teachers loved your songs at the Soros workshop," she said. "We would be so grateful to have them on tape."

I felt as though we had finally won over a reluctant friend.

Denis stopped by, and said that after much thought he wanted to change his statement of goals on his scholarship application, but he was worried that I would be annoyed. On the contrary, I was relieved. Trying to help him define his goals had been touchy, but his effort to work through it resulted in a much better essay, as well as a better sense of why he wanted to study in America. He said less about American sports and more about his future career as a teacher in Russia.

I hoped Denis would win this year. And I hoped Lena would win. And I hoped Masha would win.

23

Deeper Into the Life

Two of the new volunteers, Allison Reid and Wendy Guyot, stopped by to pick up their backpacks and say goodbye. They had come to Birobidjan for the weekend to visit their host families. With Americans around the region, our apartment was an in-town storage place and e-mail center. Wendy said there might be a message from her father. I signed on and she read it.

"Couldja print it out? That'd be great. Thanks!"

"No problem."

"Well, see you guys Thanksgiving! Oh, and tell Vera we'll call her! Oh, and dinner last night was great," she continued. "Oh, and if people call you, here's what we want you to tell everybody about Thanksgiving." She thrust a note into my hand. The group was planning a Thanksgiving reunion in Birobidjan.

Then Allison said, "Don't forget I want you to come see me a week from Sunday. Bye, you guys."

They hoisted their backpacks on over their coats and pulled the door closed behind them.

My birthday, November 6, started beautifully. We stayed in bed, luxuriated, sipped coffee, talked a little. Opened our arms and hearts and bodies to each other. Stretched. Smiled. At breakfast John gave me a sweet amber ring made in Russia and sold in a room above the local cheese-and-butter store.

In the afternoon, in the Russian style, I threw myself a birthday party in the teachers' room. Everyone came. I felt deep appreciation for their warmth and friendship.

I counted my blessings. There were many – having John in my life, my three children, John's four, my grandchild, John's two, my dear sister and brothers and father, our friends back home, our friends in Russia. I also mused over certain tragedies and failures and sadnesses. And I knew that in one sense I was in a runaway place, thousands of miles from home, building a new life that I treasured but that was temporary.

November 7 is a Russian holiday, Revolution Day. In 1997, the day marked 80 years since Lenin and his followers overthrew the Czar. There was an effort to change the name of the holiday to World Peace Day, but newspapers still called it Revolution Day. The local statue of Lenin in the town square was garnished with bouquets of long-stemmed carnations.

Once again, I was enjoying teaching. My students were energetic and fun, naive and bright with promise. Tanya Sherman and her boyfriend Sasha Lushchinsky, 20-year-old students who planned to be married after graduation, and some of the others often stopped by our apartment to practice their English.

"Is joy for me to listen to Tanya play the piano," Sasha said. "Is beautiful. My soul rise above ordinary life when her fingers move over the keys."

"I want Sasha to be a businessman, but he is really a dreamer," Tanya said.

"Can I be film star in Hollywood?" Sasha asked.

Boris Kosventsev, the director and chief artist of the Birobidjan Modern Art Museum, invited John and me to the opening of a new show in his gallery.

After looking at the new paintings, meeting the artist, and buying a small painting, we joined a few people who were sitting around Boris's office behind the scenes, drinking vodka and snacking on bread and cheese and pickles. Boris talked about his father. We had heard that his father spent time in prison, but we hadn't heard why.

"He was an actor," Boris said. "Rather a famous actor in Russia. He didn't always have the leading roles, but he was always working, in one film after another. He was much in demand.

"But in 1951, my father made a terrible mistake. Maybe it's not fair to say so, because he didn't know at the time that it was a mistake. My father starred in a film about a man who escaped from prison. The script had been approved; everything was without problem until the film began playing in the Moscow theaters. Then charges were brought against him. Two policemen came to the house, pushed my mother into the kitchen, and waited for my father to come home. When he arrived, they arrested him and took him away. According to the KGB, starring in this film was a political act against the state. He was sentenced to ten years in prison."

No one spoke.

I wanted to hear more. "Why was your father blamed?" I asked.

Boris swallowed the rest of the vodka in his glass and poured another, gesturing around the room with the bottle. People put their glasses out for refills. That done, Boris lit a cigarette and continued.

"As it turned out, after the film was released, the part my father played seemed to inspire people in a way no one had predicted," he said.

"The blame was placed directly on the head of my father because it was his part that inspired people. My father played the role of an anti-Leninist."

Boris leaned forward, waving his cigarette in our faces. "Even though the film portrayed him as the villain, the censors said he played his part – how can I say? – too sympathetically. You see, it made trouble for them – the censors – because they had approved the script.

"Ah, *Kaneshna*! (of course!)," said one of the other Russians.

"Even after he was released from prison, my father was not allowed to return to Moscow. That is how I happened to be born in this far corner of the world."

Boris leaned back and inhaled deeply, letting the smoke out through his nostrils. He seemed intent on the impact of his concluding statement:

"The fact is, it's very clear – my father was sent to prison for ten years because he was a great actor!"

John and I took a bus to the countryside to visit Allison on a bright Sunday morning. The village was a few miles south of Birobidjan, past Waldheim, on a narrow road that wound around the swamps and through potato fields, by the graveyard, and beyond the little settlement of *dacha*s owned and tended by people who lived in Birobidjan.

As we approached Waldheim, the bus stopped. An old man in the back row was clutching his chest and swaying from one side to the other, like a metronome, moaning and gasping for air. The other passengers whispered among themselves, debating whether he was suffering a heart attack or a vodka overdose.

The driver lit a cigarette, put the bus back into gear and turned off the main road. He drove the bus down a narrow dirt lane to a clinic at the edge of town. He jumped off the bus, trudged to the door, and banged on it until a man in a white coat opened an upstairs window. The driver and the man in the clinic yelled back and forth, then the driver returned to the bus. He ordered two of the male passengers to get out of their seats and help the old man off the bus. They half led and half dragged him to the door, the man in the clinic unlocked the door and opened it, and they all went inside. We sat and waited.

"He'll die there," one of the passengers said, and some of the other passengers nodded, then were silent. They were stoic, distant, uninvolved.

An hour went by. There were murmurs and whispers. No complaints. Some people slept in their seats. Others stood outside the bus and smoked.

The driver and the two men returned and climbed aboard the bus. Nothing was said about the sick man. The driver started the engine, backed the bus down the dirt lane, maneuvered it onto the road and drove on.

Continuing on the road southward, the bus passed woodlands and swamplands. The woods were pretty, even in early winter before the snow, with the stark grace of slender exposed limbs, the absolute desolation of dead, dry grasses, not brown, not gray, no color at all, just a neutral tone of frayed matter out of which rose the thin birch and oak trees. The swamps, drying under the autumn sun but with patches of ice, were speckled with black clumps that looked like some sort of bunchy plant growing in clusters around a ball of mud. These covered the lowlands like fuzzy marbles on a frayed rug.

The bus slowed for a herd of cows making their way across the road, driven by a farmer wearing quilted clothing of brown or black, dust-covered, and boots that looked held together by layers of dried mud.

Another thirty minutes south was Allison's village. The main part of the town was off to one side of the road: rows of wooden houses, a general store with a big covered porch, the school beyond. Allison lived on the second floor of a two-story apartment building.

Allison showed us through the school; it was clean and newly painted, and plants hung from the walls and lined the windowsills. In the central hallway was a small museum displaying photographs of the local leaders and war heroes who dedicated their lives to the socialist state or who served in the Great Patriotic War. This village, like every other we had seen, also had a war monument to the villagers who died in that war. The names carved in it must have represented almost every family in the village, nearly every man of fighting age. The war left millions of Russian widows, now frail and elderly.

In Allison's apartment was an old television set that didn't work and a new telephone that was one of very few in the village.

She told us that one day some little boys pushed open her door and threw a firecracker onto her floor. She identified them, and the local militia fined their parents.

Another morning, she said, a man stood knocking on her door for twenty minutes, demanding to be let in, yelling at her that she was beautiful and that he wanted to talk to her and give her potatoes and homemade strawberry preserves.

"Later I realized he was the husband of a teacher at my school," Allison said. "I hope she doesn't find out."

When the three of us left her apartment, we ran into a girl who was one of Allison's students. Allison scolded her for skipping class on Thursday.

We hiked a mile away from the village and sat in a meadow for our winter picnic, pulling off our mittens to slice bread and spread peanut butter and jam. A little further down the road, toward the western hills, was a pond where children ice skated and men cut holes in the ice and sat beside the holes to fish, talk a little and drink hot tea. The day was cold – maybe 20F, but the sun was bright.

On our return trip to Birobidjan, the old bus made another unexpected stop because the back door was rattling. The driver got off and banged on the door for awhile. Finally he decided it would stay shut and the bus made its way back to the station.

A teenage girl and her boyfriend heard us talking. When John dozed off, they decided to practice speaking English with me, and I reciprocated by practicing Russian with them; back and forth, in both languages: "Do you have a family?" "How old are you?" "Where do you work?"

We arrived at the bus station at 6:30 – time to go home and cook supper.

I liked working with my students, but they continued to whisper during class and debate the answers to tests. Was it cooperative learning or was it cheating?

After trying a variety of responses to these issues, I decided to try not taking either too seriously. When they talked to a disruptive degree, I would whistle for their attention or act interested in what they were whispering about. This amused them, but it didn't change the situation.

John and I gradually came to realize that these problems weren't just in our classes. They were school-wide, perhaps Russia-wide. College students spent about forty hours a week in class. Maybe this was partly because there was no library to speak of, and most of their information had to come from the teachers, not from reading. And they seemed to believe that if the teacher wasn't talking, they weren't learning.

After fifteen months of relatively good relations, we and Kommandant Valentina, the building superintendent, were waging war over a locked gate.

To go to class, we had to unlock the padlock on the barred metal gate separating the hallway to our apartments from the classrooms. We did this every morning, and then the gate stayed unlocked until late in the evening. Our students and other visitors were free to come down our hall and knock on our door any time.

But one morning, Valentina came out of her office near the gate and locked it. We had our own gate keys, so when I came back to our apartment during a break between classes, I unlocked it and went through to our apartment. Valentina emerged from her office and locked it again. When I headed back to class, I unlocked it.

John was doing the same thing. Each time, Valentina locked the gate after us.

That evening, John confronted her, and she told him that the militia ordered her to keep the gate locked. John didn't believe her. She stood firm, glaring up at him silently, her key in her hand. She waited for him to go through the gate and then she locked it behind him.

Valentina had just returned from an absence of several days. She said the stress over the attempted break-in of the Huelsbecks' apartment had caused her blood pressure to rise and strained her heart, and she had spent ten days in the hospital. It was when she came back from the hospital that our relationship with her soured.

Valentina was more grossly overweight than ever and she smoked three packs of cigarettes a day. She and her husband, Uri, often set up their barbecue beneath our window and sizzled skewers of pure pork fat until the outside was browned and the inside was blubbery. Then she would pop the morsels in her mouth and savor them, seven or eight blobs at a single meal, downed with two or three shots of vodka, followed by more cigarettes. We didn't think the stress of an attempted theft caused her illness. But she did.

Vera tried to stop by our apartment for coffee the next morning, but her way was barred by the locked gate. Later, in the teachers' office, John told her about the situation. Vera marched down the hall to Valentina's office and scolded her, Valentina yelled at Vera, Vera came back to the office and said, "The war has started." She told us she had returned her key to Valentina's office (where she had often gone to smoke a cigarette) and she said it was time for us to call Anatoli Surnin and complain to him.

I called his office. There was no answer. Valentina's door was wide open, an unusual situation. Valentina saw me. She had locked the gate again. I unlocked it and carried the padlock down the hall to our apartment.

I apologized to Vera for our having stirred things up, but Vera insisted that it was "a necessary move."

"Vera might even be enjoying the excitement of our contretemps," John said.

Later I returned the padlock to the gate, without locking it. An hour later, the gate was locked again.

In her village, Allison was having a problem with the man who had knocked on her door and yelled that she was beautiful. It turned out he was the village drunk as well as the husband of a teacher at Allison's school.

Allison telephoned to report that the man had returned and again yelled for her to open the door, telling her again how beautiful she was, yelling that she should not say anything to his wife, pleading with her to let him in.

This time Allison's neighbors shooed him away and warned her that he was a troublemaker. He had left a frozen fish outside her door, like a dog presenting a dead rat to its master for approval.

Vera said similar things had happened to her.

"I am neither as young nor as pretty as Allison, but when a man – a carpenter, a plumber, whoever he may be – when he finds out I have no husband, he immediately tries to seduce me."

Phil and Linda were having their problems as well. Their troubles were with the tall, lanky worker Valentina sent to replace the lock on their door after the intruder tried to open it. When the young man had finished his work, they invited him to stay for tea. Since then, he had returned to their door several times, knocking and knocking, wanting to come in – sometimes late in the evening, sometimes in the afternoon, once when they were getting ready for work in the morning.

They kept telling him, in their new and halting Russian, that they were busy, they had a lot of work to do, and would he please go away, but he wouldn't take the hint.

Harry Anderson, the Peace Corps volunteer whose scalp we couldn't help but scrutinize since delivering his hair restorer, came from Vladivostok to visit for a couple of days. He considered himself an expert in Russian ways, based on his self-proclaimed seduction and abandonment of several beautiful Russian language tutors.

"Russians don't take hints," Harry said bluntly. "You have to hit them over the head with a board to get their attention, and then use direct and forceful language, and then they might begin to be persuaded that you aren't interested in further communication."

Harry advised Allison to stand in the middle of the floor behind her locked door and start shouting, "Militia!" And Phil and Linda, he said, should stop being polite. As for us, Harry said, John and I should demand that Anatoli Surnin speak to Valentina.

Maybe Valentina wanted us to complain to Surnin, giving her an excuse to quit or be fired, we speculated.

We had other complaints. Valentina couldn't seem to get the *puele sost* (vacuum cleaner or, literally, dust sucker) repaired, although it had been broken for weeks. Also, since she had returned to the job, we could hear the roar of an ancient refrigerator in the first-floor apartment directly beneath our bedroom. The motor had been silent during her absence. One night, in order to sleep, I fantasized that the vibrating hum was a ship's motor and I was on a cruise in some southern sea.

One of the cooks told John that Valentina was using that refrigerator to stash meat and vegetables she scavenged from the kitchen. She could no longer use the good refrigerator next door since Phil and Linda had moved in.

With such perks as free meat and vegetables, we decided that Valentina was not likely to quit her job. We didn't want to complain to Surnin. We were tired of the little war of wills. After Valentina left in the evening, and after John was asleep, I crept down the hallway with my key and stole the lock.

Shopping for Thanksgiving, we learned that Russians use sage not as a seasoning, but as a medicine. We went to buy sage to make stovetop stuffing. I stopped by the table of a gray-haired woman who sold herbs and spices in the alleyway between the bread kiosk and the outdoor market. She wore thick felt boots and a grayish-brown fur coat that looked homemade from a variety of animals killed and skinned, dried and brushed, and crudely sewn together.

Since I had looked up the word for sage – *shalfeah* – I was doing the talking while John stood idly by. She gave him a worried look and asked in a hushed tone how he felt, but he was busy staring off into space and didn't notice that she was talking to him. She pointed me in the direction of the nearest pharmacy, and, in case they were out, she mentioned two other pharmacies in the area that also might have sage. But then she waved aside those instructions, shook her head and patted me on the arm.

"Tomorrow," she said. "Come back tomorrow."

Having committed ourselves to buying the sage from her, we didn't buy any at the *apteka* (pharmacy), but curiosity drove us to stop by and ask the pharmacy clerk what *shalfeah* was used for.

"Sore throat, bronchitis, coughing," she said.

I returned to the herb vendor the next morning and she handed me a package of sage.

"How much is it?" I asked.

"*Podarok*!" she exclaimed. "Gift! Your husband is sick. You need this. No cost!"

She refused to take any money for it. She assumed that if I needed sage, he must be sick. We were very touched by her concern and kindness.

When I strolled by a day later, she inquired about the health of my husband.

"Much better," I said. "Thank you *very* much."

"Go in good health," she replied, smiling.

Vera, Lena and Pavel were our closest friends. We were with Vera almost on a daily basis, and Lena and Pavel often had us for dinner at their apartment and we hosted them at ours; we went to parties together, picnics, concerts. Vera used to join us, too.

But when Lena had a dinner party to celebrate Pavel's 39th birthday, Vera wasn't invited. Looking back, we realized we hadn't all been together since summer. Lena had been gone, then we were gone, then Vera was busy with the Peace Corps training. But still, we recalled, she hadn't been along on the infamous picnic last spring either. How could we not have noticed before now that our friends had gone their separate ways?

The other people in their small circle were at Pavel's party – Tanya and Oleg, Sasha and Luba, John and I, as well as Pavel's elderly mother who had recently moved to Birobidjan from a village on Russia's far northeastern coast. But not Vera. And no one said anything about her; the silence seemed like a hole in the fabric of the party.

Other than that, we enjoyed the evening; we tried to keep up with the Russian conversation, and when we got too far behind, Lena would speak in English to get us back into the loop.

The way word traveled in Birobidjan, Vera must have heard about the party and didn't know what might have been said about her. Nothing was. But the next time we saw Vera, she volunteered the information that Lena had asked Vera for her old job back, in our department.

Lena was still at the college, teaching English to students in other disciplines, but she wanted to return to the English Language Department. She had left the department because of the feud with Larisa, the unpopular department head Vera had replaced. But after Vera rehired Vasili Ivchenko, Lena expected to be rehired as well.

John, Vera and I were in our apartment, talking, at the end of the day after classes. "I turned her down," Vera said, her foot tapping.

"Why?" I said, stunned.

"Her knowledge isn't very good," Vera said. "She couldn't teach the courses we require – phonetics, grammatics, stylistics."

This was incredible news. Lena's command of English was excellent, as good as Vera's, and her scholarly ability had never been questioned before, to our knowledge.

But instead of letting Lena return, Vera hired, along with Vasili, three new graduates: Katya Valentinovna, and two Natashas; all fifth-year students of John's the year before.

"They're young and eager to please," Vera said.

At least we realized then why Vera was not invited to Pavel's birthday party, although Lena and Pavel hadn't said a word about it. Maybe they said nothing because Lena felt humiliated and embarrassed. Or maybe she didn't want to put us in the middle between herself and Vera.

But the fact was, Lena had been gravely insulted. Could it be that she really wasn't qualified to teach in our department, by some high standard Vera wanted to set? Or was it that Vera found it easier to dominate and control the new graduates?

To make matters worse, from our view, the subjects our department required – stylistics, phonetics and grammar (or as they call it, "grammatics"), the way we had observed them being taught – were ineffective, even at times inaccurate. They didn't help the students communicate in English or understand the language. As linguistics subject material, we thought they were arcane and irrelevant. Unless Lena was really inferior as a teacher, which we didn't believe, we could only speculate that friendship was not as important to Vera as power. At least this friendship wasn't.

Then, we wondered (John and I spent hours mulling over these issues, which it occurred to us was a very Russian thing to do), why did Vera always claim that she hated being the head of the department? Obviously, power was important enough to her to sacrifice her friendship with Lena and Pavel. Or maybe she just didn't like them as much as we thought.

Or, could it be, we wondered another time, that she didn't like Lena feeling sorry for her because Vera wasn't married? Lena had once said to us how sad it was for Vera to go through life without a husband, without children.

"How incomplete her life is," Lena said, tousling little Vanya's golden curls and giving him a hug. Maybe Vera had heard words to this effect, too, and this was her way of getting even for that sense of pity.

The temperature on a mid-November dawn was at zero F. When it climbed to 15F, around noon, John and I put on layers of clothing and took a long walk by the Bira River. The wide, shallow river was still flowing in the middle, and we could hear debris bumping along under the ice in places.

The delight of the day was finding a vendor who still had a few fresh green peppers. (She must have had a China connection.) We made pizza smothered with green peppers, and the next night stir-fried chicken with green peppers.

A thin layer of snow covered the ground. Cars slid around the streets, sometimes unable, even if the driver was willing, to avoid sliding toward people walking. Many of the vendors' stalls at the open-air market were empty. But other salespeople still sat there, in their mittens, huddled behind their metal counters. The saddest ones were old women in with only three jars of jam or one small tub of homemade pickles, a few bunches of wild herbs tied with a thread, or a few packets of pumpkin seeds.

The cold deepened. I stuffed more cotton batting in the cracks between the windows and the window frames to keep out the drafts. I longed for deep snow to cover the lumpy, hard, frozen, gray earth.

Just as the temperature plummeted, the city fathers decided to lower the heating several notches, to conserve coal for the long winter. We were grateful again for the heavy homemade quilt we had bought in Vladivostok our first winter.

Vera's seventeen-year-old nephew Misha telephoned from Ussuriisk one evening. We had met him during our training and we liked him. We were surprised to hear from him, but we knew Vera didn't have a phone. At first, it seemed that he had just called to chat, but when John asked him how Vera's family was, he mentioned that her Granny was not well. It was nothing to worry about, he stressed, though Granny was ninety-four. Misha said to tell Vera he would call her at our building the next afternoon at three.

The next day Vera had a full schedule – four lectures on stylistics. But she didn't show up for work. I asked people where she was. No one knew, but by the end of the second period they all assumed she wouldn't be coming in at all.

"High blood pressure," Veronika, the secretary, said. "She sometimes has this problem."

We decided to go to her apartment and tell her Misha said he would call her at three. The day was cold and overcast, looking as though there would be more snow to cover the frozen, dry and dusty earth.

At first Vera didn't answer the door and John started writing a note. But when I knocked again and called her name, from behind the door, she replied weakly, "Yes?"

"Hello, Vera. It's Sharon. Your nephew called."

She opened the door and insisted that we come inside immediately, because she could not stand there in the chill of the dark hallway, and because in Russia it is considered bad luck to talk in a doorway. Vera looked waiflike, her frail figure covered by a cotton gown and cotton robe, huge furry slippers on her feet, her short straight hair askew from lying on the pillow, her eyes sleepy behind her glasses. She was pale, and she seemed worn and tired.

First we mentioned Misha's plan to call at three, but Vera felt too sick to get dressed and go to the college to await the call. She said she could try to reach him from a neighbor's phone upstairs.

"He mentioned your Granny," I said. "It's nothing to worry about, he said, but she's not too well."

Vera gasped. "It's a sign! I felt it!" she cried, putting her hand on her heart. "This is why I felt so tired and ill, beginning yesterday. It's Granny! I must go to Ussuriisk!"

John said, firmly, "Misha said she is not really ill, it is not serious. But we wanted you to know he said he would call. Would you like us to take the call for you? Then we can come out and tell you. Or you can call us, maybe at four."

"Yes, yes, thank you. Or maybe I'll call him, from upstairs. Yes, I may call him."

She thanked us profusely for coming, and apologized profusely, as she always did whenever she thought she had caused us the slightest inconvenience. We insisted it was no trouble, we were always glad to do anything for her.

We went home to await Misha's call, debating whether we had been wise to disturb Vera at home when she was ill.

Three o'clock came. No call. Three-thirty. Vera knocked on the door, wearing her plaid woolen cap and matching scarf, her brown winter coat, jeans and boots.

"I have bought my train ticket," she announced. "I am going to Ussuriisk on the five-o'clock train. I will return to Birobidjan on Friday."

"Have you called Misha?"

"No. I will go no matter what Misha says."

"Are you well enough to travel?"

"It is not a problem. I can sleep on the train. I must go."

At four o'clock Misha called.

When John told him Vera was on her way to Ussuriisk, he cried, "Oh, no!" He didn't want to be held responsible.

At first, I felt that we had unnecessarily created a huge problem for Vera, but John and I talked it over and decided that Vera wanted, even needed, to go. Misha's call, our visit, her own illness – she felt all these events were signs that her Granny would want her there. And it was a good time for her to go. Things weren't going well at school, there was confusion, there was the feud with Valentina over every little thing, Vera knew we were sad about Lena, the worst students were continually disappointing her, she didn't want to complain to us about them because she knew we thought they should be flunked out and she couldn't do that, and on and on. Maybe she wasn't so much physically ill as emotionally and mentally exhausted, and in need of a break.

She had wanted to go to Ussuriisk at the end of training, but her mother told her to wait until January, when she planned to go to Vladivostok for Peace Corps work anyway and her train fare would be paid. She obeyed, but instead she had gone with us to Blagoveshensk, spending at least the same amount of money but not having to contend with her mother's will.

Now Misha's call provided the impetus she needed to make the trip. She didn't return his call because she didn't want to risk being talked out of going.

We felt the weight of responsibility for alarming her unduly, but we were fairly sure it was good that we delivered the message.

Eighteen people congregated for Thanksgiving dinner. With so many, we all decided that, rather than trying to cook, we should go to the new Jewish restaurant for dinner, fourteen Peace Corps volunteers and four Russian friends. Ludmila Vinnikova and I went over there in the morning to make reservations and discuss the menu. Our Thanksgiving dinner consisted of stuffed squid, stuffed chicken skin, ground pike fish balls, cabbage salad, beef with red sauce and mashed potatoes. At the end of the dinner, Ludmila called the cook out from the kitchen, a fat, red-faced woman, and we gave her a round of applause.

Everyone came back to our apartment for dessert: homemade apple and pumpkin pies and pumpkin bread made from a big pumpkin out of the Vinnikovs' *dacha*. It was 1:30 a.m. before all the visiting volunteers went to sleep – some in sleeping bags on our living-room floor, some in an empty room next door, some with their host families. We were up again at 7 a.m. to see people off on the train.

Vera returned on Saturday. She seemed well, energized, and happy to have seen her dear Granny. The elderly woman was frail, Vera said, and she had a terrible cold, but "she's not dying this winter, I'm sure of it."

24

Faulkner vs. Chekhov

Time flowed on, swirling around interruptions and small emergencies, borne along through intrigues, gossip and minor outrages, so that nothing seemed to get accomplished – until some mighty rush swept the day's events to a chaotic conclusion, some occasionally even to completion. My sense of concentration was diminished, because the main force of life itself seemed to be the absolute certainty of frequent disruption: a knock on the door, a question, an urgent message, a little favor, an official demanding to inspect our visas once again.

The holiday season was approaching. The Huelsbecks next door received a gift from his sister-in-law and shared it with us. She had sent a dozen homemade cloth baggies containing herbs and spices, all from her own huge garden on Puget Sound.

One of the baggies was labeled "Mexican spices," so John concocted a California-style supper for the four of us, using mock-tortillas that I made with Russian ingredients. The result resembled burritos, which were spicy and delicious with fresh grated cheese.

Our Peace Corps-funded library expansion was succeeding in some ways. Teachers were using the new television set and VCR for various classes, hundreds of books had arrived in the mail and were being catalogued by John and Phil, the telephone was installed, and the college had e-mail access in the library room downstairs, the place that once had only eighty-five English-language books. Phil and Linda had written home for more books, and their Wisconsin town was responding generously.

But Anatoli Surnin had not yet designated a space for all these resources, so we were storing, in our apartment, the new TV and VCR, most of the books and all the videos we brought back from the states. It seemed like a joke – having won a Peace Corps grant for college resources, we found ourselves with more comforts of home than we had any right to possess.

Whenever the TV and VCR were needed for a class, two boys came in and carried them off to a classroom, then they would bring them back after class. Tall stacks of books leaned against our walls, awaiting the promised building of bookshelves.

Surnin made a new promise: Next month he would give us a room – in the building that was under construction next door.

"Yes, I promise you, absolutely, the new building will be ready in January!" he yelled, waving his arm at the pile of materials slowly, very slowly, being constructed into a three-story building just beyond our window.

John laughed out loud. He said, "Anatoli, that is the best Russian joke I have ever heard!"

A student, as a prank, removed the week's class schedule from the wall. There was mass confusion. Imagine a semester in which the schedule changes weekly, sometimes daily: When it disappears altogether, there's really a mess.

The Americans were nervous; the Peace Corps was paying us our entire December and January stipend early, to minimize problems expected on January 1, when the ruble was to be devalued.

The Peace Corps system was to deposit the money into volunteers' bank accounts in the local currency. When we heard about the upcoming devaluation, we tried to change half our rubles for dollars, but the bank was out of dollars, because so many Russians had done the same thing.

Pavel and Lena responded to the possibility of spiraling inflation by going on a spending spree. Lena bought a stunning long and full silvery-gray otter coat. There was enough extra fur, she said, to cut off the bottom and make herself a matching bonnet and scarf.

"Buy now, while prices are as they are!" Lena laughed, exhilarated by her own extravagance.

It's awkward when friends have a falling out with each other, especially in a circle as small as ours. We invited Pavel and Lena over Saturday night, with their two boys, along with Phil and Linda, thinking they'd enjoy knowing each other. When I called Lena, she asked who else we had invited.

"Linda and Phil," I said. "We want you to meet them."

"Not Vera?" she asked.

"Shall I?" I said, wondering what she would reply.

"Well, sometimes she is rather boring," Lena said. Nothing further.

On Saturday afternoon Vera (who had never wanted to watch movies and would much rather read or talk) came by and said she'd like to drop in that evening and watch one of the videos we had acquired: "Tom Jones." I awkwardly mentioned that Pavel and Lena were coming to dinner, and quickly asked if she'd be willing to come Sunday instead. So we talked a little more about their falling out.

This time Vera said Lena was jealous that Pavel and Vera spent so much time out on the balcony smoking the last time we had all been at their apartment for dinner. Vera said Pavel confided many things to her – problems he's having, frustrations, some difficulties in his marriage, his elderly mother coming to live with them.

We recalled another incident of that fateful evening that at the time didn't seem too important. At one point, after they'd been out on the balcony for a long time, Pavel had commented to us all how tiny Vera was, how thin she was, and he hoisted her over his shoulder and twirled her around the room to prove that she was as light as a feather.

Lena, who is not rail-thin like Vera, could not have enjoyed that moment.

Pavel, on the other hand, might not have minded making his wife a little jealous. Lena was a beautiful woman, voluptuous, with huge blue eyes and blonde curly hair, in marked contrast to Vera's boyish shape and her straight hair chopped off in a Dutch-boy cut, and – thanks to Vera's addiction to sugar – teeth that had given way to gold-colored crowns.

"But," I said to Vera, "I thought the problem was that you didn't hire Lena back into the department."

"Oh yes," Vera said. "That, too." She thought for a minute and added, "I have two lives, business and social, and business is the most important, and the department is my business. I can't let the other interfere. It would be unprofessional."

A light powdering of snow dusted the ground and was trampled into spots of ice on the walkway. Dry little snowflakes swirled along the ground when the wind blew.

During dinner Saturday night, we saw a shooting star, notable because of its size and brilliance. The eight of us were sitting at the dinner table in our kitchen; I happened to look out the window in time to see the light arc across the western sky. I glanced at John, and he had seen it too. Stunning. We looked at each other and marveled. Strange, that only we noticed it. The general conversation continued.

Sunday we had dinner with Vera. We watched the "Tom Jones" video for half an hour, and she excused herself, said she'd watch the rest later, retired to the corridor and smoked a cigarette, then went home.

The post office left a notice in our box that there were more packages for us. We collected six more boxes of books. Delivery had taken almost five months.

Snow fell all day, miniscule flakes, barely visible, but they added up. It seemed the entryway to every public building – such as the post office, which we exited with great caution carrying our books – was made of some smooth material such as marble. The snow from our boots fastened to this slick surface and it became even an even slicker glaze of ice. John and I crept across it in fear, grabbing each other's sleeves at every slippery step.

In the evening, safely back indoors, we gazed out at a black-and-white night that glistened with a stark and sparkling beauty.

The next morning, just before sunrise (around 8:30), the new-fallen snow reflected the brilliant blue of the pre-dawn sky; it took my breath away, it was such a deep, soft blue. How could a color be all at once deep and soft and brilliant? Could an artist's eye imagine such a blue?

A few days later thirteen more boxes arrived from Wisconsin and California. And we received two more boxes from the Darien Book Aid Plan. What riches!

There was one more box to go from our own mailing, and we got several boxes from a church in Missouri, and two more from Phil's and Linda's Wisconsin town. Books were spread all over our living room floor – fiction here, biographies there, textbooks and poetry beyond – and John sat at the computer logging them in, more than eight hundred so far. And the Huelsbecks' book campaign would eventually reap two thousand more, so that within two years the Birobidjan Teachers College would have the largest collection of English-language books for hundreds of miles around.

Maybe the relative slowness of time's passing was an advantage – life-lengthening: with the continual round of menial chores, incomplete comprehension of the language, hours of unscheduled time. There were ways I would later miss exactly this: the sense of stretched and endless time, the family of round little birds outside the window and time to notice them, our sensible suggestions met with great enthusiasm and then quietly ignored, the Russian language always to be studied and never to be mastered, the necessity of walking, walking, walking, everywhere we had to go.

Ever since we arrived in Birobidjan, John had started his day with a cup of coffee in bed. I didn't mind; he did more than his share of the cooking. But if he happened to wake up before I expected him to, he shuffled to the kitchen and looked sadly at the stove. That meant, "Where's my coffee?" He looked endearingly like a little boy disguised as a large man.

One of the realities of our Peace Corps life was that we lived in each other's pockets day and night. It was a cozy arrangement, loving and companionable, frustrating, joyful, annoying, sometimes overwhelming.

The students had enjoyed their prank involving the schedule. But the mix-up resulted in several Saturday classes to make up for the lost time, so we knew they would think twice before making such a mess of things again.

We tried to go to Ussuriisk to visit some other volunteers. First, we tried to buy tickets at noon for the six o'clock night train. No luck. In Birobidjan people could buy tickets only six hours ahead of the train. No sooner than that, because the train might be full.

Unfortunately, a new computer system had been installed on the trans-Siberian railway line, or so the story went.

"Come back at three," said the indifferent woman at the train station, just before slamming the dirty plastic window shut.

It seemed the new computer connection had not yet communicated to Birobidjan whether there would be seats available. On a Thursday evening in mid-December, it seemed unlikely that the train would be full, but no tickets could be purchased until the computer cleared it.

We returned at three and stood in line again. When we finally reached the window, it was the same story:

"No tickets. Maybe at five o'clock. Maybe later."

Would we be able to buy tickets before the train appeared? It only stayed in the station five minutes, and no one was allowed to board without a ticket.

"Maybe. Maybe not."

Irina Alexandrovna, who planned to board the same train to go to Vladivostok, hurried back to the college to try and find Vasili Ivchenko because of his connections in the city administration. Irina said his "friends in high places" might be able to help. We returned to our apartment to wait.

A few minutes later, Vera rushed in and cried, "Give me your passports! Give me your money! I will try to buy tickets for you! I know the ropes! I know the woman who can help!"

She took our passports and money and off she raced.

Phil dropped by. He wondered whether John would be giving the keynote address on Saturday at the college's "Second Annual Literary Conference." He had seen John's name on the schedule.

Saturday?

But, if we could get our train tickets, we'd be in Ussuriisk on Saturday, we reminded Phil; he was planning to let us leave our computer in his apartment. Had he forgotten?

"Oh, right," he said, sinking into a chair. "I didn't put two and two together! I didn't think of both things at the same time!"

Nobody had put two and two together. Vera, knowing we planned to be gone, had said nothing about the conference. No one had mentioned it to us.

John shrugged. "If we get the tickets, we'll go to Ussuriisk. If not, we'll attend the conference."

Vera returned at five. No tickets. Now the story was that thirty people were returning to Vladivostok from a conference and so the train was full. This made no sense, as thirty people would almost fill one car, but not an entire train. Whatever the story, we did not have tickets.

Irina, determined to get to Vladivostok, stayed at the train station with Vasili, hoping somehow or other to board the train. She succeeded, by sheer Russian persistence. We, on the other hand, unpacked the computer and set it up again, put the hardboiled eggs in the refrigerator, took the sandwiches out of John's backpack, unpacked our toothbrushes and pajamas, and turned on a Mozart tape.

John gave a wry chuckle.

"What?" I said. "Share it. I can use a laugh."

"I was thinking about the Peace Corps' carefully thought out Emergency Evacuation Plan," he said. I began to smile, too.

The plan begins with this advice: "Make your way to Khabarovsk . . . ."

In the first place, there was no bridge for cars across the river to Khabarovsk. The fair-weather ferry couldn't run because the ice was too thick, but cars were not allowed to drive across yet because the ice was too thin. And it was hardly possible to buy a train ticket on an ordinary day. Imagining the chaos of an actual emergency, we had to laugh! Otherwise, we'd be scared to death.

Winter Solstice. We went to the "Second Annual Literary Conference"; John and Phil delivered papers that were published in little blue books, in English and translated into Russian by Vera.

Pavel read a paper that had to do with modern Russian epitaphs and their origins in ancient Greek poetry. Vera made some comments, encouraging Pavel to expound, which he did in the most longwinded, rapid-fire Russian I've ever heard; it was very impressive. But the delivery was so dense and academic, I didn't understand a word. Vera said later that Pavel was brilliant and extremely knowledgeable in his field. When I told her I hadn't understood any of it, she said, "Pavel's concepts are not always clear to me either."

After John read his paper – a comparison of William Faulkner's American peasants, who were resentful, with Anton Chekhov's Russian peasants, who were resigned – the Russians, mainly Pavel, spent an hour challenging his premise with specific examples to the contrary. And they grilled John on what he meant by using the words "resigned" and "fatalistic." Vera sat beside John and translated the dialogue. John fielded the comments intelligently and gracefully, and the discussion ended in a friendly enough fashion. But he felt unfairly criticized.

Later Pavel said he thought John had made some good observations.

"But Russians are not resigned," Pavel said. "We are enduring. That is the difference."

One professor asked whether John's use of the word "resigned" was "positive or negative." Other comments were made as to how fatalism or resignation were merely human responses to hopeless situations. At the end of the day, we three Americans felt exhausted and strained, especially since every topic after John's and Phil's papers was discussed only in Russian. We understood a little, but not much, and the effort to keep up was tiring. Our chairs were hard. The sun through the window was dazzling, reflected off the new snow, and the room was drafty and cold.

A young student named Alexi had read a condensed version of his paper and received not a single comment from the others at the seminar. "Was that a slight? Was he offended?" I whispered to Vera.

"No, not at all," Vera said. "Alexi is a true student of Russian literature, and Pavel is his mentor."

"Then why didn't anyone comment?" I persisted.

"Well," she replied without hesitating, "because no one knew enough about his research to have anything to say."

Another graduate student, Pasha, also read.

Vera whispered summarily. "He is not a good student."

But we liked Pasha. Whenever he saw us, he would rush over to us, shake John's hand vigorously, and with a wide grin on his handsome young face he would try to speak English with us. Pasha was a believer in some new-age religion and, under the influence of the guru whose pamphlets he read religiously, he swam in the river twice a day – even when the temperature dropped to -20 F. and he had to chop a hole in the ice and swim in a small circle

"Pasha is Russian, but he doesn't look Russian," Vera said disapprovingly. "He smiles too much."

After he presented his paper, she dismissed him, saying, "Pasha is not a scholar, nor an intellectual."

Toward the end of the lengthy discussion on John's paper, Lena tried to make a comment and Vera interrupted her, then Pasha spoke, then Pavel. As soon as he could, John cut into the discussion, recognized Lena and asked her to make her comment.

Poor Lena! Either she changed her mind, or she had been about to say the same thing someone else said when she was silenced.

"Alexi made my point," she said weakly. "It was about the Russian peasants who joined the 1917 revolution. I have nothing to add."

It was a strain, being in the middle between Vera and Lena. We loved them both, but we had to choose one or the other each time we socialized. The seminar was awkward: Lena not getting recognized, Vera dominating, Pavel, oblivious to Lena's discomfort, basking in the glow of being the starring intellectual presence among the assembled scholars.

John and I and a few other Peace Corps volunteers spent Christmas in Khabarovsk at Amy Dickerson's. We felt closely connected because of our shared experiences in Russia, although we were years apart in age.

Amy said the Russian Far East is considered a "hardship post" for Peace Corps. She read the list of reasons: geographic isolation, lack of recreational and cultural activities, availability of food and goods, crime, lack of medical services, the weather, language difficulties, and unreliable water, heat and other basic utilities.

It was also a problem that many layers of Russian bureaucrats didn't really want Peace Corps here, she said; we'd been pushed on them in a sort of propaganda victory, we "missionaries for capitalism," a label that didn't set well with us liberal altruists. The ongoing problems with Peace Corps volunteers' visas seemed to confirm that possibility. The group after ours needed to have their visas renewed not once a year but every three months.

Another volunteer, Mike Hinken, agreed. Here in the Russian Far East, he wrote in a letter to us, "volunteers don't seem so much wanted as tolerated. Maybe that's what makes this post unique – we're not wanted here. You never see that in Peace Corps literature though."

The Russian Far East, with its incredible wealth of natural resources, was paralyzed by poverty. In Mike's opinion, "The nation suffers the same plight as the common man here – aimlessness, squandering of funds, corruption."

On Christmas Eve, Amy, John and I went to a back room in an old Khabarovsk building to attend a Lutheran service conducted by a German missionary named Marcus. He spoke in German and was translated into Russian by an attractive blonde woman who worked in a mime-and-drama theater. Her dark-haired daughter and two other little girls played Christmas carols on wooden flutes, hitting a few sour notes, but they were charming. Another young woman played the piano, which was badly out of tune. She sat on a sagging straight-backed chair, several inches too low for comfort, wrists bent upward, and hanging her fingers over the keyboard as she gazed nearsightedly up at the sheet music. Four women sang.

Then we walked to another building, piled our coats and hats in a large room, and went upstairs to a conference hall for a Christmas Eve potluck.

People brought oranges, wine, champagne, chocolate candy, cookies, and snacks such as smoked herring, pickles and brown bread.

Dedi Moroz came in, white cotton beard glued over red hair and freckles, and children lined up to perform and get rewarded with a small gift from his bag. One by one, they climbed on a chair and recited long poems to the amusement and pride of the large audience. Some of them had stage fright and momentarily forgot their words, but they forced themselves to a conclusion, jumped down, grabbed a toy or a candy bar from *Dedi Moroz* and fled to the safety of their mothers.

Amy, Ingrid (a graduate student from Columbia, doing research on women's roles in post-Soviet society), John and I sang "We Wish You a Merry Christmas," and Santa gave us four ballpoint pens.

On Christmas Day, we and Amy, Alice Hengesbach, and Steve Schue, another Khabarovsk volunteer, stayed at Amy's all afternoon and evening, talking, feasting reminiscing. We enjoyed each other's stories, and confessed that each of us had, at least once, thought about leaving early.

Alice said she'd had a long letter from Ryan, a young man who quit Peace Corps one day after our training ended.

"It's not like writing to someone who's never been here, who knows they don't know what I'm going through, but it's not like writing to one of you who is going through similar things," she said. "Ryan doesn't know what we're going through, but he thinks he does."

The week between Christmas and New Year's, Vera dropped by several times and our friendship with her seemed strong again. My students Sasha Lushchinsky and Tanya Sherman came with a box of candy as a New Year present and stayed to talk for three hours. Tanya brought an article from a Texas newspaper about Jewish life in Birobidjan; her family had been interviewed by a reporter on one of his stops along the trans-Siberian route from Moscow to Vladivostok. Our dean Tatyana Makedon stopped by with a box of candy and a little tiger toy in a bag, also New Year presents. Tatyana didn't look well. She had grown very thin and had dark purple circles under her eyes.

As the year drew to a close, we went with Pavel and Lena to a faculty holiday dinner in the cafeteria, and the next morning there was a children's New Year's party with *Dedi Moroz* and little presents for everyone. On New Year's Eve, we would host dinner for Phil and Linda and Vera, and then walk over to the ice sculpture in city center. The Russian custom is to stay up until midnight Moscow time, which is 7 in the morning in Birobidjan. We would break with custom and be in bed by 2 a.m.

Lena was so glad we called to wish her Happy New Year that she nearly cried. She still resented Vera's decision not to hire her and we thought she would probably never forgive her; maybe Vera didn't care whether she did.

Pavel said he had made three New Year's resolutions: "Not to drink much. Not to punish sons without serious reasons. Not to love sofa more than wife."

25

'Oy, Moroz! Moroz!'

The ice sculpture in the town square was simpler than the year before, maybe because the ice came later in the season, or maybe because the budget was smaller. Or because Oleg, the Russian teacher of Chinese, was not on hand this winter to oversee the sculpting. Rather than tall ice statues and ice towering buildings, there were squatty but whimsical animal ice sculptures and a large ice rink with strings of colored lights buried in the ice.

People scooted around on the rink night after night, dancing to rock music coming from a loudspeaker. On New Year's Eve, we heard "Back in the U.S.S.R.!" playing over the tinny speaker. People lit sparklers, danced, and chatted while their children slipped and slid and played around on the ice statues that encircled the rink. In the back of the square, the wooden slides were thick with ice. Children slid down them as fast as they could go, crashing into each other, laughing, and racing back up to do it again. We stayed as long as we could bear, until the cold came through our heavy boots, our thick socks, and felt as though it turned our very blood to ice.

Wendy Guyot was one of the new volunteers having visa problems. She came to Birobidjan with her Russian counterpart, Sveta, to get an official stamp so she could be registered in her village. Wendy saw us in the *rinok* and breathlessly told us they'd just missed the 11 a.m. train back to their village.

They were annoyed because the train they thought they were supposed to take was at 7 p.m. But at the last minute they discovered the tickets they had were for the early train, and they had just missed it.

Then they stayed at the station to try and get tickets for the later train. After waiting an hour, they got to the head of the line, only to be told by an indifferent clerk that they needed to buy their tickets at the next window because Wendy was a foreigner. They stood in that line for another hour, and when they got to the window the woman there said she couldn't sell them tickets because she didn't know how to work the new computer.

Finally a man behind them in line told them to ask for second-class tickets instead of first-class, and they did. The clerk shrugged and sold them second-class tickets, which didn't have to be issued by computer.

"Why didn't she tell us that hours ago?" Wendy wailed. The man shrugged and said, "It's Russia."

Wendy told us about problems she was having with her school's "male chauvinist director who hates Americans." She said he praised her to Peace Corps officials, but he personally harassed her at every turn. He had even refused to drive her to the train station in the next village (at –10F) until she begged him.

"He doesn't hate you because you're American," Sveta said. "He treats all the young teachers the same way."

Shopping was a daily highlight. We dressed warmly and hiked to the market for food, bread and other supplies. The *rinok* was open though everything was frozen, including the vendors. Bottles of oil were frozen, vinegar, fruit juice, cans of tomato sauce, jars of jam.

Farmers displayed on the tin counters only one or two samples of what they had to sell – a potato, an onion, a carrot or two. The rest of the vegetables were sheltered in cardboard boxes, inside burlap bags, beneath the counter; eggs too, in hopes they wouldn't freeze before they sold.

On our daily walks, I wore long johns and jeans, two pairs of socks and thick-soled, fur-lined suede boots. I also wore a rabbit-fur cap and a heavy jacket with hood, a woolen scarf and fur-lined mittens. On the coldest days, when I wore a ski mask to keep my nose warm, people grinned and pointed at me.

John, who has lived most of his life in Santa Barbara, disliked wearing mittens. Usually he went without and kept his hands in his pockets. He wore a hooded down jacket from China, a fleece cap, and heavy boots that slipped too readily on the icy sidewalks. He counted his falls: six times the first winter, but only twice the second.

Lena's elderly father, Vadim, came from the Caucasus for a midwinter visit. He was tall, large, with white hair, a once-handsome red face, and watery blue eyes. He wore four rows of military ribbons on his jacket, honors that he earned in the Great Patriotic War.

In the evenings, Vadim and Pavel played chess.

"When my father seems to be winning, Pasha starts to breathe like this," Lena said, wrinkling her nose and audibly sniffing air in and out. "My father wants to keep peace in the family. When Pasha breathes like this, my father lets him win. That is the only way he could ever beat my father." She sounded pleased.

We were in Lena's kitchen the day after the faculty party, talking, while she flattened dough for *pelmeni*, a Russian pasta stuffed with cabbage, one of Pavel's favorites.

Lena said that at the party, she found Pavel and Vera in a dark hallway, talking animatedly about literature and smoking incessantly.

Lena continued: "I was frankly annoyed. I said to Vera, 'Why don't you let me catch you kissing him?' and Vera said, 'Because I don't.'"

Although Vera's reply was ambiguous, Lena gave this account with the same air of satisfaction that she told about her father letting

Pavel win. In both cases, there seemed to be some score that was settled.

Russian wives sternly warned their husbands not to drink too much vodka. The men would go to the endless round of holiday parties, glum-faced, eat too much and talk too little, until the edict was relaxed; then they would grab the nearest vodka bottle, toast each other, and dance with single women and other men's wives. Their own wives sat sullen and impatient to go home, or they too reached for the vodka to melt the acid knot of resentment with the heat of eighty-proof liquor, to toast each other with red faces, and sing common Russian songs that throbbed with the force of their frustration.

"All night long she yelled at me," Pavel said after the party. Both he and Lena had dark rings around their eyes, their children too, and her elderly father who said nothing but looked relieved to have us drop by.

"Have some tea," Lena said to me. "I'll tell you all about it."

"She doesn't understand," Pavel said to John.

"I've been crying all day," Lena said. "Would you like sugar in your tea, or jam?"

"Have some caviar," Pavel said. "It's really good. My mother brought it with her from the sea."

"His mother always takes his side. I can't stand it," Lena said. "I'm very tired. I'm so glad to see you."

We walked alongside the river in the late afternoon – John with his camera, Lena, her father, little Vanya, and I – to the rectangular hole in the ice where people slipped into the frigid water and paddled around. Young Pasha wasn't the only one who went for a swim on a daily basis. These hardy souls swam every day, summer or winter, rain or snow, mud or ice. In winter, snow was banked on the windward side of the hole and a metal ladder was frozen in place by the ice at the edge, providing steps into the water.

Three women and a little girl walked ahead of us along the path and stopped when they arrived at the swimming hole. We greeted them and stayed while the women took off their coats and boots, sweaters and woolen leggings, until they were wearing only bikinis. Two of the women were stout and muscular, one was almost thin. They stood on pieces of cardboard in their bare feet, and, one by one, they stepped down into the extremely cold water. Each woman then pushed away from the edge of the ice. In the water, she hesitated, absorbing the shock of the cold, then she ducked her head under the water, then out again, pushed her hair back, swam back to the ladder and climbed out, each staying in for no more than half a minute, followed by the next woman, then the third.

They took their time getting dressed, assuring John they didn't mind his taking pictures, and invited us to join them there again at midnight on Russian Christmas (January 7). We thanked them for the invitation, knowing we wouldn't be there. When they finished pulling on their leggings, boots, sweaters, coats, hats and mittens, they headed back to their apartments, followed by the little girl who was apparently just along for the walk.

Early in the New Year, the temperature took another dive. The slightest breeze brought tears to people's eyes, the tears froze in trails on their cheeks; men's moustaches and even the hair in their nostrils were coated with ice.

The post office, reopened after a two-week hiatus. We collected a few letters, shopped at the *rinok*. The hard-packed snow squeaked under the sharp metal heels of women's boots. The sharpest heels gouged chips in the icy surface. Vendors' faces were chapped red from the cold.

It was the dead of winter, between semesters, and John was bored. When I sat down at the computer, he would become playful, want to communicate, interfere, say witty things. He needed attention; I needed space. Sometimes we abandoned each other on our two-person ice floe, and yet we didn't want to damage the most intimate human connection each of us had.

It was too cold to go out much. When we came home after shopping, we took off our heavy coats; sweaters and slacks were plastered to our bodies by static electricity; hair flew from our heads and clung for its life to any comb that tried to tame it.

But it was warm inside, sometimes even too warm, as though now the city fathers couldn't bear the thought of people going cold, so they cranked up the city's central heating to its maximum. One night, at 20 below zero, we tossed off our quilt, exposing our toes to the air, and drank water because the bedroom was as hot and dry as a desert.

Ludmila Sergeievna and her daughter Lena invited us to lunch. The Tsimbalyuks lived out of town, near the military installation, and seldom socialized, but now Ludmila and Lena were staying at a friend's apartment in town for several weeks. Ludmila, so distant and cold when we first arrived, had warmed considerably. Her husband, Sasha, an army doctor, was away, on duty somewhere in western Russia.

The day of the luncheon was marked on the orthodox Russian calendar as Christmas Day. Ludmila and Lena served us Russian salad (tiny cubes of beets, chopped hardboiled eggs, peas, mayonnaise), an egg-and-fish salad, stuffed cabbage leaves (rice, chopped meat), berry pie, Moldovan wine, strong tea (poured from a small pot, water added), compote. We had a pleasant conversation about travel, cultures, languages.

Lena, bright and opinionated, said, "I never want to live outside Russia. To travel, yes. But a Russian can never be happy outside Russia."

Ludmila echoed her sentiment. "A Russian can be better off in another country, have a more comfortable life, but he will never be happy."

They told us about friends of theirs who lived in Brooklyn. The man taught Yiddish; his 70-year-old mother was studying English, but his elderly father refused.

"The father goes fishing every day. He is very good at fishing, the best," Ludmila said. "He sees no reason to study English; everyone in Brooklyn speaks Russian."

Ludmila told us she dreamed of the day when Sasha would retire from the army and they could move to the warm and sunny coastline on the Black Sea, their real home, where they came from, where they still spent their summers.

Lena, now twenty, had lived in Birobidjan since she was four years old. But she never considered it her home. She loved Moscow. "Moscow is dirty and crowded. But it's a great city! People go there to be successful."

We liked Moscow, too. It's a vibrant city, with wide streets and narrow picturesque lanes, great art newly exhibited, fine shopping, tree-lined neighborhoods and inviting public parks.

Lena had also enjoyed a visit to New York City with her mother. The Statue of Liberty surprised her. "Somehow I thought it would be taller," she said. "I imagined it being so tall you could climb to the top and see all of America."

We invited the Vinnikovs to supper. Before the holidays, we had been to dinner at their apartment. Although Sasha had served wine and vodka and cognac, we decided to serve only wine. We thought Sasha might be disappointed. But as it turned out, he drank nothing stronger than tea that evening; he said he much preferred to have us come to their place for dinner. The law in Birobidjan was zero tolerance for drinking and driving. And Sasha was not only a believer in the law, he was a top city official.

While we sat at the table after supper, Sasha sipped his tea and talked about his family. Both of his parents were born in Jewish villages in Byelorussia. His mother's father, Isai, was a shoemaker. Isai and his wife and two of their children were killed by Fascists during the German occupation in the Great Patriotic War. Their third child, Sasha's mother, Maria Isaevna, managed to escape to a neighboring house where her friends helped her hide until the soldiers left the village.

Sasha's father, Aron Pavlovitch Vinnikov, left his village to join the Russian army when he was sixteen years old. "He fought the Fascists until the very last day, until the complete victory over Fascism in Europe," Sasha said.

After the war, Aron Pavlovitch and Maria Isaevna met and were married.

"When the government called young people to go and cultivate the vast territories of Siberia and the Far East, my parents went to the north of Khabarovski territory, to a small Nanai (indigenous) village," Sasha said. "My mother worked there as a nurse and my father headed a fire brigade."

Sasha was born in the village and his parents stayed there until they retired to Birobidjan. They are buried in the small cemetery at the edge of town.

In the middle of winter, as the moonlight streamed into the kitchen, sparkling from the frost ferns that laced the edge of the window, we talked about how much we enjoyed our visits to their *dacha*, which dominated their weekends in warm weather.

"In May," Sasha promised, "we will take a big fish to our *dacha* – a sturgeon from where the river flows in the western hills – and we will stuff it with onions and potatoes and smoke it slowly in the outdoor oven, over fern leaves and apple wood, and we will have a feast."

Round little birds sat on bare branches outside our kitchen window. They perched in a row, facing our way, as though we were characters on a TV screen they were watching. It was too bad the window was sealed for winter and I couldn't open it and toss crumbs to them.

According to the local newspaper, which I could read, haltingly and armed with a dictionary, it had been colder than 30 below zero at daybreak for the first two weeks of January. At midday it gusted up to -4.

"*Oy! Moroz! Moroz!*" is the refrain of a popular Russian folk song: "Oh! Frost! Frost!"

Sometimes John and I spent time tallying up how long we had been in Russia, when winter would end. We talked. We read. Most recently I had read Isabel Allende's "The House of the Spirits," May Sarton's "Journal of a Solitude," and Vladimir Pozner's "Parting With Illusions" (about modern Russia). This mixed lot was among the books that had arrived from the states.

We took the morning train to Khabarovsk, a slow unheated train that stopped at every village. Wind blew steadily from the river, increasing Khabarovsk's chill. Our first stop was Amy Dickerson's apartment. She had been traveling in Thailand and we got there before her. The apartment was bone cold.

We turned on the heat, went shopping for supplies, then burrowed under heavy quilts and spent the rest of the day reading and listening to music on Amy's CD player.

Amy arrived home the next morning, along with Daphne and Alice who had gone to Thailand with her. Too bad, they said, but the beach was polluted, the water at Penang was full of jellyfish, and the Russian tour group they had gone with were loud, drunk and obnoxious. The Russians, they said, loaded the return plane with television sets, VCRs and other foreign merchandise, better and cheaper than they can buy at home.

Traveling with other Peace Corps people, Amy said, is not really a vacation. Still, it was hard to return to frozen Russia. Amy was quieter than usual. We shopped and cooked for her that day; the next day she went to a Russian birthday party and we took the overnight train to Ussuriisk.

The train was another slow one; our compartment companions were two drunken men. They stumbled along the corridor and animatedly roused two other men and pulled them into our compartment to check us out as John and I feigned sleep on the top bunks. The men got off the train, noisily, around three in the morning; other people got in, and at about 7 a.m., we arrived in Ussuriisk. It was still dark. By mid-morning, we were on the bus for Anuchino to see our young Peace Corps friend, Michelle Kraviec.

Anuchino was a picturesque village, full of small three-story apartment buildings and little wooden houses behind board fences on quiet narrow streets.

The first people who saw us were two women in the town center's "cultural house." We had stopped by there to ask how to find Michelle. The women motioned for us to sit down. They fed us bread and telephoned Michelle. She came to take us home to her apartment. Children stared at us and yelled hello.

Michelle lived on the third floor of her building; on the first floor was Natasha and her husband and in the next apartment were her other daughter, Lena, and Lena's six-year-old daughter Dasha, and a husband who was always puttering on his car. Natasha and Lena were like a mother and sister to Michelle. Another teacher, Raisa, lived in one of the little houses, with banya attached, and they invited us over to use the banya in the middle of our stay. The banya wasn't a luxury in Anuchino, it was the main way people bathed. Michelle had no hot running water; to bathe she heated water with a big electric coil in a pail in her kitchen or headed for Raisa's banya.

John and I were invited to bathe first. The banya had a couple of wooden shelves to lie on. The top shelf was so hot that there were hats hanging on a nearby hook which some people wore to keep their heads from burning. We opted for the lower shelf instead. I ladled boiling water from a faucet over the stove into two basins and added cold water to each from the tub in the corner, and we used the basins of water to shampoo our hair and suds our bodies as we stood on boards that covered the dirt floor. To rinse, we poured warm water over ourselves, thoroughly steaming up the small space. Then, in Russian fashion, we flogged each other with a long, wetted-down bundle of oak leaves and rinsed off again. After we rinsed out the basins and made sure we had left everything in good order, we dried off in the anteroom, put our clothes back on, and hurried across the snow to the kitchen.

The dash from banya to kitchen – about fifteen steps – was enough to freeze our eyebrows and the outer strands of our wet hair. Michelle went into the banya next, quickly bathed and returned, her short-cropped hair damp and curly from the steam.

It shouldn't have surprised us – although we had been invited for 8:30 in the evening and had already eaten spaghetti for supper – to find a large table filled with food. There was nothing to do but eat another meal. Champagne first, then wine, and meat patties, roasted pork, mashed potatoes piled high in a bowl, carrot salad thick with mayonnaise and pungent with garlic, brown bread. Then tea and cakes. And a scolding for not eating more, for not appreciating Russian cooking, for not wanting to stay hours longer, though it was a school night and both Raisa and Michelle had to teach in the morning.

Raisa's husband got out his new video camera and filmed several minutes worth of us eating and talking, then insisted on showing it back to us before we left. We waddled back to Michelle's to sleep.

Michelle lived in a one-room apartment. In the beginning she was expected to sleep on a rickety old chair that folded out into a crooked bed. Within a few weeks, some students in the shop class had made her a bed, headboard, footboard and backboard all outlined with a simple but carefully carved design. On this she tossed a couple of big quilts and three giant pillows, and it served as a couch by day. Opposite the bed was a basic desk and a tall bookcase. On the walls were taped pictures from magazines and quotes from writers and philosophers. Michelle had accumulated dozens of books and tapes; we listened to music ranging from folk rock to chamber music to modern jazz.

After school the next day, we talked for hours, about writing, about Russia, about love.

"If you really know that someone loves you, then when they criticize something you do, it doesn't destroy you," Michelle said. "It's just some little thing that you might want to change." She giggled. "Or not."

Michelle was in love with someone back home and knew she would eventually marry him, and did a year later. Meanwhile, she was in a Russian village, surrounded by people who loved her.

On the third day, the three of us took a bus to Chuguyevka to visit another volunteer, Luke. We stayed overnight in his apartment. The first impression was of the smell of the toilet; the toilet was so disgusting Luke himself was inspired to take a picture of it when he moved in 18 months before and it had only become dirtier since that time.

Luke had learned to cook, after a fashion. He tossed two chicken legs in his grease-coated toaster-oven, and he peeled potatoes, cut them up and boiled them in a big frying pan on an electric burner that sat on top of the refrigerator. When the tray in the toaster-oven filled with grease from the roasting chicken, he pulled the tray out and dumped the grease over the potatoes. Later, he dumped in a can of peas. We were hungry and Luke's casserole, though primitive, was hot and savory.

A pretty blonde Russian girl, Luke's language tutor, came over for the evening. We danced and drank beer, and then the Russian girl left and we bedded down on Luke's fold-out couch around midnight.

Luke and Michelle stayed up talking for another three hours or so – he arguing the advantages of casual sex, she cheerfully changing the subject. In the morning, we all visited Luke's classes and answered the usual questions from shy Russian students: "Where are you from?" "What is your name?" "How old are you?"

Luke and his students had painted a huge world map on the wall; it was the brightest thing in the school. The students obviously liked him.

Another volunteer, during training, had been harshly critical of Luke. She told him he'd never be a teacher, not in a million years.

"I love teaching," Luke said. "I can't believe it, but I do."

In the morning, we took the bus back to Ussuriisk, the nearest train station. Halfway there, a wretched, ragged man boarded the bus and slowly stumbled toward us, taking the seat directly in front of me and turning to gaze at us with striking blue eyes, all the more striking because they were in a face so wasted and sick and ugly that it was hard to look at him. He was dirty, his skin was blotched and dry, with huge dark pores, and his nose was a sickly greenish color. His hat was an incredibly greasy fur, probably rabbit, with ear flaps bent outward as though they couldn't bear the proximity to his scabby head.

After staring at us intently for several minutes, the man reached a shaky hand into his coat pocket and pulled out a card, possibly identifying himself as a poor, mute, sick soul who needed money. We took our cue from the others on the bus who had studiously ignored him – although Russians are remarkably generous to beggars as a rule. We stared unhappily out the window, ignoring the card he thrust at us, and finally he put it away. Then he rummaged around in a torn cloth bag and pulled out a packet that he fumbled with, eventually extricating from it a used hypodermic needle.

"Move," I said in a panic to John, who had me wedged into the window seat directly behind the man. "Move. Let me out. I'm not sitting here."

We moved to the other side of the bus, a couple of rows back, and I started breathing again. I couldn't bear to be that close to a derelict armed with a sharp needle, no matter how pitiful he was. The wave of pity I felt for him was overwhelmed by the much stronger feelings of revulsion and fear. I was relieved to be out of his reach. We decided he was probably a diabetic giving himself an insulin shot, nothing for us to be alarmed about, but emotion ruled over reason.

The man ignored us after that, and he got off the bus an hour later, in another village as desolate looking as the one that had produced him.

We arrived in Ussuriisk at midday and waited around for the midnight train, getting to Birobidjan the next afternoon, glad we had gone, glad to be home.

It felt good to come back to our dormitory apartment – with its radiator heat, hot water, and a working stove. Michelle said the first winter, she complained many times about having no heat, but either her Russian wasn't good enough yet to be understood or people just thought she was a spoiled American.

By the second winter, she had made friends. They came in to her stone-cold apartment, discovered the radiator was clogged, and repaired it.

John and I liked visiting the village volunteers. In few other circumstances were people our ages greeted so enthusiastically by people in their twenties. The village volunteers' Russian language skills were much better than ours, both because the difference in age, and because they had little opportunity to communicate in English.

Some of their circumstances were primitive: they cooked on hot plates, they stayed warm under quilts when the heat failed. Sometimes they ate outdated packaged food because they had no other choice; sometimes they couldn't get eggs, meat or fresh produce. But there were also people in their villages, poorer than they were, who shared with them the proceeds of their *dacha*s: jam, canned vegetables, potatoes. They also shared *samogon*, a homemade vodka, sometimes flavored with wild berries, sometimes honey.

Mary, a volunteer who left Russia early, found that there were some things she missed about the Peace Corps life. She wrote about them in a thoughtful letter:

"The not knowing what was going to come next, even though it might be hideous and enormously inconvenient. My life here (in America) seems nondescript and predictable. I've fallen into that awful trap of 'been there, done that' and am now fighting the battle of balance between security and comfort. I'm finding everything simply too easy and unengaging. You can't go home again, at least not with the same acceptance as when you left."

26

Tending the Shallow Roots

A flu epidemic hit Birobidjan. All of the schools closed for ten days. Children were running around the *rinok*, playing in the cold, riding on the city buses.

We thought the new semester would start soon. The first week in February, Vera said. Then, she said, the second week. The eight hundred books from America were still waiting for a library room. They were stacked against the walls of our apartment, and Phil's and Linda's apartment, and more were on the way.

Sets of literature, poetry and writing books, were already catalogued and available for use. Yet most of the teachers still preferred to use their tattered old Communist textbooks. When I asked why, they said this was because of "continuity" and "building on what the students know." John and I told ourselves we were "planting seeds," and not to necessarily expect big changes at first. We told ourselves that our Peace Corps project could be considered a success, because at least our students were eager to read the books. But until space was provided for orderly access, the college was determined to keep the books out of circulation.

Although the start of the semester was delayed, Masha, Denis and Lena continued to show up weekly for their practice language and scholastic tests. Their scores continued to improve.

I woke up before dawn, slipped out of bed and made my way to the kitchen. I waited for the sunlight to see if there was new snow or just the same old snow. The bedroom window, facing north, was opaque with thick layers of ice and frost.

By now, our friends would talk to us about their family histories, many of which included the camps and prisons of Siberia and the Russian Far East. Some of them still seemed nervous and afraid that we might say something that, to them, would be embarrassing or humiliating.

The people Stalin wanted out of the way were the elite of Russia – the intellectuals, the spirited, the dissidents, children of the formerly privileged upper classes, musicians and artists and writers, doctors and philosophers, and in the case of our region, the Jews among them.

In many cases, charges were brought against people, witnesses found who were willing to testify against them to save their own jobs (at least temporarily), and sentences were handed down: 10, 20, 30 or more years of hard labor, often followed by permanent exile for those who survived.

Children and grandchildren of pioneers and convicts populate much of the Russian Far East, from Vladivostok – the end of the trans-Siberian rail line – to Magadan on Russia's northeast coast, and beyond, from the permanently frozen tundra of the Arctic Circle to the mosquito-infested swamplands and vast taiga of the interior, from Lake Baikal in Siberia to Sakhalin Island in the Sea of Okhotsk.

In one way, the people in the Russian Far East reminded me of Australians I had met years ago who were ashamed of their heritage, having descended from English and Irish prisoners who were transported to Australia after America became independent. But, as Australia celebrated its 200th anniversary, Aussies began telling their stories with pride. Family histories of suffering took on a sense of honor rather than disgrace. I thought that, in the future, something similar might happen for Russians whose ancestors suffered under Stalin's reign of terror.

The students were grouped in small classes and, in lockstep, they attended classes together all day every day for five years. It was the most intimate imaginable educational setting. Lifelong friendships were forged. Sometimes best friends drifted away from each other and formed a new pairing with someone else, but there was no escaping from the group.

I used a cross-culture exercise called "Culture Quilt" in one of my conversation classes. The task was for each student to make five "patches" (drawings) that depicted their faith, their ethnicity, their gender, their hometown and their future. Then they discussed each picture, explaining what the drawing meant. Finally, they looked for group similarities of pictures (their cultural identity) and individual differences (their personal identity).

Afterwards, they patched all of the pictures together and taped the "quilt" to the wall as an artwork.

The ten students in this class were about 22 years old. The quilt conversation, talking about their families and their values, was my most animated class of the semester. Two of the students, Irina and Sergei, discovered while doing the quilt that their Jewish grandparents had come to Birobidjan from the same village in Ukraine. Although this was their fifth year together in college, they hadn't been aware of this connection. As they left class, they were still talking about their intertwined family roots.

The quilt stayed on the wall all semester.

The last week of February was the week of slush. Snow melted, dripped, ran in steady rivulets off the tin roof of our building. The streams splattered down past our sunny kitchen window. Spring was approaching.

People in America had sent us many good books. We read "Angela's Ashes," "Snow Falling on Cedars," a short-story book called "Eleven Kinds of Loneliness," "The Lake in the Woods," "Goodbye to Manzanar," Jerzey Kozinski's "The Painted Bird,"

"Einstein's Dreams" by Alan Lightman, Milan Kundera's "The Book of Laughter and Forgetting."

Our students wanted to read the books as well. We began letting them dig through the boxes in our living room and borrow the books they wanted. They knew there were hundreds more in storage, and they were thrilled when finally the library made the first couple-hundred books available for them to check out.

It occurred to me that if they knew how to organize themselves to effectively appeal to the college officials, they might have gained access to these materials sooner. They didn't know how to do this because no one had ever introduced the idea to them. They had learned in school how to be good followers, but they didn't know how to be good leaders.

We volunteers thought it would be a great idea to teach Russian schoolchildren about civics – democracy and group effectiveness. Peace Corps volunteers could do this in their English-language classes. They could teach the basic concepts of democracy by helping the students design a structure of class leadership – with the usual offices: president, vice president, secretary, treasurer. Students could run for office, have some campaign issues, hold elections. The winners could perform duties and take leadership roles as decided by the whole class.

When issues came up, ranging from classroom management to holiday plans, from school problems to class goals, they could be addressed within the democratic structure that the students had developed. Then, when students reached the college level, and they thought they should be getting more out of their college years, they would know how to do something about it. And when they reached adulthood, they would be ready for leadership roles in the next generation.

Three years later, this idea was still in the air. A couple of volunteers had started such classes in their villages, but when they left and were not replaced, as often happened for one reason or another, the civics classes died with their departure.

John started talking about going home early. He was tired. Others had gone.

I didn't want to leave early, though I felt quite sure several members of my family would agree with John, so I couldn't seek their counsel. I sent an e-mail to another married couple who were with the Peace Corps in Afghanistan some thirty years before, Al and Patty Perrin. I wanted their support for staying.

"There are only four months left of our service and we're tired and anxious," I wrote. "John wants to leave, but I don't. I know some volunteers who had to leave the Peace Corps early because of illness, or a criminal attack, or war. They had no choice. I know others who just got tired of being frustrated or who thought they weren't given a chance to do good work.

"But it seems that those who go home early always start out talking about the reason they didn't stay. Maybe I'm just being stubborn, but I want to stay the whole time. I want to go home with a sense of a job well done, or at least a job done.

"But maybe I'm being selfish. Even though it's hard being here, I like this life."

Patty's reply:

"I have followed your Peace Corps experience with real interest. It of course in some ways reminded me of ours. I had the really terrible time at the first however. I had no job, I had no language, I had nothing to do, and I was becoming for the first time a grandmother here in the states. I wanted terribly to be with our daughter. She, incidentally, has never forgiven me. But I have never regretted staying. I have known people who quit and they have never really quite gotten past it. Don't even consider it.

"I have to tell you that coming home was terribly difficult for us. We could not settle down, we moved constantly and for about a

307

year had no idea of what to do or where. We could not go back to where we had been, we were too different and other people still the same. They had no idea of what had happened to us. And the terrible plethora of products was upsetting. Supermarkets freaked me out. I left baskets half full and ran out. I froze in air conditioning. People talked of inane things, the same things they had been talking about before we left.

"The greatest comfort we had was in each other. We ran from returned volunteer to returned volunteer. And they did the same. We still support each other in stress. We became a very special family, I suspect like old war buddies. I hope when you come home you will join this group. I do want you to come up and stay a while. We can hold hands and tell each other war stories.

"Stay the course and know you will be glad you did.

"Love, Patty"

But John was depressed, feeling trapped and negative. He said the Russian language was not for him; he wanted to return to his study of French. He said he was tired of teaching; the students were difficult, they talked too much, they cheated on their tests.

"I want to go home," he said. "I would go home, if not for you."

Finally, one night, after yet another argument, he said, "I am going home."

This time I said, "I think that's a good idea." And nothing more was said.

I didn't sleep very well that night, wondering what to do, what this would mean, how it would be if I went home too, and how it would be if I stayed on here alone for the rest of the time.

I imagined being alone, shopping and cooking, sitting alone in the evening, reading and writing, taking walks, inviting people to visit me and maybe visiting them, talking with people, but often being alone, and how it would be.

Or how would it be if I went home because of him, and what if he was no happier there, and would I feel like blaming him for being my reason for quitting? What if I didn't go with him and he discovered that he was happier without me? Did I dare risk that? Would I be happier?

What if I were to stubbornly stay here, and he really needed me? Or what if he didn't?

The next morning he asked, "Do you want me to stay or leave?"

"I want you to stay," I said.

"Okay, I'll stay," he said.

"You shouldn't stay just for me, because I don't want to be the reason for your unhappiness."

"I'm not staying just for you. I'm staying because it's too hard to leave."

He was still unhappy. We didn't know what to do about that. So we didn't do anything about it. We just kept going. "*Zhag za Zhagem*" (step by step).

But one thing had changed as I lay tossing and turning that night. Even though it was true that I wanted him to stay, I realized that I didn't *need* him to stay. I found it relieving, after all these years of marriage, to have made a decision separately from him, for separate reasons, my own reasons, and somehow to know instinctively that whatever else happened I would be stronger for it.

As it turned out, John's days of complaining about teaching were over. He finally told Vera exactly how he felt, as we three sat at our kitchen table after classes one afternoon, having coffee.

And Vera said, "John, please. Listen to me. Your presence is valuable, whatever you do." She stirred the usual four spoonfuls of sugar into her coffee and lit a cigarette. Shaking the flame off the match and exhaling a puff of smoke, she said, "What would you like to do?"

She was like a fairy godmother who could grant any wish, provided he agreed to stay.

So it was decided, in an animated conversation, what John would do. He would spend most of his time giving individual computer lessons to the teachers and he would teach only two classes in his favorite subject: American literature. It was as though Vera willed him a supply of energy and purpose. And it was good for me to regard him again as a positive force, this man I love.

27

Survival of the Fittest

Linda and Phil went to a dinner party at the Teacher Retraining Institute where Linda was a Peace Corps volunteer. The teachers insisted late in the evening that Linda offer a toast. She thought a minute and said, in English, "Here's to the fine men of Russia."

The Russian interpreter said, "Here's to Russian men, who are better than American men!"

Linda's friend seated next to her turned to her with a worried expression and said, "What about Phil?"

Maslenitsa carnival (from *maslo*, meaning butter), in the week before Lent, started as a pagan Russian holiday, a salute to the sun, a week of joy. There were bonfires, pancakes (*blini*, round, like the sun) with sour cream and butter, sleigh rides. People dressed in costumes and performed skits and dances in the park by the river. Prizes were given to the woman who had the most children (a snaggle-toothed, stout mother of nine won a large plastic thermos bottle), and the child who could recite the longest poem. In one contest, two couples came onstage, fifteen rubles were hidden by each girl in her boyfriend's clothing, and then the girls raced to find the money hidden by the other girl.

There was a tug-o-war between a long line of little boys and a shorter line of big boys; the big boys eventually won. In stilt contests, boys tried to walk on tall stilts with footholds about eighteen inches off the ground. Then they tried to climb atop another kind of stilts – eighteen-inch logs cut off evenly at both ends. To balance on the ends of the logs, the boys held on by a loop of twine nailed into each side of the log. By the third step, one log or the other slipped sideways and the boy toppled off.

Older boys stripped down to a pair of shorts and wrapped themselves around a tall greased pole. The winners were those who were able to pull themselves to the top of the pole, high enough to reach over the top, and take a bottle of champagne, or vodka, out of a net that hung just below the top, then painfully descend. The pole was greased, but it wasn't altogether smooth. The upward journey took strength and concentration; the slide down took endurance and a willingness to suffer. As the boys eased themselves to the bottom of the pole, holding onto the bottle, splinters pierced the white skin of their thighs and arms. They grimaced, hugged the pole, endured.

The day of the carnival was exceptionally warm and sunny, but the women still wore their fur coats and stylish mink hats, reluctant to put them away for another season, their most expensive tribute to glamour. The hats did look wonderful, some designed with a rim of fur at a jaunty angle, others tall in front, still others a furry pillbox shape. The fur hats combined with bright red lipstick, smoothly painted to the edges of lips and beyond, to make the maximum impression of luscious kissability.

We had heard about the carnival, but we didn't know where it would be. First we looked at Victory Square, in front of the casino, then at Lenin Square across from the post office. There, we fell in with the crowds strolling to the riverside park where tinny rides had stood buried under snow for several months and the stage had been barren for a season. The stage was out of use not only because of winter but also because the backside of the stage had been destroyed by an autumn fire. The tin soldiers that used to decorate the top of the backdrop had fallen into the flames and later been buried under the snow. Their blackened bodies still lay in the rubble behind the stage.

But the stage had been repaired, new smaller tin soldiers stood at the top of the backdrop, and the snow had melted from the rides.

They were set in motion for the carnival. Babies one and two years old were strapped into bucket seats on a Ferris wheel and set moving around in tall circles. They gazed down at their mothers and fathers with worried faces.

The Ferris wheel went round and round, the babies uttering not a sound. They sat patiently waiting for the ride to end, and held out their hands in relief when their parents unstrapped them and lifted out of the bucket.

A tin shed held bumper cars that bumped and squeaked around a wooden rink. Beneath the trees were sturdy metal benches that swung back and forth. Children sat four astride and pushed as high as the swing would go, not laughing or shouting, just vigorously swinging.

Men took deep gulps from bottles of beer and ate chunks of barbecued meat served on paper plates with slices of onion and a puddle of ketchup. Girls daintily ate ice cream from paper cups.

Boys chased each other around the crowd and yelled "Hello!" at us. Young fathers lifted their children onto their shoulders for a better view of the stage.

In one dance on the stage, a young man in peasant costume, with a white blouse cinched tight by a sash, baggy pants and high black boots, danced with a girl wearing a full skirt, apron and kerchief. He pouted, pulled away, gazed behind him at a row of four pretty girls who beckoned to him. He danced away from his partner, she cried silently, tried to lure him back; his expression changed to flirtatiousness and avid interest as he skillfully twirled and danced around each of the pretty girls, occasionally frowning back at his original partner.

Two of my students came to visit me one afternoon.

"We want to practice our English," they said.

I was amused because in their conversation class, these two girls hardly ever spoke. I put the kettle on the stove, made us a pot of tea, and served it with cookies. After spooning several spoonfuls of sugar into their tea, they began by pointing out that their nicknames rhymed: Alexandra's was Sasha and Maria's was Masha.

Alexandra and Maria had heard about the "Culture Quilt" conversation in one of my other classes, and wanted to tell me stories about their families.

Alexandra said that during the Great Patriotic War, a Russian soldier passed through her grandmother's village in Ukraine. He was starving and cold, and he kept slipping and falling in the mud, but no one helped him. Then a German tank came through, crushing plants, crops and trees. Her grandmother stepped in front of a young tree to save it, but the tank kept coming. At the last minute, a neighbor pulled her out of the way and the tank crushed the sapling.

"I do not understand why no man or woman in the village tried to save Russian soldier," Sasha said. "But my grandmother tried to save tree."

Maria said that in the 1970s her mother and her aunt had to leave their village school, not far from Moscow, and go to work in the fields every day. All they had to eat was a boiled beet between them, and a couple of cucumbers. All day, as they worked, they were forced to sing. The bosses knew if they stopped singing, they would eat the crops.

One day, Maria said, an American visitor, on a tour of the countryside, saw them working and said to the Intourist guide: "The children must be very happy here. It's lovely to hear them singing."

"My mother learn to speak English in school," Maria said. "And, I must say, she was a brave girl. My mother stand up and she say, 'We do not sing because we are happy. We sing because if we stop singing, boss will beat us.'"

Four beggar children, ranging in age from around eight to twelve, scrambled onto the old commuter train between Birobidjan and Khabarovsk. They were yelling and swearing. A man jumped up from his seat and slapped the two oldest children on the head and then knocked their heads together. They laughed at him, then the tallest boy turned around and punched the littlest boy in the face. His nose bled and he wiped it on his sleeve, held his head back to stop the bleeding, and chuckled at the ceiling as he sat there.

I attended the "Teacher of the Year" extravaganza at the Children's Cultural Center. Five teachers, the finalists, were escorted to the stage by boys from our college and seated at small tables at the back of the stage: Ludmila, a tall beanpole of a woman with a hearty laugh, short bobbed hair and a red jacket; Olga, a perky bleached blonde; Tanya, a tall willowy woman who smiled strenuously; Natasha, a plump brunette; and Isabella, a sedate woman in a well-fitted suit and french-rolled hairdo who exuded a mannered culture and spoke in a low voice.

First, each woman performed a long monologue about the joys of teaching.

Ludmila's students cheered and held up big posters after she finished. Olga's students cheered wildly and she raised her arms above her head. She had included three costumed little boys in a skit as her presentation. Tanya forgot her lines and nearly dropped the microphone. Natasha sailed flawlessly through the performance, but stood too far from the mike and, with the constant chatting in the crowd, no one could hear her but those in the front rows. Isabella could barely be heard either, but somehow she commanded such attention that everyone strained to listen.

The judges went to work to tally the scores and children from the local dance school performed in bright costumes. The judges, sitting near the stage, gave Natasha the first round and a boy from the college put a bouquet of flowers wrapped in plastic in her arms.

Then college students performed a sequence of horrible classroom situations – involving lazy hooligans, a class out of control, a gum-popping girl arriving late, a disruptive slut, mating games in the back row – and one by one the contestants reacted with a one-liner, ranging from "Throw them out!" to "It's Valentine's Day." Olga may have won this round; at least she was pumping her hands above her head as the results were announced.

Next each teacher joined a performance done by people at her school, sometimes children, sometimes other teachers.

Olga sang and danced Russian and Jewish folk songs with several teachers from the Yiddish school. Dancing children surrounded Natasha and waved flags in her direction as they twirled in their stocking feet. Tanya joined five other women and sang patriotic songs, accompanied by an accordion. Isabella's group appeared last and their somber recitation of patriotic poetry suited her entire campaign. Ludmila's extravaganza of dancing and singing children, tossing balloons into the audience, and prancing around the stage in a choreographed complexity of motion, costumes flying, was the definite winner of this round.

Then all the teachers came on stage and flowers were presented to them. Isabella took a step back as her boyish escort handed her a bouquet in its plastic wrapper. It had been just taken from a pail of water and she jumped aside as water dripped on her stylish dress. Other prizes, were awarded: a coffee pot to Olga, a spice rack to Natasha.

Finally, the big prize came out: a television set.

The top honor and the television set were presented to Ludmila as she was named "Teacher of the Year." The crowd applauded wildly.

The show lasted almost three hours and every bench was filled. Two other teachers and I, from the college, sat in the top row, in chairs reserved for special guests. Behind us a three-deep crowd of children ebbed and flowed as one group and then another took their place on stage. Eventually, three six-year-olds wrapped themselves snuggly around the backs of our seats, propped their elbows behind our necks, and finally draped themselves comfortably over our shoulders.

I felt a rush of happiness at being cozy with perfectly trusting and secure children who had never seen us before, who obviously never had a thought that a stranger might be a scary and unpredictable presence in an auditorium packed with parents and teachers and children.

In Birobidjan's classrooms, the teachers touched the children, they hugged them, and occasionally, we're told (though we'd never seen it), they smacked them. It was the hugs and the casual hands-on that we'd often seen, and children who felt secure and were comforted.

I thought it was sad that our American culture, with our heavy emphasis on individualism and self-reliance, had come to a place where we denied the basic right of human touch between teachers and children, because we were so paranoid about the possibility of inappropriate touching, of child molestation. Because of a few highly publicized problems, millions of American children were deprived of natural closeness with people who cared for them, and millions of adults were wary, afraid to touch, afraid to hug a crying child, for fear they'd be accused of nasty and dangerous impulses.

Not that there weren't problems in Birobidjan as well. The children in the auditorium were the lucky ones. These were not the children on the streets, who grabbed sleeves and purses, who begged at the kiosks, who didn't even flinch when someone hit them in the head.

Allison Reid and a teacher in her village made plans to go camping with the teacher's husband and another man. Then the teacher got sick and decided to stay home. But Allison and the two men went camping anyway.

The men drank a lot of vodka, Allison said, and she had a little vodka herself. It was cold, and the two men said they'd sleep in the

317

tent and she could sleep in the car. But in the middle of the night, one of the men got into the car with her and quietly eased the door shut.

"He sexually assaulted me," Allison said. She was extremely upset, but insisted that she wasn't physically hurt. She called the Peace Corps the next morning and reported the assault.

The loud, laughing, vibrant Allison blew into that village like a breath of life, and left a silence in her wake.

Amy wrote: "You know I've become pretty used to life in Russia, but today I had a couple experiences that opened some new windows in the culture for me.

"I was working with two very young teachers of English, showing them how to use the Internet. I explained that their students could come to the computer room to do research for assignments.

"One of the teachers replied: 'Our students don't deserve this (access to Internet). They aren't educated enough.'

"And while I'm so anxious to share the delights of the Internet with these teachers, I realize this same teacher has a more basic problem: She could really use a set of glasses; her eyes were bothering her terribly after twenty minutes of looking at the monitor.

"I've also been battling the attitudes of the ladies who keep watch over the Internet Center. One woman is hell-bent on keeping students out. She said to one of my students at 4 p.m.: 'What are you doing here so late in the day?'

"Today, she was berating a student for using the printer. When I intervened, she and I got into a shouting match (in Russian, I'm 'proud' to say). Unfortunately, that's how lowly people, like students, or Peace Corps volunteers, get any attention from people in power – by shouting.

"I made amends shortly with her, and we established that the student didn't know the rules, and couldn't, since there is no sign, and since the rules are three days old, and that, yes, maybe students should be able to print if they pay a nominal fee (they already bring their own paper), and maybe we should decide what such a fee might be.

"—Amy"

March 8 was Women's Day, a big holiday in Russia. Women are presented with flowers, gifts are given to them, their praises are sung.

Banks closed at noon, and so did the college. The faculty had a party in the teachers' room, where we raised toasts to women with champagne and vodka and ate cheese, red caviar, sweet rolls and orange slices.

We were at the bank in the morning, but it was so crowded, with people clustered in front of the two tellers, pushing and shoving and crowding each other, that we decided to come back later. After the party for the teachers, we returned to the bank, not realizing it would be closed. We could see the tellers and clerks sitting around a large table, raising their glasses in toasts. It was a day of parties.

We had been waiting for our monthly allowance from Peace Corps to be deposited in the bank. Instead, we had to borrow 1,000 rubles from Phil and Linda – who had waited in the morning line – because we would be out of town until March 15, attending our close-of-service conference. We had to leave for Vladivostok early Monday morning (also a bank holiday). We were glad Phil and Linda had withstood the crowds, in their usual determined and systematic way, instead of leaving, as we did, hoping for a better chance later in the day.

We also needed to buy some things to take to Pavel's and Lena's that evening. We couldn't go empty-handed, especially on Women's Day.

Lena was very pleased to learn that we "refused to go" to Tatyana's because we had already accepted Lena's invitation. Tatyana, our department chair, invited us just that morning to come to dinner for Women's Day. She was quite taken aback that we turned her down, but we apologized, saying we had already made plans.

"It's a pity," she said again in the afternoon.

We never knew if we did the right thing, in the Russians' minds. Maybe protocol dictated that the boss's invitation took priority, but for us, the priority was our close friends as well as the concept of a previous engagement.

I bought Lena a bottle of French cologne, with a pretty rose as a stopper, and a small box of candy (not too small, I hoped), and a bottle of wine.

Then I saw the old woman with the braided rugs. I had only seen her twice before. She sat in front of the hotel on the cold concrete wall, hoping someone would buy her homemade rugs. I had been watching for her for a long time, because ever since I had bought three rugs from her, other Peace Corps volunteers said they'd like to have some, too.

The Russians didn't seem to value homemade things, certainly not little round rugs braided from rags. The old woman had four rugs to sell, but I had no money left in my wallet so I went back to the apartment to get some.

Phil stopped by to give me a small present to take to Lena. I told him about the old woman and he thought Linda would like a couple of rugs for their bathroom, but they had to get ready to go to Tatyana's. Her son-in-law Sasha was coming with his car to pick them up.

"Maybe tomorrow," he said.

I didn't think she'd be there the next day, though maybe she would if the rugs hadn't sold. I decided to go back myself, and bought three rugs, two for Linda and one for Allison, for Women's Day. (I hadn't yet heard about the sexual assault.)

The old woman was still sitting on the wall, her stout body wrapped against the wind in an old black cloth coat, a wooly gray shawl around her head. No mittens. Her fat hands were red and chapped and the index finger of her right hand was deformed; it looked as though the end was missing, not neatly severed, but scarred and with a pointed rag of extra skin on one side of the knuckle at its tip. Her face was round and red and chapped; her light blue eyes, covered with a thin milky film, were sunk deeply into puffy cheeks.

I said in Russian that I would like to buy three rugs, and asked the price.

They were less than a dollar each, the same as last year.

I gave her three coins. The coins were new, in use only since the ruble's devaluation in January. She turned them over and over in her hand, looked puzzled, and finally showed them to the ice cream vendor standing next to her.

"*Da, da,*" the vendor said, assuring her that the coins were real and correct.

The old woman looked at me and nodded solemnly as I lifted three rugs from her lap, leaving her just one still to sell.

"Happy Women's Day," I said to her in Russian.

Then, and only then, did we make real contact. She rewarded me with a wide toothless smile, her blue button eyes all but disappearing in the crinkles of her cheeks, and she reached out her hand and patted my sleeve, bestowing on me the good wishes that are commonly expressed in Russia: "To your continuing good mood."

I tried to imagine what the small amount of money would buy that would make it worthwhile to sit on a cold concrete wall, with the air temperature at just above freezing, waiting to sell a few handmade rag rugs. Rows of women also sat near kiosks with bags of black sunflower seeds to sell. A cheap snack; Russians chewed on the seeds everywhere. Having sold their small offerings, what did the women buy? Did the rug woman buy seeds to chew and spit out? Did she treat herself to a bottle of cooking oil and a small wedge of cheese? Did the ragged men who trudged between garbage cans looking for empty beer bottles trade them for one precious beer (eight bottles for one beer)? Or did they take the bottle money and spend it on vodka? Or maybe bread?

In the bar next to the train station, the woman behind the bar, pouring beer and vodka for her customers, was drunk. Behind her, a young man, down on his knees on the floor behind the bar, giggled and drooled, watching her try to fill John's plastic 1.5-liter bottle with beer from the foaming tap. She weaved and wobbled, grinning foolishly.

For Pavel's and Lena's multi-course dinner, in honor of women, Pavel wore a tie and Lena was elegant in a low-cut purple dress and spiky high heels. She brought to the table a platter piled high with roasted chicken legs, a bowl with a mountain of small boiled potatoes.

The pride of the spread, however, was "herring in a fur coat," a huge layered Russian salad consisting of pickled herring fillets on the bottom, then chopped onions, a layer of mayonnaise, a layer of chopped potatoes, a deep layer of chopped beets, and a thick coat of mayonnaise over the entire top. Lena served huge heaping spoonfuls of this mixture, digging down deep to be sure that there was plenty of herring on each plate. We ate, we sang, we talked and talked, sitting around the table, then ate some more, sang some more – the usual Russian dinner party.

By the end of the evening, on our way home, there were drunks stumbling down the streets, occasionally breaking into song. There were drunken men, young and old, drunken women, young couples on the bus, inebriated people laughing, yelling, or somberly trudging along, bumping into walls.

Anatoli Surnin announced that he would not order bookshelves to be built in the room next to the library downstairs.

"The new building will be ready next fall," he said.

This was the same building that he had said would be ready in January. Hundreds of books were still stacked in our living room, and that many more on the way from the states, and no place to put them.

He did at least have a wrought-iron security door installed in the classroom next to the library, with a strong new padlock, so the television and VCR could be moved out of our apartment and into that room, where all the teachers could readily hold classes and use the equipment. As for the books, there was no other place for them.

In mid-March, we second-year volunteers went to Vladivostok for COS, the "close of service" conference. One of the volunteers dubbed it the "Congregation Of Survivors." A third of our group had already gone home.

We had a great time, sharing our stories. John and I didn't need much of the advice the Peace Corps gave us during the long meetings – about resume writing, graduate school applications, scholarship information. But we benefited as much as everyone else from the joy of realizing how much experience we all had gained, how strong were the friendships we had forged. For the rest of our lives, these would be the few other Americans who had shared those two years.

The hotel where we all stayed was extraordinarily shabby. As John noted, the only things that worked were the telephones and the prostitutes. One of them called our room each night, just checking.

John, amused, said, in Russian, "Wrong number," and the woman replied, "Why?" Then she asked, "Do you want woman?"

"I already have one," he said.

Not to be deterred, she asked, "Does she want woman?"

There was no hot water, no heat. Peace Corps workers brought in a few space heaters and water distillers. The temperature, inside and out, was still below freezing at night.

Some of the volunteers found it exhausting to meet and socialize morning to night after living somewhat isolated lives for so long. We fell into our beds – narrow cots – tired, and slept deeply each night.

Tony Ladd, who served in Gorin, the northernmost village for our group of volunteers, told us how he had proved his manhood over the winter.

The Peace Corps sent him to teach in Gorin, a village north of us in Komsomolski Krai, an area of the Russian Far East that remains dedicated to the old days, with many inhabitants who would like to see the Communists return to power. Deeply suspicious of foreigners, they were certain that Western elements were decadent, if not downright evil, and that foreigners were enemies in spirit, if not downright agents sent to spy on them.

The deeper into the countryside from the city of Komsomolsk, closed to foreigners until five years before, the more suspicious were the locals. It took Tony months to gain the trust of his village, and once they no longer feared him, they began to laugh at him. They called him a dreamy boy.

"He looks like an angel," one of the Russian teachers had said of him.

Tony was tall and lean. He wore his blond hair in cascading curls, and he had a sweet mouth with small teeth, and light blue eyes behind plastic-rimmed glasses. He was a beautiful dancer. His lean body would glide gracefully around a dance floor, like Fred Astaire in those old movies, as he did a flawless waltz, foxtrot, samba.

Even the village women giggled and poked each other when he tried to teach these dances to them. The older ones scarcely remembered their own dances, wild flings around the platform, stomping with their boots and clapping, while their men clattered around them, leaping in the air, dropping to the floor, feet out, leaping and squatting.

"Now that's a man's dance!" the village men would say to Tony.

But that was before Tony helped the men slaughter a pig.

Holding onto one of the huge beast's rear hooves while another man held the other, Tony forced himself not to turn his head away as a third man, with a big curved knife, slit the animal's white throat, and the pig gave a horrible loud squeal that became a gurgle as it drowned itself in a mess of blood and slime. Then the knife smoothly but vigorously opened a slit down the belly of the beast, hands reached in, pulling forth guts, and still Tony held on, willing himself not to faint or run or display a clue of the hideous disgust that sent waves of nausea almost to his throat.

Blood ran all over his hands, slippery with guts and fat, but he kept a sickly grin on his face, and still they laughed at him. They knew. But they also knew that he stayed with them in the slaughter, and that he wanted their approval.

Laughing, one of them waved the pig's ear in his face, and yelled, *Mushina!* ("Man!") *Sevodnia, Mushina!* ("Today, a man!")

Later, when the pig was butchered and barbecued and ready to be eaten, the men in the village drank vodka, and toast after toast was made in celebration of Tony's manhood.

Another time during the long winter, Tony told us, he fell through the ice into a stream, with the temperature around 20 below, and somehow he managed to walk six miles home before tending to his frozen feet.

"Some of them said then I was truly a man," Tony said. "If not the day with the pig, then the day with the frozen feet."

Amy told about going without cold water for seven weeks. To bathe, she would run the only available water, scalding hot, into her bathtub and then wait a couple of hours. To flush the toilet, she would dip a pail into the cooled water and pour.

One late afternoon, walking home from her college, she saw a small crowd of people clustered around a man lying on the sidewalk. Another drunk, she presumed. She went on her way, trudged up the five flights of stairs to her two-room apartment, and discovered a delightful surprise: the cold water was running again! She grabbed the chance for a long shower, enjoyed washing her hair under running warm water, and found her mood greatly improved.

After awhile, she went down to the office to use the phone and chat with the clerk there. That's when she found out the handyman, who had finally succeeded in repairing the plumbing problem, had dropped dead less than two hours earlier. A kindly man, old at age 61, with wild gray hair and huge knuckles, he had apparently been seized by a heart attack, fell in the snow beside the pipe, and froze to death. Passersby had mutely waited an hour for an ambulance to arrive, by which time he was probably already dead.

"I felt terrible," Amy told us. "He was such a nice man. He didn't laugh at me when I tried to speak Russian to him. He used to bring me peppers and potatoes from his *dacha*."

Another volunteer, Karen Cornfield, came to the conference with a huge black eye, a deep purple ring rimmed in green, and an accompanying swollen jaw and two loose teeth.

The gossip mill immediately went into action, and rumors were churned out, each wilder than the last. The one that stayed around the longest was that Karen and her Russian boyfriend had a big fight, both were drunk, and when Karen finally pushed him out of her apartment, he was so furious he broke down the door, came back in and punched her in the eye.

But that wasn't exactly what happened.

They were drunk, and they did fight, Karen said.

"But I didn't want him to go. So I hid the key and I wouldn't tell him where it was." She shrugged, as if: What can you expect? "So he punched me in the eye."

She still wouldn't tell him where the key was, and she grabbed hold of him to keep him from leaving, so in a fury, after clobbering her again, he broke down the door, and stumbled off into the night.

The brawl was the final incident in Peace Corps' bulging file of Karen's wild life as a volunteer. She had been moved from one village to another, and from that village to a third, and was bulldozing her way through the good will of that community as well. Not to mention the furious boyfriend and what might happen next with him. The Peace Corps decided, for Karen's own good, to send her home to the states. (Happily, she went to work for a motivational service, and was inspired to turn her life around.)

After the sexual assault, Allison went to Vladivostok. She spent hours with the Peace Corps medical officer. She wanted to return to her village. But the Peace Corps sent her back to Washington for medical attention followed by weeks of counseling. She was offered the chance to go to another site in Russia and continue her Peace Corps service. But she insisted that she return to her village or not at all. She did not come back to Russia.

Birobidjan was ready for spring. Our most difficult time was behind us: the interminable, bitterly cold winter. Our spirits lifted. We actually had learned some Russian, and we had learned a lot else besides – about patience, perseverance, acceptance. And about laughter and touching and friendship. About ourselves and each other.

The icicles hanging from our eaves froze by night and dripped by day, and sometimes one would break loose and crash to the ground.

We still sometimes got weary of the skirmishes with bureaucrats, the inconsistency and irrationality. We went to the post office to pick up another box of books, but the post office wouldn't release them without a customs clearance because the church in Missouri that donated the books labeled the box as having a value of $134. Anything over $100 had to go through customs and be taxed.

And someone from the regional administration came by the apartment and demanded money from us to add the cities of Irkutsk and Ulan Ude to our visas, just in case we happened to go there, which we didn't.

A boy about twelve years old was out in the courtyard below our kitchen window, making a snowman. He rolled a snowball around the field of deep, wet snow, with his hands, until it got so big he could hardly move it. At that point, he tried to continue pushing it forward by sitting down and shoving it with his feet, then he got up, backed away and ran towards the big snowy ball with all the force his weight allowed, and managed to shove it a little way farther.

Finally he gave up trying to accumulate more snow by rolling the ball through it, and instead picked up armfuls of snow and dumped them on top of the ball and patted them in, hurled snowballs at the big ball and patted them on, and shaped the ball to his liking.

Next he rolled a smaller ball and set this on top, then a third and even smaller ball on top of the second one. He pushed black rocks into the top ball, creating a pair of eyes. And finally, he packed on more snow, and gave shape to the snowman, arms and shoulders, a round nose, a suggestion of fat legs.

Then the boy started throwing snowballs at the snowman and he knocked off its head. When he tired of this, he put the head back on again and reinserted the eyes, making them look heavenward this time.

Satisfied, he went to the other side of the field and started rolling another snowball and he created another snowman. By now, three smaller boys stood at the edge of the field, watching him. When he noticed them, he moved back to the first snowman and kept his eye on the three. His jacket and pants, boots and mittens, were covered with the wet spring snow that molded such fine snowmen and stuck to everything, cold and icy.

The little boys started throwing snowballs at the new snowman at the other side of the field. They kept watching the bigger boy to see what he would do about it. He did nothing, only kept his eyes on them, sitting by his first snowman. They began kicking the new snowman, knocking sizable dents in its fat sides. Then one of them threw himself on top of the new snowman, knocking off its head. One of the other boys knocked off the second ball and stomped it into pieces. The third boy ran and leaped on top of the large ball on the bottom. He kicked at it with his boots, then slipped off. The second boy ran and jumped on top of the big ball and kicked it, too.

Great chunks of snow fell off the ball and the two other boys danced around, stamping the chunks into little pieces. The older boy stayed sitting near his original snowman, and watched them.

One of the little boys, standing on top of the big ball and kicking at it with his boots, managed to split the snow ball into two pieces. Then all three of the smaller boys ran around the two broken halves and kicked them into smithereens.

Then a very tall boy, older than any of the others, stepped out of a doorway into the courtyard. The little boys noticed him and stopped what they were doing and stared at him.

The tall boy bent down and with his bare hands scooped up a mound of wet snow. He quickly molded this into a wet, icy snowball and threw it at the little boys. One of them ducked and the other two moved a few steps away. He threw another snowball and it hit one of the boys in the head. The little boys backed away slowly. The tall boy stood where he was and continued bending over, scooping up snow, making icy snowballs with his bare hands and throwing them at the little boys, hitting one or another of them in the head, the chest, the leg.

They kept backing away, not running, not stopping to make snowballs, not crying out or even saying a word. Soon they were at the alleyway behind the courtyard and the tall boy stopped throwing snowballs at them.

Then they walked away and the tall boy went back inside the building.

The lonely boy left his original snowman and went over to the edge of the field to look at the mess left of his second snowman; there wasn't much to look at, just patches of mud and pieces of snow. But around the yard there was fresh new snow still undisturbed, though the sun had warmed it almost to slush.

The boy started rolling a new snow ball. He stopped often and looked around, at the alleyway, at the door where the tall boy had been, and at the other side of the courtyard. The ball gained bulk rapidly as the snow was so wet and heavy, and soon he could barely move it. He ran at it and shoved it a little way with the force of his whole body, arms, chest and legs. Then he pushed again. But he had lost his heart for it.

He left the new big mass of snow and went over to a nearby poplar tree and broke off a dead stick that dangled from a limb. He went back to his original snowman. He looked at it, smoothed its face, straightened one of the rock eyes so it looked better to him, and looked around again. There was no one else in the courtyard. The day was late and dusk was settling in.

The boy gripped the stick tightly and swung it hard, hitting the original snowman in the face. He hit it again. The third blow tore off the snowman's right eye, and the fourth blow broke its head. He hit the snowman several times, until he was tired of it and the snowman had been reduced to one large ball with a semblance of fat legs. Then the boy broke the stick in half, threw it to the ground, and walked away.

We sat at the kitchen window watching the buds on the trees open. With binoculars, we could discern that the buds on the poplars were beginning to split. And the pussy willows had sprouted their fuzzy buds. Spring, at last.

In the evening, we went to a Rachmaninoff concert, the first concert at the Philharmonic Hall for months.

28

Joy and Sorrow

On a sunny Friday afternoon in April, someone knocked on the door of our apartment. A trio stood in the hallway, huge smiles on their faces: Denis Kopul, Lena Tsimbalyuk and Masha Voroshbit.

Knowing it was considered bad luck to say anything over the threshold, I said, "Come in! Come in!" and we fell into a great group hug. Those smiles were a complete giveaway.

All three students had passed the first round in the scholarship competition. The winners would get one-year scholarships to a university in the United States. All three were going to Khabarovsk to take the all-important language and college aptitude tests. If any one of them was selected, that student would be the first from Birobidjan ever to win.

Not once since they had all applied did we detect a trace of competition between them. In fact, Lena and Masha had become best friends, and were constantly together in class, sitting in the front row where Lena had often sat alone. And Denis had eagerly filled them in to the last detail on his test experience the year before.

After seeing the students off at the train station, Lena's mother, Ludmila Sergeievna, dropped by to visit.

"Isn't it wonderful?" I said. "They're well prepared. They have every chance to win."

"Oh, Sharon, it would be wonderful," she cried. "But what would I do without Lena? She is not only my dear daughter. She is my best friend." Her usually composed face turned red and her eyes filled with tears.

I put my arms around her and John went into the kitchen and turned on the burner under the teakettle.

Though it was still cold by our standards of what constitutes picnic weather, Pavel and Lena persuaded us again to join them for a Sunday afternoon picnic by the Bira River, past the Tolstogusovs' apartment building.

Kolya and Vanya ran around the meadow gathering sticks for a fire. The earth was damp, as though it would never really dry out, and being a swamp, that was literally true in some places.

Pavel was restless. He seemed frustrated, distant, snapping at the boys, ignoring Lena, saying little to anyone.

In spite of the wetness of the wood, Pavel managed to get a fire going, in a pit he dug near the cloth that was laid on the ground. Then he walked off along the river, by himself.

Lena and Luba unpacked baskets and boxes of food – jars of various Russian salads, pickles and canned fruit, bowls of potatoes and beans, two large thermos bottles, one filled with heavily sugared hot tea. Lena unwrapped metal skewers and stuck them through cubes of marinated pork and chicken, and propped them over the fire.

"Have some tea," she said, passing around enameled cups.

Before long, Pavel returned and rummaged around in the picnic basket and found what he wanted: a bottle of vodka. He drank a gulp of it from the bottle and passed it to Luba's husband, Sasha, who also took a deep swig. Pavel was waving the bottle around and talking about Lena.

"How do I explain her?" he asked rhetorically. "She was my youthful mistake."

"He's joking," Lena said, waving away his comment. She went on talking about Pavel, telling us how lonely he was when he went to Moscow last year, how much he misses her when he goes there, for conferences on Russian literature or to do research on his doctorate.

"It's always the man who suffers in a divorce," Lena was saying. It was the first time we had ever heard the word "divorce" mentioned by either of them.

Pavel scolded her for letting a skewer of meat fall into the fire. The small bottle of vodka was quickly emptied and Pavel pawed through the picnic basket, looking for more.

"I brought two," he said.

Lena ignored him.

Pavel hoisted himself to his feet and reached down to pull Sasha up. "Let's get another bottle," he said, walking away from the river bank and toward the path back to the apartment building. (Nearly every apartment complex has kiosks where liquor is sold, theirs included.) Sasha obediently followed him. When they got to the path they put their arms around each other's shoulders and started singing a popular folk song.

"Pasha does everything wholeheartedly," Lena said.

Kolya climbed to the top branches of a tall, slender tree that arced under his weight.

"Kolya grows very fast," Lena said. "Soon, he will be a young man."

Vanya wandered alongside the river, where ice floes continued their swirling way southward to the China border. Before long, he returned, carrying an armful of pussy willow branches for his mother. Lena and Luba opened the larger thermos and poured themselves and us cups of homemade berry wine. "We must drink it, so the men won't," Lena said, smiling. She gave the skewers of pork another turn and put a little more wood on the fire. The meat was browning nicely.

In half an hour, Pavel and Sasha could be heard coming along the path, singing even more loudly than when they left. Kolya climbed down out of the tree. When Pavel reached the clearing where we were waiting, he carefully set two bottles of vodka near the picnic basket. Then he tackled Sasha who fell to the ground, narrowly missing the fire. The two men wrestled around for a few minutes, then Pavel rolled over and went to sleep, or passed out.

Vanya crept away with a box of matches and tried to start a fire on the other side of a nearby tree.

We played ball with the boys, and after a long time everyone sat around the picnic cloth on the ground and we had our picnic. Pavel woke up and helped himself to some salad. We finished off the tea, closed all of the food containers, packed away the dishes and cans and bowls, and cleaned up the area.

We walked back to their apartment just before the last light of day faded to dusk, Pavel stumbling along behind, singing as loud as he could, grabbing the women when they stopped to wait for him, Lena and Luba ignoring him. Our shoes were covered with mud from the damp and oozing ground.

I knew the next day Pavel would spend eight hours delivering brilliant lectures on Russian literature. I was still amazed at how hard he drank, how determined he was to get drunk and pass out, and how he always roared back with energy and passion for his work.

Most of the young women in the Peace Corps said they were eager to get back to America; most did not want to marry a Russian. Many Russian men were so chauvinistic that they made even unenlightened American men look reasonable. Men – and women, too, for that matter – had the attitude that women should generally defer to men, make them feel superior; men need women to take care of them; men need their egos stroked. Many of the Russian women wanted nothing more than for a man to take care of them. It was their fondest post-Soviet dream. "Pretty Woman" was their favorite movie; "Cinderella" was their role model.

"It is the dream of the Russian woman to find a broad back to hide behind," Vera once said. She, herself, of course, did not subscribe to this dream.

The Russian words for the state of being married differ for men and women. For men, the Russian word *zhenat* translates as "with wife," while for women, the word is *zamuzhem* which translates as "behind man."

And yet, it was often the women who held things together. The hard times in Russia seemed to make the men weaker, the women stronger. Women were willing to work for practically nothing, to keep life moving, to keep the family going, while men were more likely to give up. Generally speaking.

That generalization didn't hold in the case of Vasili Nikolaievich Ivchenko. He was overjoyed in anticipation of fatherhood. We hadn't seen Irina for months, but Vasili said that was because she needed to stay quiet and calm, the more so since the baby was due any day. Every day, he would teach his classes, pick up his stepdaughter after school, the two of them would shop, and then Vasili would go home and cook dinner and tend to the needs of his wife.

Vera had a horrible eye affliction and she wouldn't go to a doctor. It looked like several pink blisters or cysts on the eyeball, between the corner and the iris. She called in sick one morning and we were really worried.

"If she had grown up in America," John said, "She would still have her molars, her skin would be better, and she'd have a pair of decent glasses."

Vera had to hold a paper or book inches away from her thick glasses to read. Any skin blemishes she had, which were never terribly noticeable, she blamed on changes in air pressure and on her allergies to assorted foods such as all citrus fruits and all fish and all kinds of seafood.

Poor medical care was one of many holdovers from the Soviet Union, at least in remote areas. Medical schools continued to use outdated textbooks; hospitals and clinics were woefully ill-equipped. On the street, we saw people hobbling by with a club foot, a crooked limb that was broken and not set right, children with pitifully bowed legs, missing parts, scars. Many people had cheap metal crowns on their front teeth.

Suddenly the weather sailed into deep spring – almost 70F one dazzlingly sunny afternoon. There was mud everywhere, no hint of green yet, but the songbirds were positively rowdy and our moods were light.

Just as suddenly, our schedule included extra classes and guest appearances, at the college and in schools around town. Maybe people had started to realize we wouldn't be around much longer.

Vera stayed for dinner; her sore eye was less red and inflamed. She was as thin as a rail, and had a new and unflattering haircut. Her hair hung in her eyes – the fine, straight bangs falling straight down and constantly needing to be pushed aside. And her complexion recently had ranged from pasty white to blotched red. I was sure she was not eating right, and she seemed emotionally drawn tighter than a stretched drum. She said she didn't like being "the boss." She found it stressful.

She shared the gossip that Pavel had showed up drunk at a school function, and then realized he was too drunk to be there.

We knew about that incident, because the function was downstairs in the cafeteria, and Pavel came stumbling to our doorway and visited us instead.

Later, after he went home, around nine in the evening, Lena telephoned us and asked if Pavel had gotten drunk with us. We assured her that he had arrived that way and we didn't offer him anything more to drink. According to Lena, he went home and passed out, but not before Vasili Ivchenko, always one to gossip, saw him at the bus stop and spread the word about his condition.

According to Vera, Lena then refused to let Pavel go to a student function, in his own department, the next day. We found this hard to believe because it seemed to us that Lena didn't have that much influence over what Pavel did or did not attend.

Our director, Anatoli Surnin, made a rare appearance in our teachers' room. He looked gaunt, but he said his treatments in China – acupuncture and a fruit-based diet – were going well. He claimed he felt great, although his flashing eyes were sunken within dark circles and his skin had a gray cast.

The reason he came was because Larisa Belichenko was ready to return to work. Her cancer, she said, was in remission. Anatoli told us that he was considering a new position for Larisa, not as the English Language Department chair, but as the "Correspondent Student chair," involving potential students who would take their college courses by mail, a new program.

The consensus in our department was that no one cared what Larisa did, as long as she did it someplace else.

We were walking by the little park downtown on Shalom Aleichem Street, after having dinner in a restaurant Saturday night. We saw two tough-looking young men with close-cropped hair hassling a pair of middle-aged drunks sitting on a bench.

Suddenly one of the youths performed a reverse karate kick and kicked one of the drunks in the face with his heel. The drunk stumbled, got up, and the youth head-butted him in the face, then decked him with a left hook. He fell heavily to the ground and lay there moaning.

The boys walked away as if nothing had happened and hassled a girl walking alone on the sidewalk. The two of them grabbed her and tugged at her for a minute. She pushed them, laughed it off and walked away. They ambled off, staggering slightly.

Vasili's daughter was born April 17. But something terrible was wrong with her, and Vasili was in despair.

"I should never have taken Irina to that hospital," he said. "I thought it was the best in town, but it is worse than a prison."

Irina wasn't getting proper care, he said, and neither was the baby. "My baby, my little Galina, is too quiet. She doesn't move. Irina said she hasn't cried the slightest bit since she was born."

The hospital did not allow visitors, even new fathers, so Vasili had been unable to get inside and visit his wife and baby. "Irina is not eating well," he said. "They are not feeding her enough, and the food is terrible."

Vasili went to the hospital morning and night, for five days, with a basket of food he had prepared for his wife. She came to her second-floor window and lowered a rope to him, he tied the basket to it, and she raised it up again. Other husbands were doing the same for their wives.

"She shouldn't be standing in the window. She is not strong," he grieved. "She cries and tells me about the baby and about the conditions she is suffering."

Finally Vasili had enough of what appeared to be a state of limbo. Six days after the birth, he got up his nerve and stormed into the hospital, past the security gate, and brazenly rescued his wife and baby from the miserable place. It was a very bold thing for a Russian man to do – a defiance of authority, a declaration of independence.

He took them to a different hospital, where other doctors examined Irina, and declared her to be healthy and recovering after childbirth, but they agreed that something was wrong with the baby.

What the Russian doctors told Vasili was that Irina, at age 28, was "probably too old to have a healthy baby," "the baby was probably too big," and "perhaps time will resolve the problem."

I described the symptoms to an American medical officer who said the baby could be suffering anything from encephalitis to cerebral palsy to an injury sustained at birth.

Irina was allowed to go home at the end of the week, and baby Galina was kept in the hospital for another week after that. The doctors did a spinal tap, Vasili said, but the findings were unclear.

Vasili visited his new daughter every day. He held her in his arms, walked with her up and down the nursery, and sang lullabies to her. When the baby was released from the hospital, Vasili took on extra tutoring work so he could afford to have her quiet little legs massaged twice a week.

Late one afternoon a ferocious cold wind tore through town, rattling tin roofs and whipping tall trees back and forth. I felt brave in dashing into one store, as over the doorway a big piece of tin lay loose and trembling at the edge of the roof. The next morning pieces of roofing tile and sheets of tin were lying on the sidewalks all along the main street. But the wind, though still strong, was balmy, not cold.

Buds on the trees were swelling. The sun didn't set until after nine. Ice cream vendors near the hotel uncoiled long extension cords, ran them from the sidewalk into the lobby, and plugged in their refrigerated carts. The mood in the *rinok* lifted to a level almost of exuberance. Vendors selling pirated cassettes played their boom-boxes at a raucous level – the long-suffering egg vendors stood right in front of them – and children raced around, shouting, banging into people, their mothers smiling tolerantly. The produce vendors, no longer wearing expressions of grim endurance, called out: "Fresh radishes!" "Green onions!" "Delicious hot peppers!" I was elated to see such luxuries again.

The Russians around us not only spoke more quietly than Americans – on the buses, in the streets, in restaurants – they talked in longer segments. Our speeded-up pace of living gives us shorter commercials, and shorter speeches in our conversations in general (except, of course, for long-winded professors and politicians). But a pair of Russian women would sit and talk, very close together, and one would chatter on and on, in a soft but expressive murmur, while the other nodded and agreed or occasionally replied, then the other would launch into an uninterrupted monologue, for the longest time. (Judging by novels of decades past, and my own childhood recollections, this was more what American conversations used to be, before the media moved into our homes.)

I understood enough Russian by then to realize that they were just discussing the same trivia that makes for everyday conversation in America – the weather, their children, their mothers-in-law, the price of eggs.

Most of our Russian friends didn't have money for expensive restaurants, new cars, trips to foreign lands. But that's not to say they didn't enjoy life. They got together for dinners and evenings of singing and talking, they went for family picnics and long walks, they put on performances and played in contests, they gossiped openly with no apparent twinges of conscience. They formed strong and impassioned opinions and relished them, and didn't mind who knew how they felt.

I found them as refreshing as springtime.

Note to Peace Corps administrator:
Full receipts have been submitted for all grant funds received. All of the funds have been spent according to the plan, except for 1,507 rubles ($251) which the Birobidjan Pedagogical College Accounting Office still holds. We suggest that it be used to pay for continuing e-mail access.

We feel the project has been quite successful, in that more than 800 books have been added to our college, eight faculty members and 14 students have been introduced to computer and e-mail use, and 24 new videos are being used for English language training.

This year, there would be no new Peace Corps volunteers coming to Russia. The Russian government didn't approve their visas. I had been in touch with a young woman who was about to graduate from college in San Luis Obispo, California. She was already studying Russian. Now she e-mailed me that she was being reassigned to the Philippines. Two years before, our group had started training in West Virginia because of visa problems. But this time, the Peace Corps took "no" for an answer. The American will to overcome the Russian obstacles just wore out.

At times like this, the Russian determination to simply endure wore me down. Yet in some ways, I must admit, I have embodied it – there is comfort in stoicism.

A thin boy 10 or 11 years old was in line at a beer kiosk, waiting for the man inside to fill a two-liter plastic jug for him. The boy wore rubber boots, worn polyester sweatpants tucked inside them, and a threadbare jersey shirt. He was wet and cold and he was shivering. He turned to look at us. His eye was bruised and swollen.

Maybe he got the black eye in a fight with another boy, but more likely he had been abused, and his drunken father had sent him outside in the rain to buy more beer. His age didn't matter to the vendor; he had the money.

Sometimes Russia left me feeling exhausted. I wanted to focus on the signs of life, of hope: the small businesses that were operating, the effervescent teachers, the pretty little girls with huge bows in their hair, the college students who could recite long passages of

Pushkin and Shakespeare from memory. They were like life in the desert: They survived.

"The only hope is to escape," Natasha Ivanova, one of our language trainers, had said. "Maybe life in Russia will be good someday, but not in my lifetime and not in my son's lifetime. For us there is nothing to look forward to. Nothing."

She seized an opportunity to send her son to America for two months, on a scholarship. He studied English and lived with a California family.

"But now, we can't do enough for him," Natasha said. "His American parents have everything; we have nothing."

The lack of hope was painful. The drunken father hit his son in the eye and sent him out for beer and the beautiful mother sent her son to America for a glimpse of a better life.

Pavel said he would never let his son go to America to study.

"I want my son to be Russian," he said.

Spring graced the land at last. Here and there were patches of natural green, wild grasses and herbs. Meadow grasses, whatever grew naturally, carpeted the empty lots and parks. Here and there around town, small plots of flowers were planted for a splash of color. The birches and poplars leafed out at last, that first bright green-gold of new leaves. Dandelions sprouted. People picked them for soup and salads.

A pair of magpies was building a nest in a tall poplar by the river. They negotiated and squawked and rearranged their place just like John and I do. Their nest was huge, and it was complicated for them to carry large sticks through the maze of branches and twigs on the tree. As curious residents in a neighborhood where a new house was being built, we walked over there every day for several days with our binoculars to see how they were doing.

Then the magpies abandoned their nest. Construction for three days had not progressed and there were no signs of the birds.

We wondered if they had died, split up, moved away, or just took a few days off.

Vera took John to a clinic to have his ankle examined. He had injured it by "testing" a worn-down pair of tennis shoes on a long walk around town. (He hates to throw anything out until it's completely used up.) That evening his ankle hurt, the next day it hurt more, the day after that he could hardly walk. Vera took him to a Russian doctor who took an X-ray of the front of his ankle and declared the problem to be an injured Achilles tendon, although the pain was on the side of his ankle. The doctor constructed a plaster cast, from his toes to the middle of his shin. At first the cast seemed to help. But by the second day the joint of his big toe was swollen, red and very painful; the front of the cast was crunching the front of his foot. He was in misery.

We had thought that before we left Russia, we might take the train to Lake Baikal, two and a half days west, but there was no way he could hobble around, jump on and off trains, get in and out of Russian public toilets.

On John's birthday, April 24, our faculty feted him with a surprise champagne-and-chocolates party. They brought tears to his eyes with their sweet, warm praises – poems, songs, toasts. They lifted our spirits tremendously. Except for that swollen right foot, it was a wonderful day.

I notice that much of Russian music is in a minor key, and there is a tendency to let a musical phrase slide around. This creates a somber and melancholy mood.

After Stalin's death in 1953, the oppressive atmosphere of the Soviet Union relaxed somewhat and it became possible for Jews to form amateur cultural groups, though these had to be approved by the Communist authorities. Amateur choirs and theater groups were established around Russia, including Birobidjan. Unpolished though their performances may have been, they stood as profound indications that Jewish culture had not been stamped out. For younger people, especially, these productions announced a cultural identity that otherwise was given no overt expression.

Four decades later, in the mid-1990s, Judaism was openly and proudly supported. The Birobidjan Council of Jewish Organizations included a women's group, a Hebrew teachers' organization and a sports club. A Jewish primary school was opened.

We went to a concert where a local quartet of women sang – and when they sang the Hava Nagila, with costumed children dancing behind them, the entire audience, Russian and Jewish, clapped their hands and stamped their feet, some laughing emotionally, others with tears running down their faces; it was an overwhelmingly touching several minutes, a counterpoint to the grief they've been through in their lifetimes, and how hard things still were.

29

Nostalgic in Advance

John was all but housebound by his injured foot. He got out for brief, slow forays only. This was a far cry from the Lake Baikal trip we had thought about taking. But there's no rushing the healing process. The sore ankle had become a sore foot (at the side of the big toe, where a bunion would be), probably due to the plaster cast which rubbed on the foot, swelled it, and rubbed more. The cast came off, but his foot remained swollen and painful.

I made the rounds of the post office and the *rinok* by myself, sometimes joined by my students. One day I noticed that a round-faced girl standing behind the candy counter was staring at me. She looked familiar. Suddenly I recognized her – Natalia, from the orphanage. I called her name and her face lit up. We chatted in Russian.

"You remember me!" she said.

"Yes, of course. How are you? Are you working here now?"

The girl had turned sixteen and no longer lived at the orphanage. "I work. I have boyfriend." She patted her stomach. "Soon, I have baby."

The day was bright with high winds, clear skies, after a whirling thunderstorm that was quickly spent.

There was a knock on the door.

I opened it and there stood Denis, Lena and Masha; once again, all three were smiling radiantly.

"Come in!" I said.

John got up from his chair in the living room and the five of us stood in our tiny hallway, waiting breathlessly as though for a brilliant burst like fireworks.

Lena said, triumphantly, "We won! All three! We all three won!"

Their thrilling news sent a shiver through me.

Denis produced a bottle of champagne and Masha shyly handed me a box of chocolates. John popped the cork, Denis tore open the candy, I ran down the hall to get Phil and Linda to join us, and we had a Russian celebration.

The great news was made public at an all-department meeting.

"Our three students will go to the United States to study for one year," announced Vera, speaking from an official-looking document. "This will in no way slow their progress toward graduation, as they will continue to study their required Russian courses while they are abroad."

The long document went on to note that there were only five winners from the entire Russian Far East, including our three students. And Lena, Denis and Masha were the first-ever winners from the Jewish Autonomous Region. John, Phil and I glowed like proud parents.

Our students wouldn't find out until June which American universities they'd go to. As it turned out, Denis went to the University of South Carolina, Masha the University of Nebraska and Lena the University of Missouri. (All three returned in a year, Denis with a Southern drawl and a huge vocabulary of American collegiate slang.)

The paperwork for our grant project was done. The last report was filed. And after we had given up all hope, Surnin came through with space for the books and shelves to put them on. Work on the new building, he said, had slowed to a standstill. So at last he agreed that the room next to the library, with its secure iron grill in front of the door, could be used for the books as well as for the computer and audio-visual equipment.

Phil would take over the cataloguing and shelving of the books. He was industrious and persevering, so we knew that we were leaving our project in good hands. And, after all this time, the room that had originally been promised was finally being delivered.

Another Victory Day, another celebration of the Russians' victory over the Germans in the Great Patriotic War. There were honors for all the old soldiers, flowers, music, parades and dancing and speeches, men and women with chestfuls of medals on their old worn suits. Heads were bowed in memory of the millions of Russians who died in that war.

The day of honoring heroes seemed especially poignant in the Russian Far East, the land of exile, among people who were punished by communism as well as by fascism, with people whose ancestors perished in Stalin's gulag as well as in Hitler's war.

I had to go to the event by myself because John was still housebound with his injured foot. There might have been an internal infection, so Anna Krumpe, the Peace Corps medical officer had him taking antibiotics as well as pain killers. The place where the plaster cast had pressed was extremely painful, and hot and swollen. He was using ice packs on it and getting around with a cane. Anna mentioned septic arthritis as one possible diagnosis, but that was by phone from Vladivostok.

John was being quite mellow, considering the frustration of confinement. Maybe it was the pills. Or maybe he was becoming resigned to his forced inactivity. Beautiful spring weather continued, with clear sky, bright sun, gentle breezes.

John painted iodine in a cross-hatch pattern on his injured foot.

"No, I don't think it'll do any good," he said. "But I am doing it on the advice of not one but two otherwise intelligent Russian people."

I took a photograph of him applying this remedy. No, it didn't help.

"You should use a raw cabbage poultice," Veronika, the department secretary, advised.

The other American medical officer, the one I had talked to about Vasili's infant daughter, offered to examine her – if Vasili could take her to Vladivostok while she was still there, meaning within the next three months. I could hardly wait to share this ray of hope with Vasili .

"Of course, I have no idea what we'll find, or what I might be able to do, but if there is something that can be done for her, this would be the first step," the medical officer said.

Vasili and Irina talked it over, and the next day he said, "The trains are so drafty and cold. I am afraid it would not be healthy for the baby if we took her to Vladivostok."

It was a long time before I could find a way to think about this refusal without being overwhelmed by feelings of frustration and futility.

How could a parent be offered such a chance and fail to grab it? How could I understand such a decision? I still can't, but it caused me to begin thinking about acceptance, and how hard it is for me – and most Americans, I believe – to stop hoping until every last possible avenue of hope has been tried and has failed. Then we despair. Or then, finally, we accept the inevitable.

And I think Vasili and his wife must have already accepted the inevitable; they really did not believe in the possibility of hope for their baby. And so they saw as their primary parental responsibility to little Galina to love her unconditionally and protect her from harm.

John and I felt a distance from Vera, probably partly because we would be leaving soon, but also because of the break between Vera and Lena. Maybe there was something else, too. When we first met Vera, she was at an intense turning point in her life. She had gone to America for our Peace Corps training, and when we were sent to Birobidjan, she had accepted a new job here, too. She said they had first offered her the job five years before. She said our coming here gave her the courage to start a new life, too. Our lives here, and hers, were interconnected, intertwined.

But now she was entrenched in her role as department head, becoming ever more forceful in her opinions and ideas. She was as intense as ever, but so absorbed in the controls that it was wearying for us. Still, we loved her. We missed her. Maybe she missed us, too.

The days went by like sand in an hourglass, at a slow steady pace. There were a few more books I wanted to read before leaving, and in a sense the slow hours were a gift rather than a burden.

It was official. We would leave Birobidjan on June 12, go to Vladivostok where we would get tuberculosis tests and be interviewed, complete and sign a final report, then we would fly home on June 18 – our itinerary: Vladivostok to Sakhalin Island, Kamchatka Peninsula, Anchorage, Seattle, Los Angeles, and finally Santa Barbara.

We went to the Birobidjan welfare office to drop off backpacks full of used clothes we didn't need to take home. Long lines of people were waiting for attention: children, pregnant women, old men and women.

Being close to leaving, we felt nostalgic in advance for the warm friendships we had formed. It was wrenching to think of suddenly being gone from their lives, and they from ours. But few relationships are lifelong, in our generation, in our culture. Even relationships that span years are often transient over time, together then apart, in touch by letter and phone, silent sometimes, then connected again – permanent and temporary at the same time.

In thinking back over our lives in America, it seemed customary to distance ourselves from many of the people we saw most often – people at work, neighbors.

We chose carefully those with whom we would share our personal lives, and even those friendships were in segments of our lives, compartmentalized. Here in Russia our friendships were many-layered and continuous; connections were not separated strands but tightly woven threads that bound us in all our moods and tensions and joys.

We took the train to Khabarovsk for a last get-together with some of the other volunteers in our group – Amy, Alice, Steve Schue and Tony Ladd.

Alice and I read excerpts from the journals we'd kept in Russia. Tony read a poem about village life that went on for pages. We talked about the things we wouldn't miss: the curious stares; several strangers a day asking what time it was; the tough little street orphans who broke one's heart if not one's shins; the derelict look of streets and buildings; stumble-down drunks here and there; the bitterly harsh winters; and in summertime mosquitoes that are thin enough to squeeze through screens but that swell up and hold enough blood to make a mess on the wall if one managed to swat them.

We listed what we looked forward to the most when we got home, and John was saying, "French bread, steak, California salads, good wine, Mexican beer," and I added, "Our family and friends, a sense of privacy, walking on the beach." Amy said: "Freedom!"

We counted the freedoms we took for granted, such as the freedom to enter a building without explaining why, freedom to travel to another city without having to register with the local police, freedom to walk down a street without being randomly stopped and asked for identification papers.

A few days later, we received a letter from Alice. She wrote:

"There was always the knowledge that John and Sharon are in Birobidjan, just a three-hour train ride away. But now we will each go home, having shared a unique experience, and no longer be a consistent part of each other's worlds.

"I want to let you know how much I have appreciated, admired and enjoyed knowing you these past two years. Your wisdom with its touches of humor and reality have made me laugh and think.

"Most importantly you have always made me feel comfortable. I recognized that especially Saturday night. Sitting next to you made reading my journal aloud easier because I felt a real sense of support from your presence. Thank you. I just wanted to make sure you knew that.

"Peace and love,

"– Alice."

John and I passed the letter back and forth. Neither of us could read it aloud because we were too close to tears and our throats closed up.

We began to realize that by leaving we were not only resuming our former lives, we were being wrenched from our lives of the past two years that had given us far more than we ever expected. There would be times when I would feel an ache in my heart, almost a homesickness, for Birobidjan, for the constant interruptions, the dozens of people who needed us enough to knock on our door week after week, expecting to be invited in and stay and talk and laugh, to argue eloquently over literature, to gossip about each other, to bring us champagne and chocolate, ask us questions, take us to their *dachas* and their children's musical recitals, and make us feel warm and welcome and passionately alive.

30

At the Dacha

A sunny, cool day in June. We went to our favorite *dacha*, where the Vinnikovs let us help them in their big garden fronted by a tiny cottage.

John and I, Ludmila Borisovna, her big cheerful husband Sasha and their daughter Masha all weeded and hoed for a few hours. Ludmila was sad because some small cabbage plants they had put in two weeks before were bug-infested and dying. The rest of the garden was thriving: strawberries, young shoots of corn, beans and carrots and tomatoes.

We ate dinner after our labor, seated around a table in the cottage. The centerpiece was the special-occasion *dacha* picnic fare proudly prepared by Sasha – stuffed sturgeon smoked over a wood fire. The carp was sliced open and filled with thinly sliced onions, potatoes, liberal doses of salt and pepper and fresh bay leaves. Sasha built a fire under the iron smoker box and lay the fish on a platform over branches of cherry wood, and bake-smoked it for a couple of hours while we worked. Delicious. While we were eating, a light shower began, and on our way home in the evening the rain came down hard.

Besides teaching, Ludmila was studying for her doctorate. She was also determined to master the computer, though she had never touched one before.

John taught her from the beginning: "To make a capital letter, you must hold down the shift key and tap the letter at the same time. The shift key is on either side of the keyboard; use your little finger to press it down." With infinite patience, they plotted each step until she had mastered the basics of typing, and from there the marvels of e-mail. John went through this process, one by one, with several of the teachers. Ludmila was his best and most industrious student.

Pavel said the college administrators announced that teachers would get fifty-one percent of their salaries again this month, $102 instead of $200.

"How do people manage?" I asked him. I had never understood.

"What choice is there?" he shrugged.

Everyone's pay was late or reduced, not just teachers. With all its natural resources, vast geography and bright people, Russia was unable to establish an operating system.

On our last Sunday afternoon in Birobidjan, John and I went to a party at the Voroshbit family's *dacha* to celebrate the scholarship winners: Masha Voroshbit, Lena Tsimbalyuk and Denis Kopul.

Tall trees surrounded the old wooden house on a bend in the river west of Birobidjan. A winding pathway slanted downhill to the pebbly shore. It was a typical Russian *dacha*, though its house was larger than most, with a glassed-in porch looking out on the garden. Beyond a row of apple trees, smoke curled from a well-used barbecue pit.

When we arrived, Ludmila Sergeievna and Lena rushed to greet us.

"Our honored guests," Ludmila said as she warmly took our hands and pulled us into the house.

Right behind them was a little boy who almost ran into Ludmila when she stopped. When he saw us, he grabbed her skirt as though he was afraid she might disappear.

"Well, who have we here?" John said.

The little boy hid his face from us.

"This is Zhenya," Ludmila said. "Our new son!"

John and I stared at each other in amazement, then at the two smiling women, neither of whom had said a word to us until that moment about this major event in their lives.

"Zhenya, these are our friends, John and Sharon. Please, say hello."

Slowly, Zhenya let go of her skirt, keeping his head down, then without looking at us he turned and ran as fast as he could to the far end of the garden, where Ludmila's husband, Sasha, was tending the barbecue.

"This is a many-layered party," Lena said, as she escorted us to the sun porch where a long table was being set for dinner. "We are celebrating you, our American teachers – and our trip to America – *and* my new little brother."

Women were back and forth between the kitchen and the porch, carrying bowls of salads and potatoes, platters of chicken and ham, several kinds of cheese, jam and butter, baskets of bread, and bottles of wine, including champagne.

Lena introduced us to the women, then pointed toward the garden where the men stood around overseeing fish baking in a metal smoker and skewers of pork sizzling on the barbecue.

We looked across the garden. Zhenya stood next to Sasha, holding his hand, his attention divided between watching the smoke curl around the pork and keeping an eye on all the people.

Later, when we all crowded around the table, twenty-four Russians and John and me, Zhenya refused to sit in the chair next to his new father, preferring instead to hide behind him.

The chilled Moldovan champagne was opened – surprisingly delicious. Toasts were delivered, glasses refilled, and the party grew animated.

We spoke our halting Russian, since few of the others spoke English, except with Ludmila and Lena who invariably preferred to speak English with us. Whenever our conversation turned to English, Zhenya jerked to attention and stared at us.

Midway through the first round of feasting, Zhenya quietly inched his way around his new father, just far enough to reach a cookie near the edge of the table. He saw me watching him. He snatched the cookie, shoved the whole thing into his mouth, and went back into hiding.

When I pretended that I had lost interest in him, and I began talking in Russian to the woman next to me, Zhenya crept out from hiding and climbed up to sit on Sasha's knee, keeping his dark eyes on John and me. Sasha put a small plate of food in front of him.

Zhenya stuffed his mouth so full I was afraid he would choke, and he ate as fast as he could swallow, as though the food might suddenly disappear and there wouldn't be any more for a long time.

When he paused to take a drink of soda, I smiled at him, and he ever so slightly smiled back at me before turning his head away and saying, "*Nyet.*"

We had known the Tsimbalyuks for two years, but we knew nothing about Zhenya until that very day.

John and I had often visited the orphanage. Whenever we showed up, little mobs of children clustered around us, wanting to hold our hands, smiling into our faces. As Americans, we represented a dream they had – a dream of being adopted. Russians, we were told, seldom adopted children. Foreigners did.

We knew that Ludmila often served as translator for the orphanage when English-speaking foreigners, mostly Americans, came to adopt a child.

She began to tell us about Zhenya. Every time she went to the orphanage, her attention was caught by this little bright-eyed boy. She learned that he had spent three of his five years in the orphanage.

"I didn't want him to notice me," Ludmila said. "But I began to watch him. He looked as if he could really be a member of our family. My heart went out to him."

Zhenya seemed to know we were talking about him. He kept his head lowered, looking warily at us from beneath long lashes.

Ludmila said, "I talked with Lena and Sasha about how happy Americans were when they left with their adopted children. Finally, I told them about Zhenya. And then, Lena won her scholarship."

Ludmila said she couldn't imagine her life without a child.

"Sasha and I had always wanted a son," she said. "And soon Lena will be leaving. Well, my husband said, 'Let's do it.'"

Just two weeks before the party, the adoption was finalized and little Zhenya went home with his new parents.

By late afternoon, Zhenya was overcoming his shyness.

"When he first came to us," Lena said, "if anyone came to visit our apartment, Zhenya ran and hid in a closet."

Now content and relaxed, Zhenya sat quietly and watched everyone. He didn't seem sad. Just curious. Maybe he wasn't quite sure yet where he fit in.

"He's been sleeping better the past few nights," Ludmila said. "He feels more secure each day."

"Especially after you discovered why he was hiding in the closet," Lena said. "He thought every time someone came they were going to take him back to the orphanage."

Ludmila nodded. "We kept trying to reassure him that he was our son now, and we would never send him back," she said. But after each visitor left, Zhenya would cry and hold on to her and make her promise over and over. "Finally," Ludmila said, "he told me the reason for his fear."

"Mother, when children are adopted, their new parents take them away on airplanes," he whispered to her, clinging to her neck.

But there had been no airplane to take Zhenya away, so he did not believe he was really adopted.

"We cried until we laughed," Ludmila said. "And then we laughed until we cried."

There were tears in my eyes by this time. I wiped them away.

"*Nyet!*" Zhenya said suddenly in a commanding voice, pointing his finger at me. "*Ne Plachet!*" (Don't cry!) He handed me a cookie.

The celebration seemed like a beginning as well as an ending. I had been busy packing and saying goodbye and turning my emotional attention to the joys of going home to children, friends, life in the United States.

Now I saw clearly how much I had learned from our adventurous students and this little boy, and from Vera, and our friends Pavel and Lena Tolstogusov, and Ludmila and Sasha Vinnikov, and their children. Their endurance is fueled by a deep strength. They don't expect guarantees and comfort and security. They put their hopes in perseverance and intellect and love. I felt privileged that Russia would always be in our life, and its future would always be our concern. These friends, their children, our love for them – these are in our hearts to stay.

We left Birobidjan five days after the party.

Vera, Phil and Linda, and several of our students went with us to the train station and waited with us until we boarded the train, and stood there, waving to us, until we were out of sight.

As I hugged her goodbye, Vera had slipped a sealed envelope into my hand. When Birobidjan had disappeared behind us, I opened the envelope and read her note.

"My Dear Friends Sharon and John: Wait for me. I will come to visit you in California."

And I understood that our friendship might ebb and flow like the ocean tide, it might not always be clear and consistent, but it was not temporary. It was Russian, and would endure.

Epilogue:

Return to the Russian Far East

Three years later, in September, 2001, John and I were back in the Russian Far East. I was working in Vladivostok, training new Peace Corps volunteers. After the year of no visas, new volunteers were being approved once again. This was our third trip back to Russia, once each year since we left the Peace Corps.

Leonid, a Russian working for the Peace Corps, didn't like my suggestion.

I had told the new volunteers they could make a major contribution by teaching civics: having the children in their classes elect officers, define goals, work to accomplish them.

Russian people don't have a history of grassroots effectiveness, I said; they have always had a top-down rule. A common saying is "God's in heaven and the Czar is too far away."

Leonid interrupted me. "Wrong," he said. "It is not Moscow being too far away. The reason we don't organize is because of our lack of laws."

"But, Leonid, it could start in a small way," I said. "For example, all the people who live in a building could get together, paint the hallways, replace the light bulbs, and clean up the common areas, if they just knew how to get organized."

"No, it would not work," Leonid said. "Hooligans would mark up the new paint and thieves would steal the light bulbs. It is impossible to change this situation."

Vasili Ivchenko's daughter, Galina, now three years old, had wispy blond hair and pale blue eyes. A fragile, gentle child, unable to walk, she lifted her arms to be carried, and smiled as her papa kissed her goodbye.

Russian doctors were vague in their diagnoses: a problem with the nerves, one said; a problem with the muscles; a lack of vitamins; a congenital condition. Maybe Galina had cerebral palsy. Maybe damage was done at birth. Maybe there was no cure.

But what if there was? What if reasonable medical attention might mean that Galina could walk and run like other children?

The Russian Far East was probably 50 years behind the times in health care for ordinary people. Incubator domes were cracked, sterilizers broken. Needles lay on tattered towels ready for re-use. Broken limbs were wrapped in plaster casts. People died of curable diseases – for lack of medicine, lack of skilled physicians, lack of basic care.

The strong survived, but what about the rest? Galina was well loved. Her sister, Olga, now 12, adored her. Her *babushka* doted on her.

And Vasili called his little Galina the light of his life.

Vera came to Vladivostok for our trainees' conference. The Birobidjan Pedagogical Institute was getting two more volunteers.

Following us, the college had had five volunteers: Phil and Linda Huelsbeck; a girl named Jody who left after four months to be with her boyfriend; Rob Maher who stayed in Russia for three years, then married John's former student Katya Valentinovna and took her home to Boston; and another young man who left early after some thugs beat him up on the street outside our building.

Vera hugged us both, her body tense with nervous energy, smelling of the cigarette she had just smoked before climbing the stairs to our apartment. She was as critical as ever, as opinionated as ever. Why did we and she like each other so much? For we did, and still do.

She dug into her big black bag and came up with three round placemats – there is always an exchange of gifts among friends who haven't seen each other in a long time – and we gave her a scarf from Santa Barbara..

In our Birobidjan days, we had sat and talked for hours, several times a week, gossiping and laughing about everything from

Dashiell Hammett to Veronika's hairdo.

John would say something, give an opinion, about anything, and we would wait for Vera's invariable response: "It is not that, it is this."

He would say Lena is "a wonderful mother to her two boys" and Vera would reply, "She is not wonderful, she spoils them."

He would say Chekhov "writes so insightfully about the lives of the Russian peasants" and she would say, "He is not insightful but he has an active imagination, and furthermore the peasants are not living, they are existing."

Between then and now, Vera had come to Santa Barbara for her promised visit. She spent a month with us. She enjoyed it. We enjoyed her being there. But she was offended when a university student asked her whether she wanted to immigrate to the United States.

"Of course not!" she replied vehemently. "I am Russian. My life is in Russia. You have a very comfortable life here, I can see that, but comfort is not very important to me."

After returning to Russia, Vera wrote us a letter. "My visit to America was only good because you allowed me to live your life with you," she said. "I could never have had such an experience otherwise. It was not America I visited; it was your life."

We puzzled at the fine distinction, but it was a very good visit.

On the second morning of the conference, the summer sky was heavy and gray with thick layers of clouds. The air was breathlessly humid, but the heat had ebbed a little.

Vera came to a session I was leading for the Russian teachers. She sat near the back of the room, at rigid attention, as though she couldn't bear hearing another lecture on language teaching methodology. My talk touched on several of the issues she and I had argued about so often and so energetically – when to correct errors, how useful is grammar, how Americans can best work in Russian schools. I was trying, without much success, to get a discussion going.

The thirty teachers in the room came from Russian universities and Russian village schools, and their command of English varied from excellent to minimal. Within ten minutes Vera's foot was twitching, a sure sign that she was losing her patience.

The dense air seemed to close in on us. All of a sudden the clouds opened and the rain began. In spite of the warmth in the room, we were forced to close the windows against the slanting rain. People began fanning themselves with their programs.

I muddled through the session, the rain a steady, hostile presence. At the break, a few of the teachers gathered around to continue the discussion.

This, too, was not unusual. People who refused to say a word during class wanted to have their say during the break. I glanced around, hoping to catch Vera's eye, and maybe meet her for lunch in the cafeteria, but she had disappeared.

By noon, the rain was beating furiously against the closed windows which were creaking in their frames. Thunder pounded the sky like explosions from a long line of cannons.

Natalia Fomenko, the training director, came into the room and yelled over the noise of the storm: The conference was over for the day, there would be no more activities, the teachers were free to try and make their way back to the Primoria Hotel. Everyone scattered.

The typhoon swept back and forth across Vladivostok like a punishment. Lightning cracked across the sky, thunder rolled from the horizon and enveloped the city in noise, the rain relentlessly pounded the ground.

Rivers formed and raced through every gully and indentation, curbs were lost under sheets of water, men determined to drive their cars from one place to another sent water spraying over people slogging at the edge of the streets. Soon, streets were flooded, cars stalled in water, people picked their way through waist-deep currents, holding plastic bags of groceries high over their heads.

362

Dirt slid and fell away from hillsides. In the flooded eight-lane thoroughfare that connects Vladivostok and the north side of town, called Second River, cars rose and sailed off the road and into the raging river below.

A little girl was swept into a drainage ditch overflowing with water. Her brother jumped in to save her. He pushed her toward a woman who caught her hand and pulled her out, coughing and gasping. The little boy spun out of reach and disappeared under the muddy flowing raging river on its way to Amursky Bay. His body was never found.

In the low-lying suburb of Shamara, past the garbage dump, a small neighborhood of wooden houses, that had withstood the savage weather of the Russian Far East for one hundred years, was torn apart by the floods and the winds.

The next morning we woke to a gentle rain and found that we had no running water. Later we learned that all the water mains were turned off because of the flood. Vladivostok had no sewage treatment system; the usual process was that sewage ran through underground lines directly into the bay. Turning off the water minimized the amount of sewage that would otherwise be flushed into the flooded streets and neighborhoods.

On our balcony was a pair of covered pails full of water, an emergency supply we were glad to have. We watched the images of destruction on local television – the battered old houses, people wading across streets, a woman clinging to an empty stroller and howling with grief.

By noon the rain had ended and the brilliant sun was reflected from a glistening wet earth. Rivulets of water splashed everywhere. The roadway up the hill from our apartment had caved in, leaving a gaping hole in which heavy runoff sprayed like a fountain. On the main streets, whole slabs of asphalt were peeled away and everywhere there were deep potholes; cars swerved to avoid them, creating traffic even more chaotic than usual.

By the storm's end, twelve people had died.

Birobidjan's Jewish heritage has deep and abiding roots. Since we left, a new synagogue has been built, as well as a new Russian Orthodox church. Yiddish songs are being sung and Hebrew parables are being learned by a new generation. A new rabbi has come from Israel to make his home in Birobidjan.

I gave Vera a book, "Children of a Vanished World," Roman Vishniac's deeply moving photographs of Jewish children in Eastern Europe between 1935 and 1938, a collection lovingly selected and edited by his daughter and my friend, Mara Vishniac Kohn. Mara paired the photos with songs and poems from her childhood, both in Yiddish and English translation.

Vera shared the book with Birobidjan's Jewish community.

The Yiddish songs in it were being learned and sung by the children of the Birobidjan Jewish Sunday School. And the book was read at a meeting of the ghetto and concentration camp survivors in the House of Birobidjan Jewish Community.

Their spokesman, Lev Toytman, wrote this to Mara:

"Sixty to seventy years old people, we were looking through this book with the tears on our eyes, remembering our childhood and having a hazy recollection of the songs and nursery rhymes that our mothers sang many years ago. All of us were born far away from Birobidjan, in Vinnitsa region, Poland and Odessa. The book remarkably carried us to the distant years of our prewar childhood.

"On our next meeting, we brought our old photographs, though of course, we don't have many. Looking at the pictures we talked about our life in shtetls and about people who lived with us and perished in the Holocaust.

"We would like to express our sincere gratitude to the author and the editor for their work and for the feelings and emotions that they aroused in us."

The college had an expanded library with floor-to-ceiling bookshelves and a plaque on the wall inscribed with our names and the Huelsbecks'. There were 3,000 books. Television set and

VCR. Five dozen videos, and a set of "Seinfeld" episodes, complete with scripts transcribed by Rob during those long winter nights. There was e-mail access. But the phone bill was months overdue.

Anatoli Surnin looked better than he did three years before. He was no longer so extremely thin and his eyes didn't have that hollow look. His hair was grayer. He gave the impression of being a healthy man. He continued to go to China twice a year for cancer treatments.

Tatyana Makedon was diagnosed with cancer and she retired as dean of our department. Masha and Misha were still living in Birobidjan.

My students Tanya Sherman and Sasha Lushchinsky were married. They emigrated to Germany. Their families were still in Birobidjan. Another young couple emigrated to Israel, as have a million other Russians – John's students Stas Tarnovski and Anna Romanova. One of the Yiddish teachers at our college, Ludmila Piven, emigrated to Israel with her family. The other, Yelena Belyaeva, went to Israel to study and has returned to Birobidjan.

Larisa Belichenko, apparently in good health, was the chair of a new department, well away from the Foreign Languages Division.

Mr. Levin was dead.

Kommandant Valentina was fired after being caught red-handed stealing a crate of frozen chicken legs from the cafeteria.

Natasha Ivanova, the Vladivostok language teacher who wanted to get out of Russia, discovered a Jewish ancestor. She and her husband and teen-age son emigrated to Israel. Her friend, Katya Kostina, fell in love with an American man. She left her unhappy

Russian marriage and married the American. She and her 12-year-old-son now lived in Massachusetts.

Our three scholarship students all graduated. Denis Kopul joined the faculty at our college, Masha Voroshbit went to Moscow for postgraduate studies, and Lena Tsimbalyuk returned to the United States to work on a doctorate in education, then moved to Moscow.

Ludmila Sergeievna's husband Sasha retired from the military. They and their adopted son, Zhenya, returned to their hometown near the Black Sea.

The vehicle bridge across the Amur River to Khabarovsk was completed.

Having been robbed twice in her Russian village, Daphne Early became well acquainted with the chief of the local militia. When her Peace Corps service ended, she and he were married and he moved to America with her.

Alice Hengesbach, who speaks fluent Russian, was the Russian program officer for ISAR (Initiative for Social Action and Renewal in Eurasia).

Angela Frizzo, another Peace Corps volunteer in our group, worked at a Jewish immigrant center in Chicago. "The Russian Jews have a really hard time fitting in," she said. "They're just not Jewish enough."

Kolya Tolstogusov was growing into a fine young man, as handsome as his mother is beautiful and already taller than his father.

The marriage of Pavel and Lena Tolstogusov was as solid as ever. Lena had returned to the English Language Department. Lena and Vera were friends again. Pavel was traveling back and forth from Birobidjan to Moscow, as he completed work on his post-doctoral thesis.

Vera had stepped down as chair of the English Language Department. "I much prefer teaching," she said. "Let the department be as it may."

Asked whether she minded being so prominently featured in this book, Vera said, "I'm bursting with excitement. My wildest flight of fancy couldn't have pictured my humble self in a book; it might have been comics at most. Thank you. I think my real name will do, not that I'm so vain. As you use your real names, I am only flattered to be in such a company."

Vera's friend Faina, the part-time building contractor and hotel maid, taught herself how to use the computer, and she became the assistant manager of the Vostok Hotel.

Masha Vinnikova, in St. Petersburg, completed her first year of college. She was majoring in Chinese, which her parents thought would be very useful for carving out a career in the new reality of the Russian Far East.

Ludmila Borisovna Vinnikova had little time for her *dacha* this year. She was also in St. Petersburg, working on her doctorate. She said she missed her husband, but he was very busy, too.

"When I'm home in Birobidjan, and I want to see Sasha, I turn on the local television station," she said.

Ludmila Borisovna's Jewish husband, Alexander (Sasha) Vinnikov, had been elected mayor of Birobidjan. The city was thriving under his leadership.

*

A U.S. Department of Commerce report had this to say:

"It is perhaps its historic legacy that gives the Jewish Autonomous Region a distinctly different feel from other Russian Far East regions.

"Whereas much of the Russian Far East is dominated by passive Soviet era managers with a greater taste for vodka than serious business, the 200,000-person JAR bustles with primitive, entrepreneurial energy, and has a feel not unlike the Garment District of lower Manhattan.

"Local political and business leaders are optimistic, aggressive and creative. Because of the entrepreneurial qualities of its population, U.S. businesses will find good partners in a variety of industries."